2015

DATE DUE

This item is Due on
or before Date shown.

MONSTERING

INSIDE AMERICA'S POLICY OF
SECRET INTERROGATIONS AND
TORTURE IN THE TERROR WAR

MONSTERING

INSIDE AMERICA'S POLICY OF

SECRET INTERROGATIONS AND

TORTURE IN THE TERROR WAR

TARA McKELVEY

CARROLL & GRAF PUBLISHERS
NEW YORK

MONSTERING
Inside America's Policy of Secret Interrogations
and Torture in the Terror War

Carroll & Graf Publishers
An Imprint of Avalon Publishing Group, Inc.
245 West 17th Street
11th Floor
New York, NY 10011

AVALON
publishing group incorporated

ISBN-13: 978-0-78671-776-7
ISBN-10: 0-7867-1776-9

9 8 7 6 5 4 3 2 1

Interior design by Sue Canavan
Printed in the United States of America
Distributed by Publishers Group West

FOR MY DAD

CONTENTS

PREFACE

On September 10, 2004, I interviewed a Baghdad-based activist named Yanar Mohammed, about women's shelters she had opened in Baghdad and Tikrit. She told me that one of her clients had been raped by an American soldier and was being threatened with an "honor killing" because she had brought shame to her family. Abu Ghraib was the tip of the iceberg, Mohammed said, describing other ways American troops were abusing Iraqis and creating havoc in their country. The following month, I had dinner with a high-level congressional aide, Charlotte Oldham-Moore, who was familiar with issues handled by the Senate Foreign Relations Com-mittee. She told me that Iraqi women were being held prisoner at Abu Ghraib. I decided to find out what had happened to these women, as well as to the men and children who had been held at the prison.

In December 2004 I went to Amman, Jordan, and became the first American journalist to speak with female detainees who had been held in Abu Ghraib. Most of the former detainees I met were putative plaintiffs in a lawsuit, *Saleh v. Titan*, that was filed by a Philadelphia attorney, Susan L. Burke, and lawyers from a New York–based nonprofit organization, the Center for Constitutional Rights, against two private military contractors that sent interpreters and interrogators to Abu Ghraib. I went back to Amman in March 2006 to interview another group of former detainees and heard dozens of accounts of rape, assault, and murder from individuals who had been imprisoned in U.S.-run detention facilities.

I was not always sure whether I could trust the former detainees. They had reason to hate Americans, and they were at times aggressive during the interviews. Yet they shared information with me about their detentions, including descriptions of the physical layout of U.S.-run prisons and jails; the manner and style, as well as the language, used during interrogations; and other details that tended to corroborate descriptions provided by authors of military investigations, human-rights reports, and government documents about the prisons in Iraq.

For nearly two and a half years, I conducted interviews with Iraqi government administrators, business leaders, and engineers who had been imprisoned in U.S.-run detention facilities, as well as with U.S. Army officers, soldiers, human-rights lawyers, former administration officials, and private contractors—altogether, more than two hundred people who were familiar with the subject of my book. Official reports about the Abu Ghraib photographs, which were first seen by the public on *60 Minutes II* on April 28, 2004, made it seem as though the abusive acts were perpetrated by a rogue band of soldiers and were confined to a single prison. Over time, I became increasingly skeptical of that explanation.

On the evening of December 8, 2004, in a hotel room in Amman, I met with a thirty-seven-year-old Iraqi lawyer, Nabil, a former diplomat who had attended the UN General Assembly in New York in December 2001. ("I had an administrative job," he says.) [Like many of the people I interviewed for this book, he asked me to use pseudonyms for him and his family members for security reasons. Several of my sources had received death threats before I interviewed them. Two were killed afterward.] Nabil is a tall man with a high forehead, and he was dressed in a white shirt with cuff links, a wool vest, and wire-rimmed glasses. He was accused of having ties with the insurgency and was arrested on September 28, 2003, and held at various detention facilities, including Abu Ghraib, until May 28, 2004. A U.S. military official confirmed he was released from Abu Ghraib on that date.

Nabil's three-year-old daughter crawled around the hotel room as his wife, Siara, an engineer who says George Orwell's *1984* is one of her favorite books, plied their daughter with chocolate from the minibar. He rolled up his pants leg and showed me a red hole where electrodes had been placed in his knee during an interrogation in a U.S.-run detention facility. I told him not all Americans are like the ones he met. "We're not a nation of torturers," I said.

Yet it is no secret that some American soldiers and officers have been involved in cases of abuse and torture in detention facilities in Iraq and Afghanistan, especially since descriptions of the crimes have appeared in Defense Department documents, court-martial transcripts, and intra-government FBI memos. How did this happen?

There have been twelve military investigations and reviews of detainee abuse, and two hundred sixty soldiers have faced punishment for detainee-related incidents since October 2001.[1] Nine individuals in the military, all except one below the level of captain, have been sentenced to time behind bars.[2] Yet the scandal of Abu Ghraib and the lack of accountability among high-ranking officers for the crimes committed at the prison have affected the way the world sees Americans. Even before Abu Ghraib, the U.S. was in poor standing, according to Pew Global Attitudes Project. A Pew poll released in March 2004 showed that U.S. prestige in the world had dropped to its lowest point in five decades.[3] The Abu Ghraib scandel contributed to its further decline in the Middle East. Before the release of the photos, according to a poll commissioned by the Coalition Provisional Authority (a temporary governing authority set up by U.S. and coalition forces), sixty-three percent of Iraqis supported the U.S. presence. Three weeks afterward, only nine percent did. Americans will be dealing with the fallout from the scandal for generations to come.

Many excellent books analyzing the issue of torture, U.S. policy, and international law have been written since the Abu Ghraib scandal broke. This book, however, is more a work of reporting than analysis. I believe strongly in the principle of accountability, and the first step toward holding people responsible for their actions is finding out what happened, who did what, and, if possible, to understand the motives behind the abuse. Why did Americans mistreat Iraqis, the people we were liberating from Saddam Hussein? Were soldiers forced into these actions by officers or by some concept of military necessity? Or were they sadists whose behavior was unleashed by policies of individuals high in the chain of command? Is everyone a latent torturer? How do we apportion responsibility? These are some of the questions that are addressed in this book.

MONSTERING, NOUN.

[LATIN MONSTRUM; ORIGINALLY, A DIVINE PORTENT OR WARNING, FORMED FROM *MONERE, TO WARN.*][1] AN INTERROGATOR STAYS WITH A PRISONER, FOLLOWING THE SAME SLEEP AND DIETARY REGIMEN, UNTIL ONE OF THEM BREAKS.

—Chris Mackey and Greg Miller,
*The Interrogators: Task Force 500 and
America's Secret War Against Al Qaeda*[2]

TODAY YOU'RE GOING TO FIND OUT WHAT KIND OF A MONSTER I AM.

—Specialist Charles A. Graner Jr.,
shortly before his court-martial,
Fort Hood, Texas, January 15, 2005

PART I

THE PATH TO ABU GHRAIB

CHAPTER ONE

ROBOTRIPPING AT ABU GHRAIB

THEN I SAW THE GUARD TOWERS BELONGING TO THE PRISON.
I SWALLOWED, SWEAT RUNNING DOWN MY FACE, AND GRIPPED
THE HAND GUARD ON MY M-16. I FELT FOR THE FIRST TIME
WHAT I WOULD CONTINUE FEELING THE WHOLE TIME I WAS
THERE AND THAT I STILL FEEL EVERY TIME I EVEN THINK OF
THE PLACE—EVIL. I REMEMBER READING IN THE BIBLE THAT
DURING ONE OF THE PLAGUES OF EGYPT METED OUT BY
MOSES, EVERY FIRSTBORN SON WAS KILLED. THE PEOPLE
DESCRIBED A HOVERING PRESENCE THAT NIGHT AS A "DARK-
NESS THAT COULD BE FELT." WE WERE GOING INTO THE VERY
HEART OF IT.

—Sergeant Samuel Jefferson Provance III[3]

One fall morning in 2003, Sam Provance wandered into a small room in a building complex, the 519th/325th Logistical Support Area of Abu Ghraib. A portrait of Saddam Hussein wearing a green fedora was displayed on the entrance to the building. The mural was faded and chipped, and the plaster on the walls was peeling off in chunks.[4] The portrait, the front entrance, and much of the prison compound was still littered with trash and broken concrete left from the days of Saddam.

Inside the 519th/325th Logistical Support Area building, one section was filled with army cots and cabinets. Another area had showers and mirrors. Provance and other soldiers would wander off in different directions in the morning, brushing their teeth and shaving in open spaces and in alcoves throughout the building. That day, he had found himself alone in the room down the hall from the sleeping area. Part of the room had been blown out—in some kind of mortar explosion, apparently. He looked toward the ceiling.

"There were brains splattered across the wall. The wall was red— a really old, dark, dried-blood red. There were pieces of matter in it," he says, sitting at a table in the Hartley Inn Restaurant in Carmichaels, Pennsylvania, more than three years after the incident. "I was like, 'Oh, my God, where am I?'"

ABU GHRAIB'S WHISTLE-BLOWER

It is November 25, 2006, and the Hartley Inn is nearly empty. So is Carmichaels, a former mining town of 556 people located ten miles from the West Virginia border. Carmichaels has two restaurants, a First Christian Church, a covered bridge, a First Federal Savings, and not much else. Provance's father, who lives a mile and a half down the road, drives a garbage truck. Since leaving Iraq in February 2004 (Provance spent two and a half years with the U.S. Army in Heidel-berg, Germany), Provance has started smoking (Freeport Menthols). He has gotten a tattoo, "CAESAR," etched in Old-World script on the back of his neck (inspired by Judas Priest's singer Rob Halford, who, Provance says, has "ETERNITY" tattooed on his neck). Provance says he hopes to find a job with a private military con-tractor. If that doesn't work, he says he will try to find work as a police officer or a firefighter.

"The future is a blur," he admits.

At thirty-two, Provance has blond hair, blue eyes, and a slightly dated Goth look with a black, lace-up tunic-style shirt; "Harley Davidson boots," as he describes them, decorated with orange-and-red flames; and a silver ring engraved with a Winged Skull of Ur, a trademark image of serpents, skull, and wings that he purchased from a Temple of the Vampire Web site, on the ring finger of his right hand. He stands out among the flannel-shirt-wearing men of Carmichaels not only because of his clothes. A former student at Holmes Bible College in Greenville, South Carolina, Provance is now an avid reader of the late Anton Szandor LaVey, author of *The Satanic Bible*. Like many whistle-blowers, whether they are in the army or in the corporate world, Provance is unconventional.

Today, Provance belongs to a small group of individuals who alerted the world to the abuse of detainees at Abu Ghraib and in U.S.-run detention facilities in Iraq. From September 2003 to February 2004, Provance says he saw firsthand how detainees were mistreated at Abu Ghraib: a sixteen-year-old boy, for example, was hooded, shackled, and interrogated not because he knew anything about the insurgency but because it would upset an Iraqi general, Hamid Zabar, who was his father.[5] Provance also heard about beatings and assaults of other detainees. He reported the abuses to army investigators, but he says no one aggressively pursued the leads he provided. Out of his frustration with the military investigations, he agreed to appear on ABC's *World News Tonight with Peter Jennings* on May 18, 2004.[6]

The response from the military was swift. Three days later, Provance was reprimanded—partly because his "reliability and trustworthiness" had been "brought into question," he told lawmakers on Capitol Hill at a briefing, "Protecting National Security Whistle-blowers in the Post-9/11 Era," for the House Committee on Government Reform, in Washington, D.C., on February 14, 2006.[7]

"There were all sorts of intimidating acts against him," says Scott Horton, a human-rights lawyer and a Columbia University law professor who met with Provance in Frankfurt, Germany, in 2004. "His commander wanted to court-martial him."[8]

TIMELINE OF A SCANDAL

On August 4, 2003, the Abu Ghraib prison was officially reopened under U.S. command as Baghdad Central Correctional Facility. Within weeks, hundreds of Iraqi civilians were being held at the prison, exceeding the normal capacity of the facilities. Most of the abusive acts—or at least the ones that were photographed—took place in October and November 2003. Specialist Joseph M. Darby handed over a CD containing the photographs to a military investigator at the prison sometime in late December 2003 or early January 2004.[9] He received a Profile in Courage Award from the John F. Kennedy Library Foundation in Boston on May 16, 2005, for his actions.[10]

A military investigation into the abuses at the prison was begun after Darby turned in the photos. The images were shown on network television in April 2004. Soldiers implicated in the mistreatment of prisoners at Abu Ghraib faced courts-martial and, in some cases sentencing, as early as May 2004.

Since October 2001 military investigators have looked into more than six hundred accusations of detainee abuse in Iraq and Afghanistan, according to the Pentagon. Yet it is difficult, if not impossible, to know how widespread the problem of detainee mistreatment is. Thousands of civilians have gone through U.S.-run detention facilities or have been held by U.S. forces in Iraq, including many who were never tracked or registered. (More than 12,000 individuals were held in U.S. custody in December 2003, according to the Pentagon.) Detainees who are held for fourteen days or less, for example, were not entered into official military ledgers. Yet human-rights reports and firsthand accounts from detainees indicate that some of the worst abuses occurred not in long-term detention centers like Abu Ghraib but in makeshift holding areas such as trailers, police stations, gymnasiums, and other short-term facilities. The abuse in some detention facilities seemed almost routine.

In October 2005 Captain Ian Fishback, a West Point graduate, told members of congress that soldiers regularly beat and abused Iraqi prisoners between September 2003 and April 2004 at Camp Mercury, a detention facility near Fallujah.[11] Fishback was named a *Time* magazine person of the year on May 8, 2006, for his reporting on the abuses. Today, it is not clear how many U.S. soldiers, officers, and contractors have gone unpunished for crimes against Iraqi civilians.

Provance has not received the attention of fellow whistle-blowers Darby and Fishback—though he has much to tell. After speaking publicly about the abuse at Abu Ghraib, he was told that his top-secret clearance had been suspended and was "administratively flagged," as he tells me, and was reduced in rank. He was honorably discharged on October 13, 2006, and came home to Carmichaels. He took with him mementos from Abu Ghraib—dozens of jpegs, diary entries, unexpurgated sworn statements obtained for the military investigations, and eighteen homemade films. Segments from one of the films, entitled *The Shanksters Reloaded*, appear in a PBS *Frontline* program, "The Torture Question." ("Homemade movies of young soldiers dancing to hip-hop music that escalates into group attacks on a dummy of a prisoner, a primitive *Lord of the Flies* ritual of punching and stabbing that, if it took place in a bar, might prompt witnesses to call the police," wrote Alessandra Stanley in an October 18, 2005, *New York Times* article, "The Slow Rise of Abuse That Shocked the Nation." "In Afghanistan and, later, Iraq, these soldiers were the police."[12])

Dozens more of the films and photos have never been seen by the public. Nor has Provance spoken with the media, or anyone, really, at length about the incidents he saw at the prison—until now. The individuals he describes who were involved in the acts of alleged abuse constitute only a small percentage of the soldiers at Abu Ghraib. Yet I have chosen to write about them because their wild, druggy parties and sexual antics were not particularly unusual, at least according to people who lived and worked at the prison during that time. Nor were their actions condemned. Instead, the partying, obscene games, and simulation of violent acts shown on the videos seemed to be fairly ordinary. In this way, the soldiers were part of a broader, semilawless culture at the prison that may have contributed to the climate of abuse.

Provance sent me a computer disc of the films and photos while he was living in Heidelberg, and I brought along the CD, stuffed into a Priority Mail envelope marked with his APO return address, mailed on July 29, 2006, to the Hartley Inn. It was there he used the films and photographs to re-create the world of military police that existed at Abu Ghraib from October through December 2003, the three-month period during which the detainee abuses were photographed, and invited me to look inside the prison walls.

A DEMAND FOR INTELLIGENCE

On April 9, 2003, the day Saddam's cast-iron statue was toppled in Baghdad's Firdos Square, Provance was at Camp Virginia, Kuwait. He and the other soldiers watched the event on CNN. "We thought we were the heroic liberators and that we had won the war," he says and lets out a sigh. "We thought we were going home." The jubilation did not last. The images of Iraqis rejoicing on the streets over the fall of Saddam were soon replaced with footage of masked insurgents wielding AK-47s. In August 2003 the United Nations headquarters, the Jordanian Embassy, and a mosque, all in Baghdad, were bombed. The following month, thirty-one U.S. troops were killed.[13]

American forces at Abu Ghraib faced frequent attacks. "Small arms fire," according to a report dated September 1, 2003, and stamped with the heading, Secret/800th MP BDE, which was provided to me by an army officer, "directed at the southern side of the facility is becoming routine."[14] The following day, according to a September 2 report, "There was a mortar attack at 0055 local time."[15] In addition, an operations officer, Major David W. DiNenna Sr., said in a November 9, 2003, e-mail that detainees inside the prison walls were armed. "Prisoners make homemade shanks and weapons," he wrote. "We remove these types of weapons daily from the compounds."[16] Two soldiers were killed at the prison in the fall.[17]

As a systems administrator with top-secret security clearance, Provance worked the night shift and helped ensure that computers throughout the compound were operating smoothly. He wandered in the predawn hours through buildings where political prisoners had once been held by Saddam. In Provance's digital photos, traces of Arabic script, scratched long ago by prisoners, are visible on the walls of the buildings: "God help us," someone had written in Arabic.[18] Provance and the other soldiers at Abu Ghraib were familiar with the dark history of the prison. "We were told about women being raped by dogs and people being dissolved in vats of oil," he says.

"The place was just haunted," he recalls. "There was noise coming from places where there weren't supposed to be people. You'd be like, 'Was that real? Was that a ghost?'" He shifts his weight in the chair back and forth, demonstrating how he had looked around for signs of danger at the prison. Late afternoon sun streams through the windows of the restaurant, and particles of dust swirl in the air. "The hair on the back of my neck would stand." He reaches back and touches the top of his spine. "The darkness would descend on you. At night you would not go down the hallway by yourself because you knew something was there, and it was pissed off."

"They needed lights all the time," he adds. "We had our own generators and stuff, but the MPs [military police] didn't have enough lights or generators so they'd do like everyone else in Iraq would do: if they didn't have something, they'd go hunting for it. They came to me to cut wire off. Sometimes, they'd even steal it."

That fall, operations officer DiNenna e-mailed his superior officers about the lighting problem at the prison compound. In his e-mails he said light poles located throughout the prison were broken, leaving areas dark at night and making it easier for prisoners to attack American soldiers or to escape. In one e-mail with a subject heading marked, "URGENT URGENT URGENT!!!!!!!!" he asked for sixty-five more light sets for the prison.[19] The lack of supplies at Abu Ghraib was one of the many problems—but certainly not the biggest one—faced by the soldiers. DiNenna had a hard time getting through to superior officers and, throughout the prison, the chain of command was unclear. Day-to-day operations, too, seemed to be run haphazardly.

Officially, Brigadier General Janis L. Karpinski was in charge of overseeing detainee operations at the prison. But she lived at Camp Victory, a military installation located approximately thirty miles away at Baghdad International Airport, and was responsible for seventeen other detention sites located throughout Iraq as well. From September through November, according to a sworn statement she made in July 2004 in the presence of Major General George R. Fay, author of a report entitled "AR 15-6 Investigation of the Abu Ghraib Detention Facility and 205th Military Intelligence Brigade" (known as the Fay-Jones Report), she visited Abu Ghraib up to three times a week.[20] Soldiers who lived at the prison during that time said she did not have much of a presence.

"I never saw hide nor hair of her," said Provance. "[Soldiers] were just on their own. It was a shocking experience."

"I didn't know who was in charge—whether it was Uncle Sam, the CPA [Coalition Provisional Authority], or the Easter Bunny," says Sergeant Hydrue S. Joyner, who worked the day shift in the section of Abu Ghraib, Tier 1A, where many of the photographs were taken.[21]

During this time, extended tours of duty, which administration critics later described as part of a "back-door draft," were becoming increasingly common. At a Senate Armed Services hearing on September 9, U.S. senator Carl Levin, a Democrat from Michigan, said the announcements about sending troops back to Iraq were "very troubling news to people back in all of our states."[22] Senators and ordinary Americans were beginning to wonder when things would settle down in Iraq so the troops could come home. Among administration officials, not to mention commanding officers in Iraq, there was an intense demand for "actionable intelligence," as soldiers and officers referred to information that seemed likely to lead to the capture of insurgents. The intelligence was crucial to the military's efforts to prevent more bloodshed and to show U.S. efforts in Iraq were succeeding.

BIG GITMO IMPLANTS

Pentagon officials turned to Major General Geoffrey D. Miller, U.S. Army commander of the Joint Task Force Guantanamo, for help in finding a more efficient way of obtaining intelligence on the insurgency in Iraq. He seemed like the right man for the job. He had thirty-two years of military experience, and by his own account had overseen more than 22,000 interrogations of prisoners.[23] From August 31 to September 9, 2003, Miller and a group of thirty prison and interrogation specialists from Guantanamo toured the Abu Ghraib prison. Despite the risk of insurgent attacks and the primitive conditions of the prison compound, Miller decided Abu Ghraib should become the center of intelligence gathering in Iraq. He wrote a report and described how to make the place suitable for its new role. Much of Miller's classified report about Abu Ghraib, "Assessment of DoD Counterterrorism Interrogation and Detention Operations in Iraq," was devoted to a technical analysis of prison computer systems. He wrote about "bandwidth" and "data mining" as well as the need "to improve databases" and the demand for additional computer "terminals to meet full operational capability," and he suggested ways to help make the interrogation process more efficient. "Recommendation: dedicate and train a detention guard force subordinate to the JIDC [Joint Interrogation and Debriefing Center] that sets the conditions for the successful interrogation and exploitation of internees/detainees. This action is now in progress," he wrote. "It is essential that the guard force be actively engaged in setting the conditions for successful exploitation of the internees."[24]

"Before he left, [Miller] told me he was going to make Abu Ghraib the interrogation center of all Iraq," recalls Karpinski. She claims that Miller also made it clear she was no longer in charge of the prison. Instead, he and another officer, Lieutenant General Ricardo S. Sanchez, the top American commander in Iraq, would make decisions concerning the collection of intelligence.[25] (Major General Antonio Taguba, author of a March 2004 report on military abuse, "Article 15–6 Investigation of the 800th Military Police

Brigade," which is known as the Taguba Report, said Karpinski was a weak military leader who refused to take responsibility for her shortcomings. "BG Karpinski was extremely emotional during much of her testimony," he wrote. "What I found particularly disturbing in her testimony was her complete unwillingness to either understand or accept that many of the problems inherent in the 800th MP Brigade were caused or exacerbated by poor leadership and the refusal of her command to both establish and enforce basic standards and principles among its soldiers."[26])

Karpinski claims that Miller stated his expectations of how detainees should be treated at a September 2003 meeting in a visitor's bureau at Camp Victory. "[Miller] said, 'You have to have full control, and the MPs at Guantanamo know that,'" Karpinski tells me. As she recalls, Miller made the following observations at the meeting, describing how prisoners are treated at Guantanamo, "A detainee never leaves the cell if he's not escorted by two MPs in leg irons, and hand irons, and a belly chain. And there was no mistake about who was in charge. And you have to treat these detainees like dogs."

In early October, shortly after Miller's visit, boxes of electronic equipment were shipped to the prison. "Computers started coming in, and they just never stopped coming," says Provance. "Brand-new, state-of-the-art desktops, laptops. But there were still no lights in the guardhouse. It was crazy. It was like, 'Oh, my God. What do you expect from us?'"

Approximately twenty civilian and military members of interrogation teams, including several individuals who had been stationed at Guantanamo, also arrived at this time. "Big Gitmo implants," Provance calls them. They had a different approach to intelligence gathering. "They were a lot more aggressive," he explains. At Guantanamo, they had operated on "Tiger Teams," which included an interrogator, analyst, and interpreter. One civilian interrogator, Joe Ryan, kept an online diary for a St. Paul, Minnesota, radio station, KSTP-AM, while he was working as an interrogator in 2004. (His accounts of activities at the prison were removed from the Internet shortly after the Abu Ghraib scandal broke.)[27]

"[A former counterintelligence officer] has never done interrogations before but is a very experienced agent and has conducted a lot of investigations," Ryan wrote. "He has done a great job as an interrogator here, but by his own admission cannot run a good fear-up harsh approach. He asked me to help out in the booth tonight. I was like a peacock strutting around when we were done because I scared the guy so much he wet himself. That will get talked about for weeks I'm sure!!"[28]

A rift developed between the new personnel and the Military Intelligence officers from the 519th and 325th units who had been conducting interrogations at the prison. "I'd be at my computer, backing up the hard drive, and out of boredom they'd talk to me," says Provance, describing how the "old-school" interrogators talked about the problems they were having with the new interrogators. "They would be like, 'Apparently, we're not doing it the right way.' Or, 'They're not happy.'"

It was not just their approach to interrogations. Civilian contractors brought a different dynamic to the prison. Many had served in the military. But now they were better paid—between $50,000 and $120,000 a year, depending on the skills and qualifications of the employee.[29] "These guys were torn to pieces by the women," says Provance. "You see soldiers all around you, and then you see this brash civilian who comes in with a goatee, a Harley Davidson T-shirt and jeans, and the women are going to tear his clothes off."

One civilian interrogator from Waipahu, Hawaii,[30] a tall, dark-haired frat-boy type who wore wraparound black sunglasses,[31] was put in charge of a group of soldiers. (For legal reasons, I will not use his name.) Provance knew the soldiers from Heidelberg, where they had all lived together in the same army barracks in 2003. "These guys were imagery analysts. They look at pictures. They watch dots on a screen," determining whether the dots, or moving objects on the screen, are "wheeled or tracked," he explains. (A tank leaves tracks behind.) "They didn't get much respect."

"They were sent home because their jobs were obsolete," he says.

"They were back in Heidelberg, living it up, thinking, 'Yeah, we're party guys.' And then they were sent back to Abu Ghraib."

"People at Abu Ghraib—in the meantime—were expecting intel analysts and when [the soldiers] got there, they were like, 'What the hell is this?' So they told them they were going to be on Tiger Teams and then gave them a crash PowerPoint course on intelligence," he says. They were assigned to the 205th Military Intelligence Brigade, which was in charge of interrogations under the command of Colonel Thomas M. Pappas. They attended two-day training courses to learn how to conduct interrogations in a conference room where Pappas held daily briefings. They were not eager students. (Provance has described four soldiers and provided me with their full names and photographs. However, some of these men are still in the army, most likely in Iraq, and efforts to reach them through army officials and other avenues were not successful. For that reason, I will refer to them as Soldiers D, G, H, and W).

"[Soldier G] would fall asleep," Provance explains. "I'd walk over there, and I'd see him just slumped down like this." Provance reaches his hands out in the air and sinks his body into the chair and closes his eyes.

Pappas eventually assigned the soldiers a new role: Military Intel-ligence Security, or "Guard Force," according to an October 2003 Joint Interrogation and Debriefing Center Organization chart.[32] The soldiers were several levels below the civilian interrogator on the organizational chart. The civilian interrogator, Provance claims, "was telling them what to do."

"The only reason some of them even joined the army was to become civilian interrogators," Provance adds. "They're going to follow his every lead. They want to win his friendship."

The civilian interrogator oversaw the interrogation process. Soldier G and the others escorted detainees from their cells to the interrogation sites, which could be a cell, shower stall, stairwell, or a supply room, and stand nearby with weapons. When the detainees refused to cooperate, Soldier W claimed, as Provance recalls, the civilian interrogator would call them over to intimidate the detainees. The civilian interrogator did this in apparent violation of military rules that forbid the summoning of guards during interrogations when the tactic is used as a way to frighten suspects.

"They were his muscle. He'd say, 'Oh, you don't want to tell me that? My boys are going to get you.'" Provance snaps his fingers. "And dude gets a punch in the face."

"They were such loose cannons," he says. "Ready and willing to do whatever the civilian [interrogator]s wanted them to do."

Once, Provance recalls, he ran into the soldiers in a prison hallway. They were wearing watches and tiger-eye silver rings with Arabic script. "I asked them, 'Where'd you get those cool rings?'" he says. "One of them said, 'You know—from the prisoners.' Provance leans forward in his chair and demonstrates what the soldiers did. He holds up clenched fists and pounds them back and forth through the air like a boxer. He claims that one of the soldiers "told me straight out he and [a senior intelligence officer] beat up a guy." (Provance described this incident at the February 2006 Capitol Hill briefing.)

"A lot of people bought knives," Provance says. "Big knives— Rambo knives. Typically, we're not allowed to have those. But at that time they were kind of getting wild and crazy, and they couldn't be controlled. I wasn't their direct supervisor. But if I had gone up to them and tried to say—in the normal army sense—'You better do this,' they would have laughed in my face."

"The army as it is traditionally understood did not exist in that prison."

THE GENERAL'S SON

Seventy to ninety percent of the detainees at Abu Ghraib, according to an October 2003 International Committee of the Red Cross report and sworn statements made by members of the 470th Military Intelligence Group (May 18, 2004), the 519th Military Intelligence Battalion (May 19, 2004), and the 304th Military Intelligence Battalion (May 21, 2004), were arrested by mistake or had no intelligence value.[33]

Provance says he began to realize things weren't right when he met a sergeant with the 66th Military Intelligence Group, a woman in her forties who worked in an out-processing office. He was fixing a computer near her desk, and they began speaking about the detainees. She told him, as he recalls, that "most of the detainees had just been picked up in sweeps for no particular reason."[34]

Provance met one of the prisoners who seemed to be there for the wrong reason. He was the son of General Zabar. Provance escorted the boy from an outdoor tent in Camp Vigilante, an area of the prison, to an interrogation booth in an adjacent building. "They wanted me to put a hood on his head," says Provance. He explains how he and the boy were standing only yards from the building that housed the interrogation site. "I was like, 'We're looking at the place we're going,'" he recalls. "'Is it necessary?'"

"It's really dirty and nasty," he says, describing the hood—a plastic sandbag—he was instructed to force over the boy's head. "He was shaking and scared. I felt like a horrible person. It's ghetto." The handcuffs would not stay on his slender wrists. So the boy carried them. "They got him to the point where he was naked, shivering, and covered in mud and then showed him to his father. That's what broke [General Zabar] down after a fourteen-hour interrogation. He said, 'I'll tell you anything.'"[35]

"It struck me as morally reprehensible," Provance says. "And I could not understand why our command was doing it."

He says he had once held a different view of the army. After dropping out of Holmes Bible College, he worked as a cabinet-maker and read Roman and Greek history. He joined the army in July 1999, he says, because he wanted adventure and a life of valor and courage. The interrogation of General Zabar's son did not reflect the values of the military that he believed in. "I'm like, 'Oh, my God, this is real bad,'" he says.

In November, he says, he overheard a conversation in the dining hall at Camp Victory. One soldier told his friends at a cafeteria table how detainees were being treated in Abu Ghraib. "They would hit the detainees as practice shots. They would apply strikes to their necks and knock them out. One detainee was so scared. The MPs held his head and told him everything would be alright, and they wouldn't strike him. The detainees would plead for mercy, and the MPs thought it was funny," according to Provance's sworn statement in the Taguba Report.[36] Soldiers, Provance claims, were shown "how to clobber someone and knock him out—and what instruments to use so that they didn't leave marks."[37]

Other soldiers in the cafeteria that day listened eagerly to the stories of how detainees were being treated. "The whole table was howling with laughing," Provance tells me. "Howling."[38]

The mistreatment of detainees was apparently conducted in a cruel, yet playful, manner. "When you look at those [Abu Ghraib] photographs and you hear the testimony, nobody appears to be angry. In fact, there's laughter in the background," said a prosecutor in the court-martial of a former Abu Ghraib guard, Ivan L. ("Chip") Frederick II, in Baghdad on October 24, 2004. "It's a game, Sir."[39]

"They'd talk about their experience when the detainees were being humiliated and abused," says Provance. "It was always a joke story. It was like, 'Ha, ha. It was hilarious. You had to be there.' It would be funny if it were in a movie—in a spoof like *Naked Gun 2½*."

He puts his chin in his hand and looks across the room.

"You see these Iraqi people. It's hard to imagine they're human," he says. "They're just the stock detainee. Like a movie prop."

CELL BLOCK PARTY

In late April 2004, Provance asked Soldier W for copies of the videos he had made of their friends in Iraq. At the time, they were living in Heidelberg. "I just said, 'Oh, I don't have anything to remind me of Abu Ghraib,'" says Provance. "He was like, 'Okay. No problem.' A couple days later, he gave me a CD."

"I was like, 'Wow. I can't believe they filmed this stuff,'" Provance says. "I saw it as something credible to show people. There was truth to what I was saying."

The films may not win awards for production quality. They are characterized by a wobbly, *cinéma vérité* feel, naturalistic techniques, and lack of direction (Soldier W seems to record every last groan, grimace, and fake-scream uttered by his friends). Presented as a body of work, though, the videos provide an exclusive, inside look at the culture of Abu Ghraib and illustrate how soldiers partied, showed off, acted out violent impulses, and fell into romantic entanglements.

Provance and I move to another table at the Hartley Inn, and I put the CD in the MacBook on the table and start by clicking through several of his digital photos. In one picture that Provance obtained from an anonymous source, the civilian interrogator who is wearing a bandana, is questioning a detainee with the help of a female interpreter dressed in an army-fatigue jacket marked with a badge, "U.S. Contractor." She is holding a cigarette and a drink as if she were at a nightclub.[40] The detainee is a heavy-set, dark-skinned man identified as an Iraqi police officer named Dawod in a sworn statement made by Frederick. Dawod is squatting backwards on two, flimsy plastic chairs. The chairs are stacked together to support his weight.

"He looks scared," says Provance to me. Then he looks at the civilian interrogator in the photo.

"That's just his dark side," says Provance. "Mr. Cool Interrogator. He's wearing one of those black fleece coats. They were premium at the time. The only people who had them were officers, females, or civilians."

Females? I ask.

"The guys they were sleeping with would give them one," he explains.

Like an engagement ring, I tell him.

He laughs. "I tell you what—people fell in love really quick out there." The female soldiers, he recalls, would talk about their husbands for a period of time after they got to Iraq. "They'd say, 'Yeah, it's a hot day and, you know, my husband really hates the heat,'" he explains, describing how women put up a "fire wall" to deflect the sexual come-ons from the men around them. Weeks later, though, husbands were not mentioned. "These girls—they'd enjoy this lavish attention.

But once they've indulged, it would all backfire, and they'd find their reputations in the gutter."

"The jealousy is horrendous," he says. "Every guy is walking around with a hard dick and is like, 'Pleased to meet you, I'm Joe.'"

He pretends to expose himself.

"Everybody wants to have someone, but not everybody can have someone. There's only ten percent women. Before a girl can even get to work, twenty guys slap her in the face with their dick. It's sexual harassment. But it's so rampant, she has to get used to it. A girl in the army is going to have a reputation of being either a slut or a bitch—depending upon whether she sleeps with them or not. A guy hears about how she gave another guy a blow job, and he wants a share. It creates a lot of tension. You see things written in the Porta-John: 'Queen for a Year.' Or 'Enjoy it now, bitch.'"

The whole place had a frenetic, sexually charged atmosphere. Civilian interrogators were players, says Provance, because of their hip clothes, haircuts, and style. Not only did the civilian interrogator described by Provance have an attractive girlfriend (a female soldier), he had a certain way of treating detainees. "He is very aggressive," according to sworn testimony in the Taguba Report. "He generally yells in their face, and throws the table in the room."[41] Soldiers looked up to the civilian interrogator, explains Provance, and tried to follow his lead.

A crude, sexualized atmosphere is apparent in the films, which were recorded in a prison cell in a Logistical Support Area building for Military Intelligence and Military Police that was located north of Tier 1A.[42] Provance's friends converted the cell into a party room with fluorescent lighting, narrow cots, and a strip of yellow flypaper hanging from the ceiling. A green, flower-print carpet covers the floor, and desert boots and tennis shoes are stuffed under the cots. Plywood is nailed onto the wall, covering the barred window and the door. GNC Lean Shake containers are stored on a shelf.

Here, the soldiers danced at night and shouted out lyrics from OutKast's "Hey Ya! (Shake It Like a Polaroid)." In one video, two men are swaying back and forth in front of the camera. Another time, a soldier wearing a Key West T-shirt flexes his biceps for the camera and moves his hands though the air in a graceful, wave-dancing gesture. Soldier W, off camera, lets out a guffaw that sounds like the bark of a seal. "Hey Ya!" plays as soldiers dance and spin around in a circle in the prison cell, which is decorated with snapshots of friends and family. Much has been reported on the criminal behavior of soldiers at Abu Ghraib. But until now few—if any—detailed, documented accounts of sexual relations among soldiers and between soldiers and female prisoners have appeared in the press. Sexual relations between guards and prisoners, even when consensual, are against military and prison regulations, and the alleged behavior of the soldiers reveals an unmilitary-like aspect of the prison that was part of the climate of abuse.

In the fall of 2003, claims Provance, an officer was spying on women in the showers. Another officer, he says, brought in prostitutes. Frederick also said he heard that "people in the Hard Site [an area of the prison, Tier 1A] were pimping the females out for a dollar," according to a sworn statement he made before a military investigator at Camp Arifjan, Kuwait, on November 3, 2004.[43] Meanwhile, Soldier G, who appears in the videos as a man with huge pecs and a tiny waist, used to shave his pubic hair and leave piles of it in a canteen cup in a public space. "He was trying to be all Mr. Pimp Sexy," Provance explains.

Frederick described a November 2003 incident in a shower with a female detainee who was about eighteen years old. She "reached over and stuck her hand down my pants and touched my penis," he said. She "let me put my hand down her pants. I put my hand down her pants and barely touched her vagina," he said. "She tried to get me to hug and kiss her, but I wouldn't so we left the shower."[44]

An intelligence officer, Lieutenant Colonel Steven L. Jordan, provided a sworn statement at Camp Doha, Kuwait, on February 24, 2004, that was included in the Taguba Report. In an unredacted version (a military source who asked to remain anonymous gave it to me), he talked about a female detainee who gave birth at Abu Ghraib.[45] Her name is included in the document, but it has not been previously disclosed to the public. In December 2003, Frederick said he saw her with an American soldier—not Jordan. "She kissed him on the mouth," Frederick said, "and he kissed her back."[46]

Meanwhile, Provance claims that soldiers stocked up on sticky, eight-ounce bottles of Robitussin by the caseload from drugstore.com and drove in convoys along one of Iraq's most dangerous roads to purchase the cough medicine from the Army Shoppette at Baghdad International Airport. "They would clean it off the shelf," he recalls. The syrup is thick and sweet, and it smells both fruity and medicinal. They chased it down with two tablets of Vivarin: "Robotripping." It's a cheap high—like LSD (I've been told)— except more jangly.

"I can't feel my feet!" says a soldier in one of the videos. Someone else laughs—a crazy, frantic laugh. They would lunge at each other and press their fingers against each other's throats, holding their thumbs down hard on the arteries, Provance says. One guy would cut off someone's air supply until he thrashed around. Then the same guy would do it to himself.

One video, "Booty Crook Ben," is apparently inspired by a Mystikal song, "Pussy Crook," that plays softly in the background. "Stop that fucking running and bring that ass over here/Bitch touch your toes," Mystikal raps in the background. "I cut you up when I'm climbing on you." (In July 2002, recording artist Mystikal [aka Michael Tyler] was charged with the rape of a forty-year-old woman in Baton Rouge, Lousiana, according to the Associated Press, in an assault that was videotaped.[47]) In "Booty Crook," Soldier H is sleeping on an army cot in the dark cell. His hands are tucked between his legs, and he is curled in a fetal position. Soldier W stands next to him and pretends to masturbate. He climbs on top of him and humps him furiously.

Provance remembers how his friends used to joke around and set up Booty Crook scenes in the prison cell. "It was just like this comedic character. 'Oh, don't go to sleep. The Booty Crook is going to get you,'" says Provance. "I always thought it was weird, too. I was like, 'What's the point?'"

"Those guys are crazy," he says and laughs.

In another video, two women are sitting on a cot in the prison cell. "Now these guys have been dancing all night, trying to impress these girls," says Soldier W, who acts as the narrator. "See that girl on the left—she's impressed."

"That girl on the right," Soldier W continues, describing a woman in a long-sleeved, white T-shirt and striped jogging pants with her hair pulled back in a ponytail. "She's not impressed," he says. "Everyone wants to get close to her."

Later, Soldier W realizes (or fantasizes) she is interested in him and carries on a quiet, one-sided conversation that she does not seem to hear. "Are you serious?" he says. "Do I really want to come over and have sex with you right now? No, I don't. Thank you." Another soldier climbs on top of her and thrusts his hips up and down. Eventually, the screen goes black.

"It's depression, isolation, boredom," Provance says, trying to explain the speedy mating rituals at Abu Ghraib. "Girls were looking for security. For men, it's just a buildup of desire. You really get down to instincts and the danger of it."

He cracks his knuckles.

"It's very competitive among the men. You got a woman—you're one of the elite. It's King of the Hill."

In another video, Soldier H is wearing a U.S. Army jacket as he shouts out lines from a rap song. The camera pans across an open spiral notebook, showing words scrawled in black ink, slanted sideways and crammed together. His songs explain what is like to be a soldier in Iraq, and they are raw, torn-from-the-pages-of-a-journal-style musings on the predicament: "Do I actually have a choice for my placement?" he says. "I don't want to face it."

"All they do is pay," he says. "All I do is give/I'm so fucking tired of living in this pattern." He says he wants to "kick the shit out of Iraqis." Then he talks about "mortar rounds."

"Now when they land, I don't even turn around," he says.

"I'm looking at my cock. Shellshock."

He turns a page in his lined notebook. "Don't let—'How are

you?'—be the first question you ask." He stares straight ahead and pretends to address a woman who is greeting him after he returns from Iraq.

"BITCH!"

In another video, a soldier calls out, "Abu Ghetto. Ghetto Abu." Someone shouts, "Everybody's drunk. Everybody's out of control." On the screen, Soldier W holds up a sleeping bag and punches it. Soldier H says something to the camera. "He says, 'This is what happens,'" Provance explains as we watch.

Several soldiers pound their fists into a black backpack resting on two piled-up mattresses on the floor. One soldier holds the backpack down and hits it four times. Two other soldiers take turns hitting it. Another holds it up like a punching bag and everyone slams fists into the material. The sound track for the video is by rapper Lil Jon of the East Side Boyz. The song is called "I Don't Give a Fuck."

What are they doing? I ask.

"They're definitely pretending it's a person," says Provance. "That's the crazy thing about it. And they're all equally enjoying it."

Misogynist, brutal rap music provides the sound track for several videos. It would show a misreading of the situation at Abu Ghraib, however, to say Mystikal lyrics compelled the soldiers to participate in the alleged abuses. In fact, it seems to work the other way around. As men who are drawn to violence, or the simulation of it, they chose to listen to music that expresses and celebrates those impulses.

In an opening scene of another video, "The Shankesters," filmed on November 3, 2003, a soldier is wearing tight shorts and a beige T-shirt. He has muscular legs and thighs, strong arms, and short, cropped hair, and he is pulling apart a collapsible wire chair with a swatch of fabric attached to it. Within seconds, the chair is transformed into a human dummy.

"Hey, y'all," says a soldier, off camera. "Tell him why you mad."

Soldier H is barefoot, and he is wearing silver dog tags. He has a heavily tattooed right shoulder and arm, stubble on his upper lip and chin, short, brown hair, and thick eyebrows. He is naked from the waist up, and he absentmindedly strokes his chest with his fingers. He says, "We're all mad."

Soldier W stabs the dummy with a six-inch knife. "Through his tit!" a soldier calls out. Another kicks the dummy. Soldier W stabs it three more times.

A soldier says, sarcastically, in mock-sympathy, "Oh. Did he stab him?"

Soldier W loses his balance and nearly falls over. He steadies himself and kicks the dummy again. His face is scrunched up, and his eyes are narrow. His right arm is stretched behind him. He kicks harder. Then he hands the knife to another soldier. They are both smiling.

In another video, one of the soldiers addresses a human dummy—again, it's the collapsible chair. "Nobody can hear you scream now," the soldier says. Someone smashes the chair in the corner and breaks it into pieces. A 2003 OutKast song, "The Love Below," comes on, and Andre Benjamin (aka Andre 3000) croons like Frank Sinatra as soldiers slash other human dummies with knives. "That's some good cuttin' music right there, boy," says one of the soldiers.

Provance is holding a silver dinner knife as he watches the film, and he uses it to identify the soldiers on the screen. "He's actually wearing a top-secret badge around his neck," he says, pointing to one of the men. "Crazy." He shakes his head and again laughs. The simulated violence on screen may be disturbing to some viewers. For Provance, though, it seemed more like he was watching a video of a summer vacation or a high-school graduation than witnessing a series of disturbing acts. He misses his friends.

Meanwhile, on film, a soldier says in a high-pitched voice: "Oh, oh, oh, shit!" He slices a knife in the air. Another soldier opens a switchblade. "See what happens when you fuck with the wrong cat?" He flips out the blade. Meanwhile, a third soldier is sitting on a cot. His legs are spread apart, and his hand is touching his crotch. The camera lingers on his groin and then shows the knife slicing through the air.

THE DARKEST CHAPTER

The afternoon light is fading, and Provance puts the dinner knife on the table. Across the street, the electronic time and temperature displayed in front of the First Federal Savings Greene County Bank flicker between "4:47" and "64 degrees." A plastic Santa, covered with blue tinsel, decorates the window of a hair salon, Mary's Cuts, and an American flag is hanging on a pole a few yards away from the Hartley Inn.

For Provance, settling down in Carmichaels has not been easy after his experiences in Iraq. "If I go to a bar, I wear flannel. If I put on this jacket—" He looks down at the Coney Island Varsity decal and shakes his head. "Here, difference is bad."

Living with the specter of the past has been difficult, too. He talks about writing a book called *Seasons of the Abyss.* "Abu Ghraib would be the darkest chapter," he says. He wants to have ABU GHRAIB tattooed in Arabic on the back of his neck—underneath the word, CAESAR—though people tell him he should put that part of his life behind him.

"When I came back here, I got twenty-one questions. People were trying to tell me they know more about Abu Ghraib than I do. I'm like, 'You work at Value City.' One of them—well, she was like, 'There are people who want to get on with their lives, and there are people like you who want to keep bringing this shit up.'"

"I'm like, it's not just Abu Ghraib. It's a bigger issue. It's about what's been happening. It wasn't just a few bad apples or an outbreak of sadism. It was policy. The scandal photos were exploited, and they were encouraged. Those MPs thought what they were doing was acceptable. So acceptable that they would use them as wallpaper for their laptops. It wasn't just mischievousness. A kid goes over there and busts glass out"—he points to the First Federal Savings across the street—"and he's not going to take a picture of himself doing it and mail it to his parents."

"Imagine being in Colonel Jordan's shoes: an aide to Condi Rice comes and sees you and says, 'Your work here is being looked at by our government's highest people.' Those people used the scandal to their advantage to misdirect attention away from the real abuse and the damage. Generals were shooting at the feet of the interrogators and telling them to dance. But for all eternity, the only thing people are going to say is, 'Oh, it was that one little girl.'"

He is describing Lynndie R. England, the soldier who became the symbol of criminal wrongdoing at Abu Ghraib. There were individuals higher in the chain of command who were responsible for the abuse, he says. Yet they were not punished for their involvement in the criminal acts. It was not the first time he had become disenchanted with army officers. He was frustrated by an administrative roadblock when he decided to enlist in the army as a reservist. Several years later, in 2003, he says, he ran into problems with an officer in Camp Virginia who reprimanded him for not doing the officer's laundry. Like many whistle-blowers, Provance has a keen sense of injustice. At Abu Ghraib, he says, he felt offended by the officers who did not take his reports about detainee abuse seriously and failed to treat him with respect. It is clear he did not approve of the soldiers who mistreated the prisoners. But it is the behavior of the officers that can throw him into a rage.

He glances out the window of the restaurant. He looks angry. His words may sound harsh, or perhaps unchivalrous, when he describes women in the army. But similar observations could be made of the male soldiers—at least in his version of the events that transpired at the prison. The soldiers were objectified as "muscle" and got lavish attention (boxes of fancy computers and visits from administration officials); they indulged themselves (beating detainees and treating it as a joke); and found their reputations in the gutter (their names appear in the army reports on detainee abuse and some, like England, are serving time).

Electronica music is playing from the speaker of the MacBook on the table. It looks like a rave party on the screen—only the guests have gotten high on Robotussin and Vivarin instead of the usual party drugs. A soldier swings strands of electrical lights over his head as if he were lassoing a wayward calf. Other soldiers are tripping as they wave strings of tiny, colorful electrical bulbs in the air. The lights flicker in the dark prison cell and create a mesmerizing neon glow. "Look at that shit, man," a soldier says in a mellow voice.

"I always tell people Abu Ghraib was *Apocalypse Now* meets *The Shining*," Provance says. He puts his elbows on the table and stares at the light display. "A surrealist combat zone with the horror and haunting of *The Shining*."

The culture at Abu Ghraib that Provance describes so eloquently–with its Robotripping, raunchy videos, and Mystikal soundtrack—is only part of the picture. There was also a political dimension to the scandal. That culture exists thousands of miles away in the conference rooms and policy sessions of Washington, D.C.

CHAPTER TWO

THE TORTURE MEMO

The people who work in the Eisenhower Executive Office Building on Pennsylvania Avenue, next to the West Wing of the White House, stand out for their seriousness even in a city not known for its *joie de vivre*. Yet the building itself has a rakish charm, with exterior walls made of granite and cast iron, its architectural roots in the French Renaissance. Inside, it has the feel of a slightly seedy, Old World–style Gramercy Park hotel. Attorney Timothy E. Flanigan, a senior administration official, worked on the second floor of the building from 2001 to 2002. He had acted as deputy of the Justice Department's Office of Legal Counsel in the first Bush administration[1] and was an advisor during President George W. Bush's campaign—along with a young legal scholar named John C. Yoo—steering Bush on legal issues that came to include the Florida recount.[2]

As a White House legal advisor, Flanigan, forty-nine, and his boss, Alberto R. Gonzales, serving as White House counsel, were responsible for analyzing issues ranging from domestic security law to international war crimes statutes in the wake of the 9/11 attacks, wrote *Washington Post* reporter Dana Milbank on January 30, 2001.[3]

The *New York Times's* Elisabeth Bumiller described the place where Flanigan worked as "Legal Central in the administration's campaign against terrorism."[4] Indeed, he had taken up the subject of terrorism as part of a small group of legal experts that included Gonzales; David S. Addington, a counselor to Vice President Dick Cheney; and Yoo, who was at the time a thirty-five-year-old deputy assistant attorney general at the Justice Department's Office of Legal Counsel. Unlike many legal issues that Flanigan had dealt with in the past as a presidential advisor, this one was neither dry nor abstract.

Flanigan was living with his family in Great Falls, Virginia, on September 11, 2001. That day, he huddled with other advisers in the White House situation room and wondered what would happen next. He had personal cause to worry about a future attack—fourteen reasons, counting all his children. A graduate of Brigham Young University, Flanigan has been included in publicity materials as a participant in Federalist Society activities.[5] He has a broad face, a slightly heavy build, a receding hairline, and a penchant for dark suits, white shirts, and ties. In the hot, sticky summer following 9/11, Flanigan, Gonzales, and Yoo, along with other high-level officials, worked on advising the president on legal dimensions of some of the most important new counterterrorism policies. During that time, Flanigan would find himself soaked in sweat, waiting outside the Eisenhower Office Building, as the manholes on Seventeenth Street let off steam in the afternoon heat.

"The overall response to the war on terror was a very dramatic realignment of thinking in the government as a whole," Flanigan tells me in a telephone interview on December 22, 2004, from his office at Tyco International, where he had taken a position as a senior lawyer. "We moved away from viewing a response to terror as a sort of one-off, criminal-law approach, where you're dealing with a discrete number of defendants, to viewing this as a broader line of attack that would require a higher level of coordination between the FBI and the CIA."

The Office of Legal Counsel's Yoo, a chunky Harvard graduate with smooth dark hair parted on the left side, also found weaknesses in the criminal-justice approach to terrorists. He believed a more vigorous effort, led by the president, was required. Yoo and his Office of Legal Counsel colleagues "went into overdrive," as he wrote in his book *War by Other Means: An Insider's Account of the War on Terror*, attending meetings with officials from the FBI, CIA, the Pentagon, and the State Department in which they discussed the treatment of detainees in U.S. custody.[6] (Full disclosure: I am a plaintiff in a lawsuit, *ACLU v. NSA*, which Yoo wrote about in his book.[7]) The subject of detainees—and interrogations—was difficult and emotionally trying.

Yoo was working in his office in the Robert F. Kennedy Building in Washington when the first United Airlines jet flew into the World Trade Center on September 11, 2001. His friend, Barbara Olson, the wife of Solicitor General Ted Olson, was killed that same day when the American Airlines jet that she was on crashed into the Pentagon. Most of the participants in the detainee-policy discussions had—like Yoo and Flanigan—experienced the terrorist attacks firsthand. They wanted to stop al Qaeda in its tracks.

"It's not a cops-and-robbers exercise," Flanigan says. "If you arrest Bin Laden and bring him back to the U.S. for trial, and he gets a lawyer who tells him to shut up—that's a problem. If we believe a future terrorist attack is possible, or that Bin Laden has information that could prevent the event, then we need to find out what he knows. The focus has got to be on getting the information we need to protect American citizens. If you view this as war—and not as a normal, criminal-justice matter—then you are going to have a somewhat different approach. You can be more forward-leaning. You're not going to provide everyone with a lawyer."

DEFINING TORTURE

The new approach to capturing and detaining terrorism suspects led to a reinterpretation of laws that banned torture. "When I joined the administration in the summer of 2001," Yoo wrote, "I never anticipated having to detail the precise meaning of torture in military and intelligence interrogations."[8]

On August 1, 2002, Jay S. Bybee, head of the Justice Department's Office of Legal Counsel, signed a memo that provided a narrow definition of torture: interrogators could do what they wanted as long as the intensity of pain inflicted on suspects was less than "that which accompany serious physical injury such as death or organ failure."[9] Yoo is widely acknowledged as the author of the document, which later became known as the "Torture Memo." "Our intent in the Justice Department's original research was to give clear legal guidance on what constituted 'torture' under the law, so that our agents would know exactly what was prohibited, and what was not," Yoo wrote.[10] In fact, the memo created conditions under which almost any type of physical duress could be inflicted on detainees during interrogations.

How could such a legal opinion make it through the vetting process of the Justice Department? Critics of the administration say the Torture Memo was passed along through back channels within the department and approved in a clandestine fashion, wrote Yoo. Yet there were no objections to its conclusions or demands for a revision, he claimed. "The opinion went through the normal processes of review," he wrote. "No one urged us to make any significant changes in the opinion and I do not recall anyone disagreeing with the basic conclusions of the opinion."[11]

Specific types of interrogation methods "were discussed by the administration and then blessed," Flanigan tells me. "Nothing was approved that had not been done to U.S. troops during training."

It is true that the Torture Memo did not go through extensive revisions. But it is a stretch to claim that no one disagreed with its conclusions, especially as events progressed and it became apparent that the administration intended to go forward with plans to exclude certain prisoners from the protections offered by the Geneva Conventions, which says that detainees must be treated in a humane fashion. On January 19, 2002, the secretary of defense issued a memorandum for the chairman of the Joint Chiefs of Staff stating the following: "The United States has determined that Al Qaeda and Taliban individuals under the control of the Department of Defense are not entitled to prisoner of war status for the purposes of the Geneva Conventions of 1949."[12]

It was a major policy development, and many individuals in the administration found fault with it. "It will reverse over a century of U.S. policy and practice in supporting the Geneva Conventions and undermine the protections of the law of war for our troops, both in this specific conflict and in general," Secretary of State Colin L. Powell wrote in a memorandum to the counsel to the president and the assistant to the president for National Security Affairs one week later. "It has a high cost in terms of negative international reaction, with immediate adverse consequences for our conduct of foreign policy."[13]

Secretary of State Powell was not the only one who was surprised by the opinion of Yoo and the Justice Department lawyers. On February 2, 2002, State Department legal advisor William H. Taft IV wrote a memorandum that was addressed to the Counsel to the President. His memo included a paper entitled "Status of Legal Discussions re Application of Geneva Conventions to Taliban and al Qaeda" that discussed the opinion of Yoo and the lawyers that "our conflict with al Qaeda, regardless of where it is carried out, is not covered" by the Geneva Conventions. In addition, the paper stated, lawyers from the Defense Department and the White House supported the conclusion.

Taft provides a brief summary of their reasoning:

"This conclusion is appropriate for policy reasons because it emphasizes that the worldwide conflict with al Qaeda is a new sort of conflict, one not covered by GPW [Geneva Conventions on Prisoners of War] or some other traditional rules of warfare."[14]

Taft disagreed. He said that it was important to recognize that the Geneva Conventions apply to the conflict in Afghanistan because it shows al Qaeda and Taliban detainees will be treated "in the way that we intend to treat them."

"It demonstrates that the United States bases its conduct not just on its policy preferences but on its international legal obligations," Taft wrote. "Agreement by all lawyers that the War Crimes Act does not apply to our conduct means that the risk of prosecution under that statute is negligible. Any small benefit from reducing it further will be purchased at the expense of the men and women in our armed forces that we send into combat."[15]

Taft's opinion—and the views of Secretary of State Powell—were not shared by the president. On February 7, 2002, President Bush issued a memo to the vice president, the defense secretary, and intelligence-agency directors about the importance of garnering information from terrorists fighting for the Taliban and al Qaeda.[16] At a press conference on the following day, Defense Secretary Donald Rumsfeld said, "The reality is that the set of facts that exist today with respect to al Qaeda and Taliban were not necessarily the kinds of facts that were considered when the Geneva Convention was fashioned some half a century ago."[17] For this reason, argued Rumsfeld and other administration officials, harsh interrogation techniques may be used on certain types of prisoners.

Nevertheless, Yoo, Flanigan, and other supporters of the new policy on detainees said the harsh interrogation techniques were not supposed to be used on Iraqi prisoners. The soldiers at Abu Ghraib behaved abhorrently and contrary to official policy when they mistreated detainees in Tier 1A. "Stripping someone naked and putting them in forced positions and dogs barking requires a different mindset," says Flanigan. "That is someone who has a perverted sense of what is appropriate."

"The war in Iraq was understood from the beginning to be a conventional war in which Geneva Conventions applied," Flanigan says. "What happened in the Iraqi prisons was a direct violation in that guidance. I can't understand why prison officials would ignore clear guidelines. Someday someone may prove that there's a direct relationship between the guidance provided for the war on terror and Iraq. Until someone proves that link, I have to shake my head and say, 'You've got to be kidding.'"

Yoo reinforced the notion that the harsh techniques were intended only for a certain kind of terrorism suspect—and certainly not for Iraqi civilians. The acts of humiliation and mistreatment depicted in the Abu Ghraib photographs, he explained, were not permitted under any circumstances. "The pictures of the appalling abuses at Abu

Ghraib, which emerged in the summer of 2004, allowed some to jump to a conclusion—one that was utterly false—that the Pentagon had ordered the torture of Iraqis," he wrote.[18]

In October and November 2003, more than a year after the Torture Memo was issued by the Office of Legal Counsel, Specialist Charles A. Graner Jr. was overseeing detainees in Tier 1A at Abu Ghraib. Yoo has claimed that administration officials have nothing to do with the abusive acts committed at Abu Ghraib. Yet the techniques that were used on the Iraqi prisoners had been approved for al Qaeda suspects by Yoo and the other officials. In fact, Graner was apparently responsible for the implementation of some of these techniques, a list that included, as Yoo wrote, "limiting a captured terrorist to six hours' sleep."[19] Graner and England also forced the detainees to exercise—a technique cited by Yoo. Among soldiers, the method is known as "smoking" a detainee, or making him exercise to the point of collapse. Many of these techniques are depicted in photographs taken with Graner's 5.0. megapixel Sony. The pictures range from smudged, dark images of men standing in the prison hallway to vivid portraits of abuse that took place in well-lit corridors.

England is photographed holding a naked detainee with a strap wrapped around his neck like a leash. Other naked detainees are placed in a human pyramid and, according to court documents, Specialist Megan M. Ambuhl observed "a group of detainees masturbating, or attempting to masturbate, while they were located in a public corridor of the Baghdad Central Correction Facility." A detainee is photographed standing in a cell with his arms draped along the prison bars. His head is covered in a hood. A naked prisoner is reaching his arms across a bed frame in a dark room. A pair of women's underpants is pulled over his head, and light reflects off his arms and back. An interpreter is standing next to naked prisoners shackled together and lying on the floor in a wide hallway bathed in yellowish light.

The Torture Memo was presented as evidence at Ambuhl's court-martial for detainee-related misconduct in October 2004. Her lawyer claimed there was a connection between the memo and the abuses that occurred at Abu Ghraib: "It should be noted that, accepting the fact that the actions depicted in the photographs at the prison were wrong, the Attorney General of the United States stated otherwise."[20]

The Torture Memo was withdrawn in December 2004, a few days before Gonzales's confirmation hearings to become attorney general. "DOJ replaced the memo with a superseding legal opinion in an effort to satisfy the administration critics, who were having a field day attributing the Abu Ghraib photos to the 2002 legal memos," Yoo wrote. "Since the legal conclusions in the new memo were basically the same, this exercise in political image-making may have seemed worth it simply to ease Gonzales's confirmation. The 2002 memo was, in effect, rewritten in 2004 to take out language about what torture was or wasn't, to placate the sensibilities of those who didn't like seeing the law of torture and harsh interrogation even discussed," he wrote. "Nothing of substance about the law had changed."[21]

Flanigan distanced himself from the Torture Memo during Senate hearings while he was being considered for the job of deputy attorney general in the following summer. But he has never backed off from its premise. "The entire focus was avoiding torture," he tells me. "Not as a game like, 'How close to torture can I get?' We wanted to stay away from it. No one was interested in inflicting pain for the purpose of inflicting pain. The only thought was that if we used these techniques, it would save American lives."

Flanigan, Yoo, and other lawyers focused on legal aspects of the terror war in Washington in the months after the attacks of September 11. Thousands of other men and women across the country signed up to join the army or were receiving military training as reservists in the expectation that they might soon be needed on a battlefield in a distant country. One of them was a young woman from West Virginia.

CHAPTER THREE

LYNNDIE IN LOVE

The IGA supermarket in Fort Ashby (population 1,354) is boarded up, and an Authorized West Virginia WIC Vendor sticker on the front door is faded and peeling. Two boys ride their bikes near the store. One pops a wheelie. A hawk flies low overhead, and insects buzz in the still, eighty-seven-degree air on this August 2006 afternoon. Kansas's "Dust in the Wind" blares from the radio of my rental car: "All we are is dust in the wind. Nothing more than dust in the wind." Three decades after its release, the song resonates here in the parking lot.

"How many people pay attention to the cashier in the grocery store?" says Lorraine Boles, seventy-one, who works across the street at Fort Ashby Books. "I have a slight picture of one of the girls who worked there—the one I think was Lynndie. She had a pretty smile."[1]

I came to Fort Ashby because I wanted to find out about Lynndie England, who was serving thirty-six months at the Naval Consolidated Brig Miramar in San Diego for detainee-related abuse.[2] In the midst of the global scandal of Abu Ghraib, England had remained frustratingly silent about her role at the prison. Since her arrival at the brig, she had received only two visitors—a civilian lawyer and a legal associate who claimed to represent her (they didn't).[3] Not that others had not tried to get in touch with her. England receives requests every week from journalists for interviews, says her civilian attorney Roy T. ("Tuck") Hardy. Yet no one had spoken to her. I figured the best thing to do was to ask her parents, Terrie and Kenneth, if I could talk to their daughter. Their mobile home is down the road from the IGA in a dirt-and-gravel patch of land situated off Route 46, behind a sheep farm, next to the windowless Roadside Pub. On summer afternoons, the trailer park smells faintly of manure. Terrie, Kenneth, and England's two-year-old son, Carter Allen (the child of Graner), live here in a $200-a-month rented trailer.[4] England's sister, Jessie Klinestiver, her brother-in-law James, and their two-and-a-half-year-old daughter, Allee, live in a mobile home yards away. It is hard to tell which trailer belongs to the Englands, so I choose one at random and then see a cooler that says CSX—the name of the railroad Kenneth works for—next to the front steps.

A skinny woman clutching a pack of Bronco Lights answers the door. Terrie, forty-six, a former housekeeper with Dawn View Center, a retirement home down the road from the trailer park, looks at me. She has pale eyes, deep etches in her face, and three gold rings on her left hand. She stands in the doorway for a moment, smoking, and I show her a magazine article I wrote about female soldiers killed in the Iraq war. She invites me inside the trailer.

ECHOS OF ABU GHRAIB

The one-stoplight town of Fort Ashby has a frozen-in-amber quality that makes it seem like a small town in the 1970s. The main hangouts are 7-Eleven and Evan's Dairy Dip. And a Cumberland, Maryland, radio station 106.1 WKGO ("Go 106.1") plays not only "Dust in the Wind" but other mid-1970s hits. I heard Heart's "Magic Man" three times in twenty-six hours while I was in town.

The Fort Ashby Public Library is located near the IGA parking lot. It is the site of a Brown Bag Program for low-income families. One August afternoon, more than twenty men, women, and children stop by the library and pay $5.00 for a month of subsidized groceries. They carry away cardboard boxes full of applesauce cans, soup, cooking oil, KitKat bars, Pace salsa, and other items. The median family income in Fort Ashby is $32,375, according to data provided by librarian Cindy Shanholtz, who helps coordinate the Brown Bag Program.[5] But many survive on less. Kenneth makes $1,500 a month as a railroad utility worker when he doesn't put in overtime, says Klinestiver, twenty-seven. She is heavily pregnant with a second child and dressed in an oversized T-shirt and a navy baseball cap. Nobody in the England family, including both sets of grandparents, parents, and children, has a bachelor's degree. Klinestiver has made it the furthest. She did half a semester at Potomac State College in Keyser, West Virginia, hoping to study accounting, before she dropped out. Meanwhile, the men in their family work the night shift—Kenneth at CSX; their younger brother, Josh, twenty-one, at Wal-Mart; and Jamie at Pilgrim's Pride, a chicken-processing plant in Moorefield, West Virginia.[6]

England and Klinestiver wore their hair short while they were growing up in the trailer park. They played softball and joined Future Farmers of America. And they used to watch *Where the Red Fern Grows*, a film based on a Wilson Rawls novel about a ten-year-old boy and his two hunting dogs in the Ozarks during the Depression. The video still sits on a shelf in her parents' trailer. "We love animals—cats, dogs," says Klinestiver. "We're real tender with them."

They roughhoused with Josh, though, and they never wore makeup. They didn't want "to be all girly pretty," says Klinestiver. Instead, they played cops and robbers, carrying pop guns and shooting them off as they ran through the tall grass. "Lynndie was always the cop. That was her big thing," says Klinestiver. "That didn't work out too good."

England's ticket out of the trailer park was the U.S. Army. She signed up at age seventeen in a Pittsburgh recruiter's office in December 1999.[7] She did it over the protests of Terrie. "I joined because I wanted to. And I wanted to pay for college," England says. (I had several lengthy conversations with England over a two-day period in the brig in August 2006—her first interview in prison and to date her only print interview.) "I didn't think there would be a war. But I was ready to go if there was one."

Long before England was deployed to Iraq, Terrie tells me, she and her sister worked the same shift as cashiers at the IGA. England met a stock boy, James Fike, and fell in love. He is five foot, seven inches tall, and he has dark brown eyes and a steely gaze.[8] They got married in March 2002.[9] Like many people in eastern West Virginia, England and Fike applied for jobs at Pilgrim's Pride. At the factory, England made $10.50 an hour, more than twice a cashier's wages. Moorefield is more than an hour's drive away from Fort Ashby. So they carpooled. For a while, Fike rode a shuttle bus that was operated for workers who live in distant villages and towns.

Fike worked in Breast/Debone, and England worked in Marination.[10] The plant is located on South Main Street, a narrow, two-lane road clogged with logging trucks, motorcycles, and Chevrolets, across from an antiques store called Tony's Flea Market. In front of the store, a dusty ceramic chicken and a $25 chicken-shaped glass serving platter are displayed on a small table. People around here say they're tired of chicken. Dorinda Barr, a Dollar General Store cashier and a former Pilgrim's Pride worker, says she won't eat the stuff—not "on the bone." (She doesn't mind chicken fillet.)[11] It is not hard to see why. Black smoke pours out of steel pipes at the plant and, depending upon which way an orange windsock is blowing, the place smells like gasoline fumes, decaying carcasses, or a Tender Roast.

Nevertheless, the factory jobs are coveted because of their high wages. Working conditions can be rough, though, and former employees say they have little influence over how things are run at the plant. As a mixer in Marination, England noticed that discolored, unhealthy-looking chicken parts were being sent down the line. She told her supervisors, but they ignored her. Her sister recalls her walking over to her station and taking off her smock.

"I said, 'What are you doing?'" Klinestiver says. "'We've only been at work for an hour.' She said, 'I quit,' and walked out the door."

"I didn't like the way management was doing things," England explains. "People would take the good chicken off and put the bad chicken on. Management didn't care."

It was worse in Live Hang—located in Pilgrim's Pride Moorefield Fresh Plant next door. During her shift as a cashier at the nearby Dollar General Store, Barr describes the plant's slaughterhouse. Workers grab the chickens, fasten hooks on their claws, and hang them upside down from a conveyer belt, she explains. Then chickens are transported to the "kill room," where, Barr says, "They go through an electrical shock. There's a big saw where their necks go across." Workers in "Live Hang" earn an extra twenty-five cents an hour—a compensation for occupational hazards they face. "You get pooped on when you work there," she says.

A People for the Ethical Treatment of Animals (PETA) activist was hired as a plant worker and conducted a secret, eight-month investigation of the plant from late 2003 to early 2004.[12] The workload in the slaughterhouse was intense, the anonymous PETA investigator explained in an article entitled "What the Investigator Saw: Eyewitness Testimony From PETA's Investigation into a Pilgrim's Pride's Chicken Slaughterhouse." Yet managers rarely made an effort to cut back on their requirements, he wrote, or to reduce the number of chickens supposed to be slaughtered. Workers simply couldn't deal with the large volume of poultry. So they took the chickens from the conveyer belt and threw them in a large bin or hopper.

"Sometimes, this would cause animals at the bottom of the pile to suffocate," he wrote. Workers also used the chickens to get back at coworkers.

"In some instances, live chickens were discarded in this manner merely to create extra work for an unpopular person who had been assigned to [pick them up]," he wrote. Workers jumped and stomped on the live animals, soaking the room in blood. Yet the supervisor did not seem bothered, telling workers to curb their behavior only on the days when they were being watched by inspectors. "Don't kill the birds in the improper way because we have inspectors here today," a supervisor once told workers, according to the PETA investigator.

There were other incidents reported by PETA:

On November 13, 2003, approximately two hundred live chickens "were slammed against the wall" by employees. "Several hours later, many of the birds were still alive."

On November 17, 2003, a worker "twisted the neck of a live chicken until the head popped off; he then used what remained of the bloodied body of the chicken to write graffiti on the wall."

That same day, a worker "intentionally squeezed two live chickens so hard that feces squirted out of them. [He] directed the feces into the eyes of seven other live chickens, exclaiming, 'They shit all over us every day.'"

A worker also "used a concrete-filled coffee can to crush live chickens, and the chickens did not die instantaneously."

"Echoes of Abu Ghraib in Chicken Slaughterhouse," Peter Singer, a bioethics professor at Princeton, and Karen Dawn, the head of an animal advocacy group, DawnWatch.com, wrote in a July 25, 2004, *Los Angeles Times* article. "In both Baghdad and Moorefield, West Virginia, a simple cruel dynamic was at work," they wrote. "When humans have unchecked power over those they see as inferior, they may abuse it. Slaughterhouse workers do not expect to be chastised for hurting animals. And the American soldiers at Abu Ghraib clearly did not expect punishment, or they would not have posed for photographs."[13] Several employees were fired after the PETA investigation. But no one was prosecuted.[14]

Klinestiver says the employees did more than beat the animals. During her job orientation, a supervisor stated the ground rules of the factory: no sexual activity with the chickens. Klinestiver says she was surprised to hear the announcement. Then, after she started working at the plant, she heard stories from coworkers and began to understand why she and other new employees had been warned about mistreating the animals. "They told me that people there actually fucked chickens," she says. "They'd grab the beaks and rip them apart and make them bigger. Then they shoved their sexual parts into their beaks. Besides being overly gross and sexual, it was like morally wrong."[15] (Efforts to reach the factory workers who spoke about the sexual abuse were not successful, and the claims could not be substantiated.)

Klinestiver and England were both shocked by the behavior of coworkers at the plant. And England had even protested shoddy plant standards. She was a whistle-blower.

"A lot of people complained about it," England says defensively when I point this out to her. "It wasn't just me." Did it ever occur to her, I ask, to protest the following year when things seemed wrong on the job at Abu Ghraib? She looks down at her hands and doesn't answer.[16]

MEET CHARLES GRANER

After leaving her job at Pilgrim's Pride, England, twenty, got a job as an army administrative clerk in Cresaptown, Maryland. She processed the paperwork of Graner, thirty-five, for the 372nd Military Police Company when he arrived in November 2002. That fall, he used to follow her out to the smoking area when she went to have a cigarette. He didn't smoke, though. He just wanted to see her.[17] "He was funny, the jokester," she recalls. "Was he too old for me? I didn't think about it at the time. He acted like he was three years old." He may have been childish at times. Other times, he was raunchy and bad to the bone. "An outlaw," she calls him. Their affair started in March 2003 while they were stationed in Fort Lee.[18]

"After Lynndie joined the army and was working as an orderly in the U.S., she didn't know anybody. She was a really quiet girl," Karpinski tells me. "Enter Charles Graner. He's much older, and he's full of himself. He's just got that kind of personality."

"She was blown away," Karpinski says. "She felt like someone was finally talking to her. Paying attention. He seemed far more experienced and worldly than anyone she knew. It only took a few, short conversations. She was enamored with him."[19]

"Graner was the total opposite of Jamie [Fike]," says Klinestiver. "Lynndie told me, 'He's real open. He likes to do stuff. Wild stuff.'"

England brought Graner home to speak with her parents in early 2003. With a foul mouth and pierced nipples (they saw those later), he did not make a good impression. "If he showed up on my doorstep, he'd get shot," says attorney Hardy. "This is West Virginia."

Graner walked into the Englands' trailer and looked around at the three-bedroom unit with a linoleum-covered floor, the living room decorated with a painting of a red covered bridge and a framed print of a deer. Two plastic fly swatters and a wooden plaque bearing the message "I [heart] Kentucky the Bluegrass State" hung from a paneled wall in the kitchen. "I said, 'Charles, you're more than welcome to sit down,'" Terrie recalls. He remained standing. "We were just like, 'There is something wrong with this guy,'" says Klinestiver. "I don't know what. Maybe when he was born, something fell out of his ear that was supposed to be attached to his brain."

Terrie says she took an instant dislike to him. "I told him, 'You're nothing but trying to get into my daughter's pants,'" she recalls. "He said, 'No, ma'am, my intentions are honorable.' He was blowing smoke up her ass. I said, 'Here's the door and don't let it hit you on the way out.'"

Graner has admitted to beating his former wife, Staci Morris, and dragging her by her hair across a room. He was accused in a federal suit, *Horatio Nimley v. Charles A. Graner*, filed on May 25, 1999, in the U.S. District Court for the Western District of Pennsylvania, of injuring an inmate, Horatio Nimley, while Graner was working as a prison guard at Pennsylvania's State Correctional Institution—Greene. On June 29, 1998, according to the suit, Graner and another guard hid a razor blade in a side dish of mashed potatoes that was served to Nimley. He bit down on the razor, slicing the inside of his mouth, and bled profusely.

Less than four months later, according to the suit, a guard slammed Nimley's arm in a narrow opening, known as a "pie hole," in his cell door. Nimly shouted in pain. Then, according to the suit, Graner heard the commotion and ran up a flight of stairs and headed for the cell. He was accused of hitting Nimly's arm, which was jutting out of the slot in the prison door, four times with a baton.[20]

PORN VACATION

In March 2003, England went with Graner and another soldier to Virginia Beach. Their friend took a picture of England performing oral sex on Graner. In addition, Graner took a series of pictures as they engaged in anal sex, showing the progression of the sex act, "minute by minute," says Hardy. Graner photographed England as she placed her nipple in the ear of their friend, who had by that time passed out in a hotel room. Graner was photographed as he exposed himself near their friend's head while he was asleep in the room.[21] Soon it became their new game: whenever Graner would ask her to, England would strike a pose.

"Everything they did, he took a picture of it," says Hardy. "She was asked why she let him. She said, 'You know, guys like that. I just wanted to make him happy.' She was like a little plaything for him. I think the sexual stuff—and the way he put her in those positions— was his way of saying, 'Let me see what I can make you do.'"

After the Virginia Beach trip, they rented a car and drove to see her family in eastern Kentucky. Terrie, Kenneth, and her paternal grandfather were hunting turkey together in Daniel Boone National Forest. For years, the Englands had visited the park. England even named a male cat, Boone (pronounced "Boonie"), after the place, says Klinestiver. That day, England sat with Graner and her parents at a picnic table. She asked Graner to show the Virginia Beach pictures. He handed a packet to Kenneth. Her father opened the envelope, looked through the pictures and handed them to Terrie. "'He said, 'You might not want to show them to your dad,'" Terrie recalls.

Terrie looked at the photos and could not believe what she saw. The photos depicted nudity and sexual scenes. "I was really bent out of shape," she says.[22]

Graner flaunted his affair with England, and the photos were passed around among the soldiers in their unit. Military rules forbid soldiers from taking lewd photographs. Also, England was married to Fike. Her affair with Graner violated army rules.[23] Neither England nor Graner got in serious trouble, though. Several weeks later, they got ready for their deployment to al-Hilla, Iraq.

During this time, men and women in Detroit, San Diego, and other cities were being recruited for civilian support jobs for the army, including positions as interpreters in Iraq. Some of the people hired for these jobs seemed to have a less-than-professional manner, according to former interpreters who worked in Iraq. They would all end up together at Abu Ghraib.

CHAPTER FOUR

UNDER CONTRACT

Detroit has one of the largest Arab-American populations in the country, according to recent U.S. census data, and suburban Dearborn is 30 percent Arab American. It is a prime recruiting hub for military contractors who are looking for bilingual employees. The need for such workers has increased steadily over the years.

In the late 1990s, the Vice Chief of Staff of the army began to recognize that additional linguists were needed for the U.S. military operating in the Balkans and elsewhere. At that point, according to the Fay-Jones Report, officers began to set up a plan to contract out the linguistic tasks, and private companies began to get more heavily involved in the work.[1] One company, Titan, had previously held a $369 million contract to supply civilian translators and is now owned by L-3 Communications. Their contract was extended in 2006 and was at that time worth $1.05 billion, according to Joe Walker, a spokesman for the army's Intelligence and Security Command.[2] The army could not function without the help of contractors. They have been acting as interpreters, fixing meals for soldiers, paving roads, delivering mail, and otherwise assisting American troops dating back to the Revolutionary War. The number of military contractors, however, has reached its peak in the most recent conflict. A U.S. military census report released in December 2006 shows that 100,000 contractors are now operating in Iraq.[3]

How much of the military's investment in the private sector has worked out as a savings for the government—and for taxpayers, of course—is unknown. The only studies that have been done, says Brookings Institution senior fellow P.W. Singer, author of *Corporate Warriors: The Rise of the Privatized Military Industry*, are those that have projected savings (and have been conducted by contractors). "The simple fact is that it is not clear that outsourcing always saves money, either in general industry or specific to military services," he wrote. "A RAND report on the private provision of professional military education programs in the U.S. found no cost savings."[4] Government contracts with private companies are awarded through a formal process. Government contracting officers announce requests for proposals in publications like *Defense Daily* and put the word out among colleagues. It's a small world. Many contractors spend years in the military before joining the private sector. Titan's executive vice president of operations, Lawrence J. Delaney, is a former assistant secretary in charge of acquisitions for the air force, for example, and three of Titan's senior vice presidents have served as officers or in high-ranking military positions.[5] Contractors present a formal bid, and government officers choose the best offer. But when demand for contractors increased significantly in the weeks and months leading up to the Iraq war, the contracting system went into crisis mode.

"Government contracting officers were under tremendous pressure to meet multiple demands in a tightly compressed time frame," said Larry Allen, executive vice president of a nonprofit association of government-contract companies, Coalition for Government Procurement, at a September 2004 Senate Democratic Policy Committee hearing. "[Government contracting officers] turned to companies with which they had existing contracts and which had well-established reputations."[6]

Meanwhile, things were reaching a breaking point in Iraq as soldiers found they were not able to communicate with the people around them. One marine who is now a student at American University, Lance Corporal Rajai Hakki, says he was the only Arabic speaker among 500 military personnel who had been deployed with him to Iraq in 2003.[7] The pressure was on private military contractors to provide translators and interpreters in Iraq. Four thousand were needed.

COMBAT PAY

Detroit, February 2006. It had been three years since private military contractors have begun recruiting dozens, if not hundreds, of local Arabic speakers for jobs as interpreters in Iraq. Broken bottles lay in the gutter along West Warren Avenue. Shards of glass are smashed into the cracks of the pavement. The storefront window of a real-estate company ("WE BUY & SELL HUD, Banks, Auctions, Houses") is held together with masking tape.

Inside the real-estate company, one former recruiter for a private military contractor, Haider Al-Jebori, a forty-two-year-old man with sunken eyes and thick eyebrows, sits at a computer. He is learning how he can rescore his personal credit rating with the aid of a company called Credit Technologies. I sit near the front door and wait for him to finish his computer lesson. Real estate is a new venture for Jebori. Before dealing in properties, he and a partner, David Ayoub, a Chaldean-American businessman who was born in Baghdad, had served as foot soldiers in a large-scale campaign to hire interpreters for the army in Iraq. They founded a company and printed a set of business cards, "Bridge Recruiting, Inc., Translators in Iraq," in Arabic and English with an Iraqi and an American flag flying next to each other.

A copy of a local newspaper, *Detroit Middle East Arabic Chaldean Newspaper*, is folded on a table in Jebori's office. The newspaper has a full-page ad on the front: "If you speak Arabic, this is your chance to start a career as an Army Linguist." As a recruiter, Jebori had placed ads in the newspaper while he was looking for candidates to recommend as interpreters. At the same time, Titan placed ads in another local newspaper, *The Arab American News*, edited by a Lebanese American journalist, Osama A. Siblani. Titan National Security Solutions recruiters said in their advertisement that they were looking for "bilingual Arabic/English speakers," offering compensation up to $157,000 for employees who are "willing to travel/relocate worldwide and to live in a harsh environment."

Ayoub and Jebori referred more than 600 job candidates to a private military contractor. Twenty-five individuals were hired. For each person hired, Ayoub and Jebori made $1,000. It had seemed like an easy way to make money—but, Jebori says, it was not worth the investment required. Bridge Recruiting folded after several months. As a subcontractor for the private military contractor, Ayoub and Jebori could not find enough people for the interpreter jobs.[8] The private military contractors faced a similar problem in securing employees—on a larger scale. Even with the high wages, they were not easy jobs to fill. Among those hired were former construction workers, computer technicians, security guards, and assembly-line workers.

"I saw people who cannot spell Bob. B-O-B," says Walid Hanna, an Iraq-born director of Michigan Community Financial Services in Sterling Heights, Michigan, and a former interpreter in Iraq. "I saw translators who didn't even understand English."[9]

"They were so desperate very early on to find people who could speak English and Arabic," Karpinski tells me. Officers began to turn to local Iraqis as their guides and interpreters. "They were paying them three hundred dollars a week so there were a lot of people who wanted these jobs," she says.

There was a semiformal system in place for hiring local interpreters: military personnel interviewed Iraqis who spoke English and were willing to work as interpreters. Once interpreters were cleared by the U.S. military, a representative with the private military contractor made a job offer. Afterward, the private military contractor paid the salary of the local hire and, at times, arranged for their travel within the country. In reality, the process was more haphazard. "One of the officers would call the [company] coordinator and say, 'We need a couple more linguists,'" Karpinski says. "And they'd say, 'Your best bet is if you find one, tell me, and I'll write up the contract.' So they're hiring these people—not vetted, not cleared."[10]

Abdullah Khalil, a former truck driver in Vienna, Virginia, who worked for a private military contractor in 2003, recalls speaking with local hires in Iraq. "They would see someone riding a donkey, and they make him a translator," he says. "The only thing he knows how to do is ride a donkey."[11]

Many of the interpreters were unqualified because they did not have adequate language skills. Some were not suited for the jobs—period. They held virulently anti-Baathist views, according to former interpreters and soldiers, and were prone to violence.

Many of the people working in Ayoub's office, Michigan Community Financial Services in Sterling Heights, are Chaldean. Many of the people they recruited were Chaldean, too, or had a personal stake in overthrowing the Saddam Hussein regime. Chaldeans and other Iraqi Christians, including Assyrians and Syriacs, constitute roughly 3 percent of Iraq's population of 26 million people. The Iraqi Christians suffered decades of oppression under Saddam. Their religious affiliation was stamped on their national identification cards, and they were discriminated against in various ways: the use of the Assyrian language, Aramaic, for example, was discouraged. Even worse, Chaldeans and other Iraqi Christians were executed and imprisoned. Many of them fled to Europe, the U.S. and other parts of the world, seeking refuge from the persecution they experienced under Saddam. In the United States, Chaldeans have settled mainly in the Midwest, which has the largest concentration of Iraqi Christians outside the Middle East. (The 2000 U.S. Census shows 34,500 Chaldeans, Assyrians, and Syriacs live in Michigan.)

Seeds of sectarian strife existed in Iraq before Americans arrived. The entire country could fit into the space taken up by Colorado, Kansas, Oklahoma, and Texas. And it encompasses a variety of ethnic and religious groups. Roughly 80 percent of the population is Arab, including a mix of Shiite and Sunni Iraqis. Roughly 15 percent are Kurds. They live in northern Iraq. Many of them hope someday to establish their own nation. The remaining 5 percent are Turkmen, Chaldeans, Syriacs, Assyrians, and assorted Christian sects.

In a March 2006 speech at Freedom House, a nonprofit, Washington-based organization that promotes democracy, President Bush said Saddam had crushed his opposition and tried to destroy ethnic groups.[12] In the 1980s, Saddam targeted the Kurds. He sprayed villages with chemical gas, slaughtered men, women, and children, and removed thousands of people from their homes. Afterward, he encouraged Arabs to take over the Kurdish houses and farms, creating the conditions for fierce hostility among the groups. And when Shiites tried to rebel against his regime after the 1991 Gulf War, they were slaughtered.

Conflict among the ethnic groups, especially between Shiites and Sunnis but also with Iraqi Christians, Kurds, and Turkmen, is one of the biggest problems facing the new Iraq. Tension among various groups from the Middle East is also apparent in Detroit and the surrounding area. I ask Jebori if he had advertised for interpreters in *The Arab American News*. "Baathist," Jebori says, referring to the publication. He spits the word out as if he has a bad taste in his mouth. "They support Saddam."[13]

"Of course I'm not a Baathist," says *The Arab American News's* Siblani, who is a leading expert on Arab-American issues and is profiled in former *Wall Street Journal* writer Paul M. Barrett's book, *American Islam: The Struggle for the Soul of a Religion*. "When Saddam Hussein bombed Kurdish villages in the 1980s, we were the first to come forward and condemn the attacks."

Siblani and others at *The Arab American News* have been critical of the Iraq war, however, and their position has been unpopular with Jebori and individuals in some Arabic-speaking circles in the Detroit metro area. "Removing Saddam Hussein was one of their priorities—regardless of the cost," explains Siblani.[14] Jebori's description of *The Arab American News*, for example, hints at his own political views—and animosities—and may have influenced his judgment in referring job candidates for the interpeter positions. It may have led him, for example, to recommend individuals who were also strongly anti-Saddam and anti-Baathist. As professional interpreters, civilian employees were expected to maintain distance and impartiality while they were translating for the American troops and not let their personal opinions or prejudices creep into their work. Unfortunately, the interpreters were not always able to conduct themselves in a professional manner, according to soldiers and civilian contractors who served in Iraq. Once unstable interpreters were put in positions of authority over Sunni Arabs in detention, the situation became explosive.

VICTIMS AND THEIR OPPRESSORS

Some U.S. Arabic speakers, acting as interpreters, were responsible for assisting individuals who once had been their oppressors and were now detainees in U.S. custody. Many of the conversational exchanges between U.S. interpreters and Iraqi detainees were fraught with tension, prejudice, and suspicion. And they were conducted in a language American soldiers couldn't understand.

"There's already a prejudgment," says Yemen-born Marwan Mawiri, who worked for a private military contractor as an interpreter from 2003 to 2004. He says many interpreters who had Chaldean and Kurdish backgrounds saw Sunni Arabs as criminals and aggressors.[15]

Before getting hired, Mawiri explains, he had been supporting his wife and their three-year-old son (they have since had a second child, a girl) on a $30,000-a-year salary as a case manager for the Arab-American Community Center for Economic and Social Services, an organization that provides a job-works program for the unemployed. He saw a help-wanted ad for interpreters in *The Detroit Free-Press*, called a toll-free number, spoke with a company representative "for two or three minutes," he says, and was invited to their offices in Virginia. Almost immediately, he was offered a job.

"If you were to give [civilian interpreters] a proficiency language test, at least fifty percent would never pass," says Mawiri. He says he never took one. "The job is lucrative, and it pays. No one will say he don't know how to translate."

After interpreters were hired, they didn't seem to get much guidance. Former truck driver Khalil, for example, says he spent a short time on U.S. military bases, learning about "insects, bombings, and ambushes" before going to the Middle East. Nobody, he says, told him about how to be an interpreter, or how detainees should be treated, or how international law and human rights should be followed in the combat zone. "The contracting system failed to ensure that properly trained and vetted linguist and interrogator personnel were hired to support operations at Abu Ghraib," according to the Fay-Jones Report.[16]

"If the linguist is Kurdish, and the accused is Arabic, there's already a bias," Mawiri said. "If he is an Arab, a Sunni, he's a terrorist. He's a motherfucker. That's the word that comes out of their mouths. And not just one or two linguists. Many said it. If it's a Kurdish detainee, they say, 'Oh, these people have suffered for so long. That's why they're stealing.' Or, 'No, that can't be—.' It doesn't take a rocket scientist to figure out what's going on."

One morning, Mawiri recalls, he and a group of soldiers went on a routine visit to a village near Kirkuk to speak with local leaders about fixing a water well in the area. Mawiri's roommate, a heavyset American Kurdish linguist in his fifties, also employed by a private military contractor, decided to come along. Mawiri knocked on the door of a tribal leader's house. Nobody answered. Three villagers walked past. Mawiri looked over at them and asked if they knew where the tribal chief was. The villagers shrugged.

"[The other interpreter] shouted out, 'They're fucking lying!'" Mawiri says.

The interpreter charged toward the villagers. The soldiers cranked up their weapons. "They're about to shoot people," explains Mawiri. "The villagers don't know where the chief is. Not everybody knows where the chief is. Maybe the chief is out of town. I ask them a question, and they give me an answer. I translate the answer. That's all we're here for. [The interpreter] says, 'Well, they're Arabs.' I mean—he hated Arabs so bad. He would do anything to hurt them."

"He and the other translators were Americans," Mawiri says, grabbing his belly with his hands in a fit of agitation and hiking it up as if it were the folds in a baggy sweatshirt. "But they had more allegiance and loyalty to their tribe and family than to the military. When they got there, the Kurdish linguists became lobbyists for the Kurdish cause. The Shia linguists became linguists for the Shia cause. Kurds were turning in Arabs. Turkmen were turning in—you know—whatever. Shia were turning in Sunnis. Excuse my language, it was a cluster F. And who got burned? American soldiers and Arab Sunnis."

TORTURE FOR PROFIT

Birmingham, Michigan, attorney Shereef Akeel says he first heard about the abuse of detainees at Abu Ghraib in March 2004—several weeks before the scandal broke. He had developed a reputation among Arabic speakers in the Detroit metro area and received a visit from a man who said he needed legal help. The visitor, a forty-two-year-old car broker, walked into the office and told Akeel that he had been beaten and tortured at Abu Ghraib. They talked for a long time about what had happened at the prison "The American personnel knew that it was a free-for-all," says Akeel, recalling what he had heard from the former prisoner.[17]

Akeel soon joined forces with Burke and her legal team, a group that has included Jonathan Pyle and Judith Chomsky, both of Philadelphia; Jennifer M. Green of the Center for Constitutional Rights; and Riva Khoshaba of Washington. On June 9, 2004, lawyers filed the suit *Saleh v. Titan* in federal court in San Diego and held a press conference at the National Press Club in Washington. The suit in various filings, has named four individuals who worked for private contractors; Titan Corporation, a company that sent approximately 4,000 interpreters to Iraq; and CACI PT Inc. and CACI International, Inc., which sent up to sixty employees to Iraq to work as interrogators at various times between August 2003 and August 2005. The suit accused the interrogators and interpreters of torture, rape, and murder and asked for an unspecified amount in damages.[18]

A lawyer representing CACI, John F. O'Connor, said in a statement posted on the company Web site that the lawsuit tries "to twist and invent facts in an attempt to dictate the United States' policies in Iraq, and to defame and extort financial compensation from CACI." In addition, CACI posted a September 27, 2006, statement on its Web site. "No CACI employee has ever been charged with any misconduct in connection with incidents at Abu Ghraib." "CACI assisted the Army with gathering much needed intelligence in an effort to save lives and safeguard our troops during dangerous and hostile wartime conditions."[19] Titan spokesman Evan Goetz refused to comment about the lawsuit but said the company would "vigorously defend against allegations that Titan committed any wrongdoing."[20]

On August 11, 2004, Akeel traveled to Iraq and interviewed approximately twenty other men and women who had been held at Abu Ghraib. Akeel says he thought it was important to see events at the prison through "the detainees' eyes." That year, staff members of *Michigan Lawyers Weekly* named Akeel a "Lawyer of the Year" for his work to help "tortured Iraqis put Abu Ghraib horrors behind them."[21]

Akeel and Burke were not the only ones who watched events unfold in the Iraq war and the global war on terror with its increasing reliance on private contractors, botched reconstruction projects in Iraq, and reports on detainee abuse and thought about turning to the U.S. courts for a remedy. More than forty cases involving rendition, abuse and torture, including *Saleh v. Titan*, have been filed since 2003. *Saleh v. Titan* and a copycat suit, *Ibrahim v. Titan*, are the only civil actions accusing private contractors of torture and abuse in Iraq. These cases are being closely watched because if they succeed in winning fees for their plaintiffs and fees for the lawyers involved, other cases will doubtless follow.

The *Saleh v. Titan* legal team has relied both on the Alien Tort Claims

Act of 1789, which was originally designed to combat pirates on the open seas, and the Racketeer Influenced and Corrupt Organizations Act (RICO) of 1970.[22] Both have been used by human-rights groups to hold U.S. companies responsible for wrongdoing in other countries. For these reasons, *Saleh v. Titan* has been applauded by human-rights lawyers and activists who see them not only as a recourse for Iraqis who have suffered in American custody but also as a way of uncovering the truth behind a government policy that may have led to their torture.

Saleh v. Titan is an especially complex case. For the Alien Tort Claims Act, Burke had to show that the contractors did, in fact, harm the detainees. RICO, meanwhile, is the "workhorse" of the suit in that it allows for the tripling of damages and attorneys' fees, according to legal experts. It's also a lot trickier. For RICO, Burke had to establish that the contractors conspired with government officials to torture detainees in order to increase their profit margin. One of the complaints in the lawsuit concerns employment practices.

"They didn't take any caution in who they hired," explains Burke.[23] Many of the interpreters seemed ill suited for their jobs, and the slipshod hiring practices and training, she says, contributed to the mistreatment of detainees. Military officers seem to agree that contractors were not always adequately prepared for their duties before they arrived in Iraq. In the Fay-Jones Report, for example, Fay wrote, "The contracting system failed to ensure that properly trained and vetted linguist and interrogator personnel were hired to support operations at Abu Ghraib."[24]

In some cases, Burke says, the contractors ended up treating the detainees in a horrific manner. The complaints in the lawsuit, as Judge James Robertson of Federal District Court in the District of Columbia wrote in his June 29, 2006, opinion, include "allegations of nearly unspeakable acts of torture and other mistreatment by interpreters and interrogators."[25]

Not surprisingly, Burke's legal team—and their strategy—has detractors.

Angela B. Styles, a former administrator for federal procurement policy at the Office of Management and Budget in Washington, says she believes it will be hard for the lawyers to prove a profit motive was involved in the torture. "By being cruel and torturing people you're going to increase profits?" she says on the telephone and lets out a laugh. "It's necessary to say it. In order to prove their claim, they have to have a profit motive. But it doesn't seem to be logical. This case doesn't look like it was written to win."[26]

A research fellow at New York University School of Law's Center on Law and Security, Christian Lucky, agrees that certain passages in the complaint are jarring. "It reads strangely. You think, 'Gosh, they conspired to commit torture in order to get more business?'" he said. "I have to go through the looking glass and say, 'What is their business model?' Then you think, 'This is a company that does interrogation services. They are saying, 'Look, torture will help you, Pentagon. We tortured this guy, and we found this information out.' You ask yourself, 'What is their motivation—patriotism? No, profits.'"[27]

Civilian contractors played a key role in the operations at Abu Ghraib. Some appeared in the infamous photographs and may have contributed to the abuse of detainees. And it was civilian contractors, in fact, who helped turn the Iraqi prison into a U.S.-run detention facility in 2003.

CHAPTER FIVE

THIRTY MILES FROM CAMP VICTORY

SADDAM HAD HIS KILLING CHAMBERS AT ABU GHRAIB AND THE SAND WAS LIKE DUST, ASHES, AND IT WOULD JUST PUFF WHEN YOU STEPPED ON IT. I WONDERED, "DID SADDAM CREMATE PEOPLE?"

—Ken Davis, 372nd Military Police Company,
September to December 2003, Abu Ghraib Prison.
"What Was Asked of Us," by Trish Wood[1]

General Karpinski, fifty-three, is five feet, eight-and-a-half inches tall, with a sturdy frame and long, blonde hair she wears pulled back in clips. On a July 2003 morning she stood near a lake at Camp Victory and felt the cool air blowing across the surface of the water. The lake was smooth as glass. Suddenly, several gray, plate-shaped flounder broke the surface of the water and flung their bodies in the air.

The fish flew six feet high, twisted their bodies in the desert sun, and then slid back into the water. Then they did it again. "I wondered, *Why would the fish jump like that?*" she tells me more than three years later over a cup of tea in an airport café in Newark, New Jersey.

Flounder are bottom-feeder fish. Yet they were leaping toward the sky. The 130-degree heat and the gray-green water, choked with weeds, must have been unbearable. "I wondered, 'Are they boiling alive?'" she recalls. "'Are they popping out so they can save themselves?'" They were behaving in a way that seemed perverse and unnatural—apparently in response to the extraordinarily difficult circumstances in which they had found themselves. After watching the specacle, she climbed in a military vehicle and headed thirty miles away to check on the troops at Abu Ghraib.[2]

THE HAUNTING OF ABU GHRAIB

Major combat operations in Iraq were officially over on May 1, 2003. Administration officials, lawmakers, and military leaders in Washington spoke about a political and economic campaign to help Iraqis ease the transition from a despotic regime to build the foundation for a democratic government with a vibrant civil society and respect for human rights. In Baghdad, though, Iraqis had more pressing needs. The electricity kept going out. Looters ransacked abandoned buildings and held up stores and bakeries, and mothers kept their children home from school because they worried about their safety. American troops tried to prevent excessive violence by maintaining a presence on the streets. They were also looking for weapons stored in farmhouses and basements and trying to develop ties with tribal leaders to help rebuild their communities. At the time, there were semi-frequent "Elvis sightings," or reports on Saddam Hussein's whereabouts, during their frantic search for the former dictator.

By the late summer and fall of 2003, American soldiers began to arrest an increasing number of Iraqi civilians in their efforts both to find Saddam loyalists and to weaken the insurgency. During one twenty-four-hour period in August, said U.S. Army spokesman Colonel Guy Shields at a press briefing on August 18, 2003, in Baghdad, coalition troops conducted fifteen raids and detained 124 individuals under suspicion of criminal activity or attacks on coalition forces.[3] As the number of arrests went up, so did the number of people held in detention facilities. It was not long before the prisons and jails were filled beyond capacity levels. Americans needed a place to keep all the prisoners.

At an August 2, 2003, conference on prisons, Captain Errol A. Huffman, a military official who had been helping to set up new detention facilities in Iraq, described Abu Graib as a crucial part of the new criminal justice system. According to a Ministry of Justice report, "Financial Overview: Iraqi Correctional Services," fourteen facilities had been designed to hold the rapidly growing prisoner population. Because of its location, size, and existing facilities, Abu Ghraib, which had been undergoing a $1.75 million, six-month renovation managed by private contractors, was considered to be the main detention center.[4]

The Abu Ghraib prison—with its five separate building complexes, eight guard towers, and a fifteen-foot wall surrounding the premises—was in better shape than most of the other prisons that had been functioning under Saddam. The cells, some of them measuring three feet by three feet, were located in low-slung, creamy white buildings that can be seen in digital photographs in a Joint Forces Intelligence Command document, "Abu Ghurayb Prison Complex," that cited an October 2002 CIA report as its source.[5]

Showers and toilets, dining halls, medical stations, and even a printing press, were available along with other facilities needed for prisoners and staff. In addition, Abu Ghraib was located in a central part of Iraq, twelve miles northwest of Baghdad, according to a Joint Interrogation and Debriefing Center report presented at the prison in October 2003,[6] making it easier for Americans to transport detainees there after they had been captured in various parts of the country. According to a military report shown to me by an officer who worked at the prison, Abu Ghraib was "the largest and most suitable prison site for dangerous and long term criminals within the country of Iraq."[7]

In fact, it would have been hard to find a worse place for the largest American-run prison in Iraq. The infrastructure was there for a reason: Saddam had kept up to 30,000 prisoners at Abu Ghraib. A Coalition Provisional Authority officer argued against using it as a central holding facility for Iraq prisoners under American control, saying, "It was no different than going into Dachau and saying, 'We're going to use this as a prison facility.'"[8] A United Nations official visited the prison and said it should not be used for Iraqi detainees, and a human-rights researcher agreed, writing a paper entitled "The Ghosts of Abu Ghraib" in order to alert U.S. officials to the problems of setting up operations at the prison.[9]

There was no escaping the ghost of Saddam. His portrait appears in several places on the prison grounds: in one mural, he is smiling and wearing a white uniform; two swords are crossed above his head, and four white doves flutter beside him.[10] It was a reminder of his dictatorship—a time when the prison supposedly had rape rooms, torture chambers, and gallows. As many as 4,000 prisoners were executed at Abu Ghraib in 1984, according to an October 2003 report by the American military. One hundred twenty-two prisoners were executed in February and March 2000, and 23 were killed in October 2001.[11]

Saddam had burned some of the facilities, trying to erase the horrors of the past.[12] But the hanging ropes and the death chamber remained. Military contractors, Coalition Provisional Authority officials, and officers who were planning the renovations expressed concern about its history and how that would influence public opinion in Iraq. "Unfortunately the Abu Ghraib prison complex includes a building where death sentences were carried out," according to a July 2003 army report, "Abu Ghraib Prison." "An appropriate memorial is being considered for the site and attempts will be made to include ideas and desires of human rights groups and organizations representing former prisoners."[13]

Abu Ghraib posed more than a PR problem. It was situated in the middle of the Sunni Triangle. Some of the people who lived in the area were raising funds for an armed resistance against American troops. Others were stockpiling ammunition, grenades, walkie-talkies, and weapons to be used in building homemade bombs and launching attacks on Abu Ghraib.

"The Prison," as Abu Ghraib was known, was hastily planned, quickly rebuilt, and understaffed—mainly by soldiers who were poorly trained for their jobs or did not want to be there. Karpinski held a bachelor's degree in English/Secondary Education from Kean College of New Jersey, and she had no foreign language skills.[14] She was a corporate consultant for executive training programs based in Hilton Head, South Carolina, where she lived with her husband and an African grey parrot, Casey.[15] On August 5, 2003, Karpinski became responsible for overseeing the opening of the prison and assuring it ran smoothly.

NATURAL DEATH

The Baghdad Central Confinement Facility (BCCF), as Abu Ghraib was officially called, was divided into three camps. Each of them could hold several hundred detainees. Camp Ganci was named after a firefighter killed in the terrorist attacks of 9/11[16] and was designed to hold thieves, looters, assailants, and individuals accused of petty crimes. The prisoners were held in large tents until they had a chance to appear before judicial hearings. Camp Vigilant was designed for foreign fighters who opposed the new government in Iraq. Yet this camp, too, was overrun with small-time criminals and people who had gotten captured in raids—with few foreigners or terrorists among them.

Another area, which was known as the Hard Site or Tier 1A, was designed for "high-level" detainees accused of supporting armed resistance against coalition troops. This section looked like an American prison. There wre two levels, as shown in photographs, each with a long hallway flanked by prison cells on both sides. On the upper level, it was possible to stand in a hallway and look down and see what was happening on the ground floor.[17] Detainees arrived by military vehicle, and, within two weeks of the prison's reopening, five hundred individuals were being held in razor-wire pens. Despite the months of planning, though, the military staff and prison facilities were unprepared for the influx of detainees. One of the prisoners, Abdul-Sattar al-Kashani (he asked me to use a pseudonym for security reasons), a thirty-seven-year-old salesman for an oil-and-petroleum company, was injured by an IED (improvised explosive device) on August 4, 2003, in Mosul. His left leg had to be amputated, and his arm was severed below his elbow. Three and a half years after the incident, the flesh covering the stump of his arm pulsates, fontanel-like, when blood pulses through his arteries, and he walks with a battered wooden crutch held together with four screws and a busted rubber stopper. He had been accused of setting off the bomb and was taken to Abu Ghraib on or around September 4, 2003. He says he was surprised by the primitive quarters of the prison. After he arrived, he says, he found himself left alone on a patch of sand and gravel. "I was just lying there in a mattress in the sun," he tells me in a March 2006 interview.[18]

American soldiers and officers lived in concrete buildings. Prisoners like Kashani lived in tents that left them vulnerable to enemy attacks on the prison. On August 16, 2003, six detainees were killed when "three mortar rounds were fired into the Abu Ghraib prison," according to an October 2003 Joint Interrogation and Debriefing Center report. After the attacks, according to the report, instructions were provided for treating Iraqi and American victims. "In the event US casualties occur—perform immediate first aid," states the PowerPoint presentation. "In the event detainee casualties occur—MPs will direct all assistance where and when necessary."[19] In other words, Americans should be treated promptly if they are wounded. Iraqi victims may be treated differently.

During this time, the medical staff at the prison was limited. A medical officer from Ashley, Pennsylvania, talked about the situation with an investigator from the U.S. Army Criminal Investigation Command (CID). [The army investigative unit was founded in 1918 as the Criminal Investigation Division and is still known by its original acronym.] According to the officer's July 11, 2004, sworn statement, which is included in an agent's Investigative Report, the medic "examined between 800—900 detainees daily" in the Medical Section/Operations of Baghdad Central Corrections in August 2003.[20] The prisoners were dirty, hungry, and dressed in tattered prison or hospital gowns. Many needed medical attention. "Joint doctrine and policy defines a requirement for medical screening of all detainees," according to the Fay-Jones Report, portions of which were cited in the Office of the Surgeon General of the Army's "Final Report: Assessment of Detainee Medical Operations" (April 13, 2005). "This requirement was not being met at Abu Ghraib. Additionally, there was an absence of medical documentation for some detainees, and a general absence of a centralized management system for medical evaluations. The report also concludes that medical personnel are . . . found to have some degree of responsibility or complicity in the abuse that occurred at Abu Ghraib."

Some of the medical personnel working at Abu Ghraib in the fall of 2003 were upset over the treatment of detainees. Three of these individuals said they felt "conflicted" about their roles in assisting detainees who were being interrogated at the facility in the fall of 2003. They described their "concern about the lack of mental health services for detainees, especially the children," according to the army surgeon general's report.

It may seem surprising to some people in the U.S. that children were being held at Abu Ghraib and in other U.S.-run detention facilities in Iraq. Yet dozens, and perhaps even more, have been held in U.S. custody, including one child that did not survive. In the spring of 2003, a child died of tuberculosis while being confined at Camp Cropper, a detention facility that is located at Baghdad International Airport, according to a physician who is cited in a footnote (#30) in the army surgeon general's report. The physician had previously complained of having inadequate medical supplies to treat detainees, even "getting into arguments" with his commander over the situation. The lack of supplies had severe consequences; the physician described "one child hemorrhaging from his cavity TB and dying." Afterward, the physician developed a medical therapy for TB patients, relying on a series of drugs to treat the disease among the prisoners.[21]

Steven H. Miles, MD, author of *Oath Betrayed: Torture, Medical Complicity, and the War on Terror*, says the death of the juvenile could have been easily prevented. "TB is identified in the Geneva Conventions as being so endemic in prisons that you have to screen for it," he tells me. "But the U.S. was not doing that. So you have a child dying without treatment because of our failure to comply with Geneva standards in U.S. facilities."[22]

Given the conditions at detention facilities, it is perhaps not surprising that prison officials at Abu Ghraib were barely able to process all the detainees or maintain records on their arrests. According to a February 2004 International Committee of the Red Cross report on the treatment of detainees in Iraq, there was no "satisfactorily functioning system of notification to the families of captured or arrested persons, even though hundreds of arrests continue to be carried out every week."[23]

There was no standard procedure for the discipline of prisoners, either. "Minor offenders are forced to kneel in front of the guard tower," according to a military report, "Baghdad Central Correctional Facility," which examined the custody and control of detainees. "Major offenders are segregated by being handcuffed to the inside of a connex with the doors open."[24] In many cases, the detainees were not interrogated or questioned about the insurgency. Instead, they languished in stifling heat, praying and reading the Koran aloud. Some did not survive. According to an August 11, 2003, CID report, "Several detainees with pre-existing medical conditions died while in BCCF [Abu Ghraib] due to the nature of the prison complex."[25]

On August 11, 2003, according to government documents, a detainee identified as Wathik Salah Mihdy asked an American officer for help because he was having chest pain. He was "staggering and falling over himself," said the sergeant. The officer checked Mihdy's vital signs and sent him back to the compound. Thirty minutes later, Mihdy was dead. A group of prisoners gathered around his tent, chanting prayers, then picked up his body and carried it around the prison grounds. The cause of death was listed in an autopsy report as "Myocardial Infarction." In other words, a "natural death."[26] That same day, a group of detainees brought the body of "a 65 inches tall, 180 pounds (estimated) Iraqi male who appears to be older than 50 years" to American guards, according to an October 2, 2003, Armed Forces Institute of Pathology Autopsy Examination Report. "He appeared to have been dead for some time," it added. His cause of death was listed as "cardiovascular disease."[27]

Two days later, a group of detainees carried to the prison gate the body of a "thin, muscular 70 inch tall, 150 pounds (estimated) [man] whose appearance is consistent with an estimated age of 40–60 years," according to an October 24, 2003, Armed Forces Institute of Pathology Autopsy Examination Report. Cause of death: cardiovascular disease.[28] At 10:30 PM on August 20, 2003, a detainee was discovered to be "unalert and unresponsive," according to his August 21, 2003, death certificate. Ten minutes later he was "pulseless, unresponsive, and not breathing." He was pronounced dead of "myocardial infarction" at 11:00 PM.[29]

Within a twelve-day period, from August 8 through August 20, 2003, five men died of heart attacks at the prison. One prisoner, Najem Abed Mohamed, who was "approximately 55-65 years old," had diabetes, according to a June 4, 2004, CID report, and had been taking daily medication. His condition was aggravated by a two–day hunger strike in which he refused food, water, and medication. In the autopsy report, his death, too, is described as "natural."[30] Another detainee, Dham Spah, was pronounced dead on August 16, 2003, after an eight-day hunger strike. Like the others, he died of "Myocardial Infarction," a "natural death."[31] On August 20, a detainee helped another prisoner, Emad Kazen Taleb, to a medic because Taleb had been "gasping for air," according to a CID report. Still, he "was breathing and had a pulse." He died shortly afterward—another "natural death," according to a military report.[32] On September 3, according to a Situation Report (STRP) an army officer showed me, one of the detainees attempted suicide.[33]

Records of medical examinations of prisoners are hard come by. It is therefore nearly impossible to find out what the condition of the prisoners were when they arrived at Abu Ghraib and, therefore, whether their deaths were caused by mistreatment, harsh prison conditions, or preexisting medical problems. Recently, however, an American physician, Allen S. Keller, director of the Bellevue/NYU Program for Survivors of Torture at New York's Bellevue Hospital, was given a chance to examine two former prisoners and interview them about their incarceration. His report is the first forensic evaluation in the U.S. medical literature of former Abu Ghraib detainees who claim to have suffered from mistreatment.[34] Keller provides a detailed picture of what the detainees experienced at Abu Ghraib and how the American soldiers and interrogators, as well as the difficult living conditions at the prison, may have contributed to the death of a prisoner at the camp.

Keller spoke with one former detainee, a thirty-one-year-old police officer identified as B.R., approximately two years after his release from Abu Ghraib. They met in Amman, Jordan, in February 2005. (A producer for *60 Minutes Weekday* requested that Keller examine B.R. as part of their efforts to investigate the crimes at Abu Ghraib.) Over a six-hour period, B.R. provided his medical history and described what happened to him and to his sixty-three-year-old father, a local tribal leader, while they were detained at Abu Ghraib in the winter of 2003. They lived in "a large canvas tent with wooden plank floors," wrote Keller. "They were given two blankets, one to put on the wood and one to cover themselves with," he wrote. "'It was a very light blanket and it was very cold,' notes B.R." His father was "repeatedly interrogated." Afterward, he had bruises on his body.

"One evening, about six weeks after his arrest, B.R.'s father began experiencing shortness of breath and chest/abdominal pain. Prior to imprisonment, his father had no known medical problems. B.R. reports that he repeatedly notified a U.S. military guard that his father was sick and asked for a doctor, but was repeatedly rebuffed and threatened with solitary confinement," Keller wrote. "After several hours and multiple requests, the guard finally sought medical care. A nurse came to the tent, took his father's blood pressure and gave him a pill, but did not examine him or ask him any questions. The pain continued over the next several hours. As B.R. held his father in his arms, his father stopped breathing and died."

"B.R.'s father likely died of a myocardial infarction. While B.R.'s father had no knowledge of prior cardiac disease, the mistreatment B.R. reports his father suffered would have exacerbated the chances of him having a fatal myocardial infarction. B.R. reports that no military investigators spoke with him concerning his father's death."

Keller examined the autopsy report for B.R.'s father and an army investigative report about his death. "The cause of death listed on the autopsy report was 'atherosclerotic cardiovascular disease resulting in cardiac tamponade,'" he wrote. "The manner of death is reported on the death certificate as 'natural.' The timing of the events reported by B.R., including when his father was brought to the gate in the blanket (apparently already dead), is consistent with what is in the investigation report. However, the army's investigation report does not mention any of the events B.R. reports occurred prior to the death of his father, including alleged mistreatment, repeated requests for medical care, and the reported inadequate medical evaluation. A subsequent army memorandum notes that "The investigation did not conduct interviews of those witnesses who found the victim and took his body to the military police guards. There was no effort made to interview the alleged brother and son of the victim who were reportedly present at the prison at the time of death."

"B.R.'s father's death appears to be an example of at least an inadequate medical investigation," wrote Keller.[35] A similar conclusion was reached by an army investigator on another case. Military investigations into prisoners' deaths were often cursory and incomplete; some reports were less than eight pages long. In a May 22, 2004, memo to the commander of the Fort Belvoir, Virginia-based headquarters of the CID, for example, a special agent said the investigation into detainee Najem Abed Mohamed's death was "operationally insufficient and was administratively insufficient."

"The investigation did not conduct a crime scene investigation or explain why such an examination was not conducted," wrote the CID agent. "The investigation did not conduct any interviews of people with the victim at the time of the incident. A medical person mentioned in a narrative summary provided by a U.S. Army medical personnel alleged the victim had a preexisting medical condition aggravated by a self-imposed hunger strike, the investigation did not obtain any medical records or conduct interviews to substantiate the information."[36]

The deaths of Mihdy, Spah, Mohamed, and other prisoners—whether by hunger strike, diabetes, or some other cause—will likely remain a mystery. It is clear, though, that conditions at Abu Ghraib were harsh. Perhaps not surprisingly, many of the prisoners were threatening to riot. Some were getting help from the outside.

A SCENE OF CARNAGE

In August and September, insurgents were starting to infiltrate the confines of the prison by posing as contract interpreters, janitors, and food-service workers. Approximately three hundred contractors were working on the renovations of wings five through nine at the prison, according to an army report on policy and procedures at Baghdad Central Correctional Facility. "None of the contractors are badged, and they are not individually escorted within the facility," according to the report.[37] It was easy for them to roam the prison grounds. One civilian contractor worker, a Sterling Heights, Michigan, interpreter named Leonard Acho, tells me that spies were able to infiltrate the prison while he was working there and that he and others were put on alert and told to watch out for suspected insurgents or collaborators. "Nobody was allowed to bring phones in there," he says. "It was my job to look for them."

"We got bombed heavy," he says, descrbing the dangers they faced from insurgents outside the prison walls. "It feels like it's right on your head."[38]

An official with the Iraqi Reconstruction and Development Council, an organization that had been created by the Pentagon in February 2003 to assist in temporary governance, warned about ties between insurgents and prisoners. In a November 12, 2003, memo (Subject: "Smuggling of messages from VIP Abu Ghraib Prisoners"), the government official said drivers employed by a private contractor that delivered meals to the prison were "exchanging letters between suspected terrorists" and "high ranking Ba'athist and other dangerous prisoners." During this time, the attacks on the Americans living inside the prison had become increasingly accurate.[39]

Prisoners, soldiers, officers—everybody at the prison—were frightened by the violence. On September 17, 2003, the night a supervising officer Lieutenant Colonel Jordan arrived at Abu Ghraib, there was a mortar attack. It was unsettling, but, luckily, nobody was hurt. The following morning, Jordan explored the compound and tried to figure out ways to make the prison safe from future assaults. He was especially concerned about two soldiers, Specialist Lunsford B. Brown II and Sergeant David Travis Friedrich, who were responsible for the prison's communications system. Most of the soldiers lived and worked in cement buildings that helped protect them from enemy attack. Brown and Friedrich, however, operated out of a makeshift office in a utility tent that was located outdoors.[40]

Brown, twenty-seven, was a former football player with a broad chest and a booming voice.[41] He had studied political science at North Carolina Agricultural and Technical State University in Greensboro.[42] He and his wife, Sherrie Wheeler Brown, gave birth to their daughter, Amber, in June 2003 while he was stationed at Camp Victory.[43] He could hardly contain his excitement over Amber's birth, as Sam Provance recalls. Brown climbed up on one of the guard towers and shouted out the news of his daughter.[44] That summer and fall, Brown worked as a driver for Colonel Pappas. Brown had a calm demeanor as he drove their vehicle along the Iraqi highways, checking for snipers and homemade bombs. "A real hero, not some movie actor, or some comic-strip hero," wrote a soldier, Specialist Sean E. Welch, about his friend Brown on the Fallen Heroes Memorial. "By far the most intimidating and yet gentle man I have ever had the pleasure of meeting."[45]

After seeing the tent where Brown and Friedrich worked, Jordan asked Colonel Pappas if the two soldiers could work in an old laundry building roughly fifty feet from the tent. The building was under the control of the Coalition Provisional Authority, and apparently Colonel Pappas did not have the authority to allow the soldiers to work there. The request was turned down, Brown and Friedrich remained in the tent. Jordan put sandbags around it. They hoped for the best.[46]

At 9:54 PM on September 20, two mortar explosions killed Brown and Friedrich while they were in the tent. Provance, Jordan, and another officer went to the area a few days later to clean up the remaining debris. "What worried us most of all was what we knew was waiting for us—the scene of the mortar attack, where our buddies were blown across the prison grounds," Provance wrote. "We were not just being sent on a mission, but a noble mission," he explained. "We were to pick up where our fallen comrades had left off, carrying on their work, facing the same dangers they had, and if we got ourselves killed, we would be joining them in that place." Most of the area around the tent had been cleaned up by the time they arrived. Brown's belongings had been carted off, along with the personal effects of Friedrich. The tent was in a shambles. One mortar shell had punctured the tent's canvas, leaving gaping slashes in the sides. Shrapnel had torn thousands of tiny holes in the material. Provance stood inside the tent, transfixed by the sight. "Beams of light crisscrossed beautifully through all the holes," he wrote. Brown and Friedrich did not have a chance. The hardest part—for Provance and Jordan—was the fact their friends' deaths could have been easily prevented.

"The whole time that they were being attacked for months, constantly exposed, they were just feet away from an empty building, where they would have been more than safe—the same place where we were now moving it all to," Provance wrote in an e-mail to me. "I inquired as to why they hadn't moved in sooner, and what I was told was even more unbelievable. They said that they had in fact requested this same move much earlier, but that the man in overall charge, my brigade commander, had denied that request."[47]

On the Fallen Heroes Memorial Web site, a page is devoted to Brown. One posting says:

DEAR DADDY,

I am sorry you never got to hold me in your arms but I heard you kept me close to your heart. Although I never met you, I love you so much and I am very proud of you. You will always be my hero.

Love your baby girl,

AMBER[48]

The sense of frustration and anger, as well as grief over lost comrades, was palpable among the soldiers at Abu Ghraib. Their requests for backup support and resources were often ignored. They faced hundreds of malnourished, frustrated detainees on the prison compound every day. At the same time, they were threatened by an enemy that moved in darkness beyond the prison walls. As Provance stood in the utility tent where the two soldiers had died, he says he tried to imagine "the shock and madness of what it must have been like." Then abruptly, one of the officers, "in a strictly business tone, ordered us to take it all down. I didn't want to, still being hit with pangs of sadness and now feeling such an odd attachment to this decrepit tent, but we had a job to do. It was also still daylight, and once the night fell, the last place you wanted to be was anywhere outside."[49]

PART II

WAR CRIMES

CHAPTER SIX

COUNTERINSURGENCY OPERATIONS

On the morning of September 24, 2003—five weeks after the suicide bombing of a United Nations compound in Baghdad killed twenty-three people, including top envoy Sergio Vieira de Mello, signaling a more intense phase of Iraqi insurgency—a group of American soldiers burst into a villa near the banks of the Tigris River in Samarra. After the team rushed in, one of the soldiers pointed his rifle at a woman, Selwa Abdullah, who lived there (she asked me to use a pseudonym for her and her family to protect their safety) and prepared to arrest her and take her to prison. Two of her adult daughters and her two-year-old grandchild began screaming. Selwa, and everyone in the villa, was terrified—and with good reason. A different group of soldiers had raided their house four months earlier, and Selwa remembered vividly what had happened that night.

On May 24, the soldiers had stormed across the villa's marble floors, rifled through family photographs, and searched inside a French cabinet. They confiscated the family's life savings and seized Selwa's husband, Sherif, who had been trained as a mechanic and, under Saddam Hussein, had risen through the Ministry of Commerce ranks until he became a director. Ever since her husband's arrest, Selwa, fifty-five, had lived in fear that the soldiers would come back to interrogate her or search the house again. But she never suspected they would take her away, too. "My daughter started shouting and screaming, 'Why are you taking my mother? You took my father!'" Selwa remembers.[1] Selwa was eventually taken to a series of U.S.-run detention facilities, including Abu Ghraib, and was released without charge on January 20, 2004.[2]

On December 7, less than a year after being arrested, Selwa sits in a room in Le Royal Hotel in Amman, across from twenty-eight-year-old Riva Khoshaba, an Assyrian-American attorney who was born in Iraq, an interpreter, and me. Warm and outgoing, Selwa quickly puts us at ease. Wearing a stylish black jacket and dripping with gold and jewels, she looks like the kind of woman you might see in a specialty food store on New York's Upper West Side, bustling around the place and filling her basket with spicy sausages and boxes of tea. She has creamy skin and hazel eyes, and she appears rested despite the fact that, two days earlier, she had embarked on a risky journey through war-torn Iraq to meet us at the hotel. She tried to come to Jordan directly, but she found the border closed in the wake of a recent explosion. So she drove to the Syrian border, which was also closed, and spent the night. The next day, she made it here. Through the interpreter, she tells us the story of her family and the events that led to her arrest.

Sherif had worked for the Ministry of Commerce for decades. They met when she was eighteen and he was thirty-four. She wasn't exactly thrilled. "I thought he was too old," she says. He was tall, dark, and "Italian-looking," though, and he won her heart with romantic gestures. He would tell her how much he missed her when she was away, and he used to sing for her and recite poetry he had memorized. She can still quote the Bedouin verse he told her during their courtship: "Your sweat is like pearls that sparkle," she recalls.

In the late 1990s, Sherif received an award from Saddam Hussein for a water-management system he had devised and had his picture taken with him. But, Selwa insists, Sherif was not close to Saddam.

"He worked for the government, and we supported [the regime]. But my husband was not important at all," she says.

REALITY CHECK

Were the former detainees like Selwa exaggerating their abuse? Were they remembering things wrong? (Many of their stories had a nightmarish, hallucinogenic quality.) Worse, were they lying? There might be financial rewards for those who are plaintiffs in the lawsuit. As I was introduced to various "torture victims," as members of the U.S. legal team described Selwa and other clients, I occasionally wondered if I was being duped.

"How do you know they're not lying?" I ask Nadia (her name has been changed for security reasons), one of the Baghdad-based members of the legal team, as we sit in an airy hotel café, with Alanis Morissette playing over the loudspeakers. At a nearby table, a tribal sheik (and putative plaintiff) eats pistachios and spits shells into a saucer. "When I sit in front of you, you don't know if I'm telling the truth," she says. "But when you look into my eyes, you find out. Of course, sometimes you get confused. It's natural. But when you depend upon your feeling, you can tell."[3]

While I was in Amman, I hired Ranya Kadri, a "fixer" who works for the *New York Times* and the *Washington Post*, to translate my interview with Selwa. Kadri, a kickboxing aficionado, has a reputation for being tough with customs officials, nosy hotel butlers, and journalists. ("John Burns is afraid of me," she tells me, half-jokingly, speaking of the *New York Times* correspondent who won a Pulitzer Prize in 1997 for reporting on the Taliban.) Before the interview, she pulls me aside. "Are you sure she's not trying to trick you?" she asks. "I've seen it happen before. They use fake death certificates and everything."

After speaking for nearly two hours about her detention, Selwa steps out of the small conference room for a break. Kadri and I walk together into a hotel bar, and Kadri turns to me and says, "I believe her. She says she likes Saddam Hussein and other things she knows she shouldn't say. She's the real thing."

AN INTERROGATION IN SAMARRA

Frank Gregory Ford, fifty-two, a former California National Guard sergeant who served in Samarra in May and June 2003, led the raid—a group of ten soldiers—on Selwa's villa in May 2003. Ford explains why they arrested Sherif. "He was considered Saddam Hussein's right-hand man," explains Ford, who served in the military for thirty-two years and has worked as a Coast Guard medical corpsman. (He is a retired corrections officer at Folsom State Prison in Represa, and he now lives in Sea Ranch, California.) He explains that an "in-house" source (someone who worked closely with the American troops at the local military installation), as well as an Iraqi who had known the family for decades, told them about Sherif.[4]

A military official based in Baghdad who was not authorized to reveal detailed information about the suspects spoke to me under the condition that he remain anonymous. He says Sherif "was listed as a Baath Party member." One of his daughters, Siara, a thirty-two-year-old civil engineer and the wife of Nabil, had been a mistress of Saddam Hussein, the military official claims. On the telephone in Baghdad, he read passages to me from an investigative file about the family. Selwa, says the military official, "was believed to be involved with financing and organizing insurgent activities."

Selwa says she knew nothing about the insurgency and that she was framed. She believes a tenant living in a property that she and her husband owned "snitched on us. We have a saying in Samarra," she says. "Everything is forgiven except wealth."

When the troops arrived at the villa, Sherif was asleep. "I said in English, 'My husband is a very old man,'" she recalls, explaining how she had asked the soldiers to treat him gently. Instead, the troops forced Sherif out of bed and took him to a military vehicle parked neaby and then returned to the house. Ford rummaged through a French cabinet and found photos of Sherif, including at least one that showed him shaking hands with Saddam. Ford also found three plastic bags filled with stacks of U.S. dollars. Then Selwa, as he recalls, burst into the bedroom, screaming, "Don't take my money!"

Selwa and her family owned farms and three money-exchange shops in Baghdad. After the fall of Saddam, she explains, they had taken their earnings and stored them in their house. Some of the money had been kept in the bedroom cabinet. But the bulk of their life savings (a total of $315,000 in U.S. dollars and $12,000 in Iraqi dinar) was wrapped up in paper and hidden underneath a slab of meat in the freezer. It was confiscated by the American forces, according to Ford and Selwa. (The seizing of assets, says Ford, is standard practice during raids, especially when suspects are accused of providing financial support to the insurgency. Many of the former detainees I met, however, said money and property taken by American troops was not returned after they were released from U.S. custody.)

At about 1:30 in the morning, several hours after arriving at the villa, Ford helped bring Sherif back to army headquarters at a local police station, a crumbling, two-story building with jail cells on the top floor and offices downstairs. The building had an interrogation room with metal hooks attached to the ceiling where prisoners were once hung by their arms. Ford tried to show people living in the area that he and the American soldiers were different from the Iraqi officers who had once terrorized suspects. He decorated a conference room, a "salon," as he called it, with a Persian rug and invited tribal leaders over for tea. In this way, he tried to encourage them to cooperate with the American forces and to help track down the insurgents who lived in the area.

That night, Ford says, he was pleased they had captured Sherif, a valuable suspect—a government official who apparently knew Saddam supporters who lived in the vicinity. Ford knew they would need to use a sophisticated method of interrogation if they wanted Sherif to reveal information about the insurgency. "He was a crafty old guy and smarter than we were," he explains. But that night, the interrogation methods seemed anything but subtle. One of the intelligence agents in the military unit started shouting insults at Sherif. "He said, 'Hey, your daughter's a filthy slut and right now she's being screwed by Saddam Hussein,'" recalls Ford. Things only got worse. Sherif was taken to

Ford's salon. One of the interrogators—a Greek American, as Ford recalls—rolled up a newspaper and immediately started beating him. Afterward, the interrogators began asking Sherif questions. Every time they got a wrong answer, Ford says, they would hit him again. Sherif had said that he suffered from high-blood pressure, and Ford monitored his vital signs during the interrogation. His blood pressure shot up to 220/180. "It was completely through the roof," Ford recalls. Sherif looked like he was going to have a stroke.

"I said, 'Look, I think you need to take a break,'" Ford recalls. (Ford, who sees himself as a whistle-blower, claims the soldiers abused other prisoners at the police station, too. Yet an army officer who is familiar with military investigations into Ford's allegations but is not authorized to speak about the subject with the media tells me that Ford's "claims of detainee abuse were unsubstantiated."[5])

Sherif looked over at Ford. "He said, 'If you leave me here, I will die,'" Ford recalls. Ford stayed with him that evening. The interrogations continued after that, and Sherif continued to dodge their questions despite the abusive treatment. Eventually, he was sent to Abu Ghraib. It is difficult, if not impossible, to know for certain whether Sherif had the valuable intelligence that Ford and military officials believed he had, or whether he was simply the party functionary that Selwa claimed and had nothing of importance to share with Military Intelligence agents. (After speaking with individuals on both sides, I suspect the truth lies somewhere in between.) The outcome of his arrest is not in dispute, however. On April 6, 2004, nearly a year after his arrest, Sherif was killed in a mortar attack at Abu Ghraib.[6]

In the fall of 2003, after Selwa and Sherif were arrested by U.S. forces, approximately one-third of Iraqis said there were circumstances in which attacks against U.S. troops could be justified, according to Brookings Institution's Iraq Index. Yet American commanders, administration officials—and certainly the American public—had only a murky understanding of the opposition forces and the insurgency. U.S. officials consistently referred to the individuals who were attacking coalition forces as "terrorists," wrote Anthony H. Cordesman, a national security analyst at a Washington-based think tank, the Center for Strategic and

International Studies, in a December 2004 paper, "The Developing Iraqi Insurgency: Status at End—2004," and showed only a limited understanding of their enemy:

> The U.S. failed to come to grips with the Iraqi insurgency during the first year of U.S. occupation in virtually every important dimension. It was slow to react to the growth of the insurgency in Iraq, to admit it was largely domestic in character and to admit it had significant popular support. For all of 2003, and most of the first half of 2004, it referred to the attackers as terrorists, kept issuing estimates that they could not number more than 5,000, and claimed they were a mixture of outsider elements and diehard former loyalists. As late as July 2004, they were still talking about a core insurgent force of only 5,000, when many Coalition experts on the ground in Iraq saw the core as at least 12,000-16,000.

American military officers who assisted in the arrest and interrogation of Sherif seemed unable to obtain the intelligence they were seeking from him, at least according to Ford. Meanwhile, military leaders and administration officials had flawed and incomplete knowledge of the insurgency and seemed unable to come to grips with the widespread popularity of the movement against the U.S. occupation—despite indications from the population. "It largely ignored the warning provided by Iraqi opinion polls, and claimed that its political, economic, and security efforts were either successful or would soon become so. In short, it failed to honestly assess the facts on the ground in a manner reminiscent of Vietnam," Cordesman wrote.[7]

Not surprisingly, military leaders became increasingly concerned about their failure to untangle the inner workings of the insurgency and their inability to ward off attacks from enemy forces. Partly as a result, individual iterrogators were under tremendous pressure to obtain information about enemy attacks from the terrorism suspects who were brought before them. During this time, another member of Selwa's family, her son-in-law, Nabil, was arrested.

"WE ARE ABOVE THE LAW"

Shortly after I interviewed Selwa in Amman, I met with Nabil, Siara, and their daughter in my hotel room. He tells me he is looking for work as a lawyer in Damascus so he can support his family. Along with the hole in his knee from the electrodes that he says were placed there, he has injuries from beatings he received while in U.S. custody. His spine is crooked, and he has scars on his knees and elbows. He was arrested on September 28, four days after Selwa was imprisoned, and taken to a detention facility near Baghdad International Airport and placed in a room with four American men.

"They said, 'You used to visit different countries in the world as a VIP and you have diplomatic immunity. This does not mean anything to us. And we will prove it to you. You may have heard much about the concepts of democracy, liberty, religious tolerance, and human rights. These are idioms and slogans. Throw them behind you,'" he recalls.

He stands up and shows how the interrogator grabbed a handful of air and pretended to throw something over his shoulder. The language used by the interrogator, at least according to Nabil's version, sounds like it was stolen from a B-movie script. But it seems to capture the spirit of the interrogation that was conducted—and the confidence of the men who were asking him questions. "He said, 'We are above the law. We can do whatever we want. We have no limits. We are above the rules. We are above even President Bush. No one has power over us. And if someone dies, it is simply part of the interrogation. That's just the way it is.'" Nabil makes a fake sad face, imitating the interrogator. Nabil throws his hands in the air—just as he says the interrogator had done—in a sign of mock despair.

Afterward, someone put a hood over Nabil's head. The same *concerto*, as he describes the men in the room, interrogated him fifteen more times. He was questioned repeatedly about his Baathist affiliation. When he could not provide the answers they wanted, they would beat him and then leave him lying on the floor. He remembers how someone would touch his fingers and toes with the tops of their boots as he lay on the ground to see if he was still alive. One winter day, he says, he was forced into a zipped-up, one-piece suit that was doused with water. Then someone put him in front of an air-conditioning unit.[8]

Officials in Washington may have been underestimating the insurgency in Iraq. Many of the soldiers and commanding officers who were working in Sunni-dominated areas, however, were realistic about the threat. They fended off attacks on a daily basis. Some of them began to consider using more aggressive interrogation tactics on the people they hauled into police stations and detention centers. In the fall of 2003, during the time Nabil says he was beaten and shocked with electricity in a U.S.-run detention facility, similar incidents seemed to be occurring in other parts of Iraq. In a disciplinary action involving the abuse of a detainee, for example, a staff sergeant with the 104th Military Intelligence Battalion, 4th Infantry Division, in Tikrit, 100 miles northwest of Baghdad, testified that a climate of unlawful behavior prevailed at the detention facility where he was stationed. It was hardly surprising, he said, that detainees were mistreated.[9]

On November 6, 2003, the sergeant had received a written reprimand for not properly supervising an interrogation in which a detainee was beaten, according to a memo issued by the Department of the Army. The detainee, who is identified in military documents only as MP2496, had been accused of killing Americans. On September 23, 2003, the day of his interrogation, he was wearing a dishdasha (a formal robe), sandals, handcuffs, and ankle shackles. He was beaten on the soles of his feet and across the buttocks with a three- to four-foot-long, natural-wood-colored riot baton, according to the military documents, and was forced to crawl on his knees across the room. "My right knee has 3 open wounds ranging in size from 1 inch to 1.5 inches across," he told military investigators in a sworn statement on October 1, 2003. "My left knee has two open wounds approximately 1 inch across. These wounds make daily prayer difficult."[10]

Beating and humiliating prisoners is not, of course, standard operating procedure in the army. At the Tikrit military installation, where approximately 700 Iraqi prisoners were living in desert tents, though, conventional rules of warfare were not always followed, according to the sergeant. "Comments made by senior leaders regarding detainees such as 'They are not EPWs [Enemy Prisoners of War, who are protected by the laws of war]. They are terrorists and will be treated as such' have caused a great deal of confusion as to the status of the detainees," said the sergeant in a November 9, 2003, memo for his commander.[11]

There was another problem. Many of the individuals who were brought to the detention facility where interrogations were conducted, which is also known as the ICE (interrogation site), were not terrorism suspects. Instead, they were family members of a "targeted individual," as a suspect was called by the military. The family members were held in U.S custody in the hope that the suspect would turn himself in so that the innocent individuals would be released.

"Personnel at the ICE regularly see detainees who are, in essence, hostages," explained the sergeant. "They are normally arrested by a brigade based on accusations that may or may not be true, to be released, supposedly, when and if the targeted individual surrenders to Coalition Forces. In reality, these detainees are transferred to Abu Ghyraib prison and become lost in the Coalition detention system regardless of whether the targeted individual surrenders himself. In hindsight, it seems clear that, considering the seeming approval of these and other tactics by the senior command, it is a short jump of the imagination that allows actions such as those committed by [redacted] to become not only tolerated, but encouraged." In addition, the sergeant said, a captain had asked him to compile a "creative 'wish list'" of methods that they would like to use on detainees. In August 2003, a sergeant submitted the list and kept a copy on a computer desktop. "It is not unreasonable to think that curious soldiers may have seen the document and read the text," he wrote. Here are items on his "Alternative Interrogation Techniques (Wish List)":

Phone Book Strikes
Low-Voltage Electrocution
Closed-Fist Strikes
Muscle Fatigue Inducement[12]

These are techniques the officer wanted permission to use on detainees and were apparently not going to be implemented unless they were approved by superior officers. But the soldiers who may have come across the wish list on the hard drive of the computer, as he explained, may not have been so formal about the whole thing. In any case, none of these interrogation techniques—whether wished for or implemented, impulsively done, or carefully calibrated—seemed to work. American troops still had no idea where the vast majority of insurgents were hiding, or who supplied them with money and weapons, or how to prevent them from attacking in the future. Meanwhile, Iraqi insurgents exploited the U.S. failure to collect information about their activities.

"Iraqi insurgents and other Islamic extremists learned that U.S. intelligence is optimized around characterizing, counting, and targeting things, rather than people, and the U.S. has poor capability to measure and characterize infantry and insurgent numbers, wounded and casualties," wrote Cordesman. "They exploit these weaknesses in dispersal, in conducting attacks, [and] in concealing the extent of losses."[13]

U.S. interrogators did try to obtain information from the individuals in their custody, as Nabil related in his descriptions of his treatment. The harsh methods were apparently ineffective, however, in finding out anything useful from him. It is possible that he did not know anything about the insurgency—or that he simply refused to reveal any information. In any case, the interrogatons were not successful. Nabil was released from U.S. custody on May 28, 2004, eight months after his arrest, without being charged with a crime. He was given a twenty-dollar bill and a five-dollar bill. In the hotel room in Amman, he sits on a luggage rack and opens his wallet, pulling out the two bills, still crisp, clean, and neatly folded, the American soldiers had given him. "I will never forget their generosity," he says, dryly, and put the bills back in his wallet.[14]

American soldiers and officers in Iraq were under pressure to obtain intelligence from suspects like Nabil. He and many other individuals accused of being involved in insurgent activities were interrogated in holding facilities and then taken to Abu Ghraib. It was the intelligence-gathering center for U.S. forces in the fall of 2003 and was also one of the most chaotic and poorly run U.S.-run detention facilities in Iraq.

CHAPTER SEVEN

THE NIGHT SHIFT

NO GOOD INTELLIGENCE IS GOING TO COME FROM ABUSIVE PRACTICES. I THINK THE EMPIRICAL EVIDENCE OF THE LAST FIVE HARD YEARS TELLS US THAT. AND, MOREOVER, ANY PIECE OF INTELLIGENCE OBTAINED THROUGH THE USE OF ABUSIVE TECHNIQUES WOULD BE OF QUESTIONABLE CREDIBILITY. IT WOULD DO MORE HARM THAN GOOD WHEN IT INEVITABLY BECAME KNOWN THAT ABUSIVE PRACTICES WERE USED. AND WE CAN'T AFFORD TO GO THERE.

—Lieutenant General John F. Kimmons, U.S. Army Deputy Chief of Staff for Intelligence, September 6, 2006[1]

Staff Sergeant Ivan Frederick was the six-foot, two-inch son of a Virginia coal miner and worked as a corrections officer at Buckingham Correctional Center in Dillwyn, Virginia.[2] He was accustomed to rough environments. But when he and a group of about twenty soldiers, including England, Graner, Joyner, Darby, and Specialist Sabrina Harman arrived in Hilla, a city fifty-eight miles south of Baghdad, in June 2003, he was taken aback by the condition of the barracks. It

was an abandoned date factory that looked like an airplane hanger—
only it was "screaming hot" and inside the factory, he said, "Birds
would shit on you."[3] He and Graner set up a tent next door to the
warehouse and became roommates.[4]

During the day, the soldiers trained Iraqi police officers and
helped supervise a local jail. At night, they got drunk. Graner came
up with an idea for a theme party: "Naked Chem-Light Tuesday."[5] A
Chem-Light is a light stick that contains a substance made of
hydrogen peroxide solution and fluorescent dye. It is packaged in a
small plastic tube. Once the contents spill out, it glows for hours.
Graner pulled down his shorts, poured the contents of a chemical
light onto his penis, and then walked around and showed everybody.
Another time, Frederick recalled, Graner wrote the words, "Po
White Trash," on the back of a Hummer. Graner, Frederick, and the
others faced long stretches of boredom—hours, days, or weeks on
end. Hilla was "a relatively calm area with rare mortar attacks and a
friendly civilian population," according to a transcript of Frederick's
2004 general court-martial.[6] Like other soldiers, they played pranks
as a distraction.

In July the soldiers took schoolboy antics to another level.
Harman, twenty-seven, a former pizza deliverer from Lorton, Virginia,
got hold of a dead goat and a cat and, with a friend, sliced the bodies
up. She and other soldiers used the cadavers for experiments. One soldier pretended to have sex with the goat head (someone took a picture). They also shoved the cat head on top of a soda bottle. "They used
to put sunglasses on it, and they'd put the rifle up next to it. They'd put
a cigarette in its mouth," England tells me. "They did the same thing to
the goat, too." The animal heads never seemed to rot, she recalls,
because they were shot full of chemicals. Joyner remembers the incidents with disgust. "That cat-head garbage," he says. "I told [Harman]
if I saw it again, I was going to cut *her* head off."

Harman was apparently unfazed, keeping the cadavers for weeks,
either outside or in a recreational room, "depending on what they
wanted to do with them," England says.

"It was funny," England says. "So funny."[7]

In October 2003, England, Graner, Harman, Joyner, and the other soldiers headed for their next assignment: Abu Ghraib.

ATTACKED FROM ALL SIDES

Twenty soldiers, including England, arrived at the prison compound on an October day. "On their way to the prison, they hit an IED. It didn't hurt them. But it was a real 'welcome to Baghdad' moment," General Karpinski recalls. She gave a short speech after their arrival and then greeted them individually. She remembers five-foot, one-inch England. Karpinski towered over her when they shook hands. It was only a brief touch. "But I felt fear," Karpinski says, recalling how England and some of the other soldiers seemed to have "a need for physical touch and for someone to comfort them—as if they were saying, 'Make this stop making me crazy.'"[8]

England was assigned a job in an administrative office. Graner, Frederick, and Joyner reported to Tier 1A and Tier 1B. Regardless of where they were at the prison compound, they could hear the sound of mortars. The three men all had similar jobs, tending to the needs of the detainees, although they had different shifts. Frederick and Graner worked from 4:00 PM to 4:00 AM.[9] Joyner worked 4:00 AM till 4:00 PM.[10] Like many soldiers at the prison, Frederick, Graner, and Joyner were expected to assist intelligence officers and civilian contractors in their efforts to find out information about the insurgency from the detainees. The soldiers were supposed to tire the detainees out before the interrogatons and lower their defenses, for example, by forcing them to exercise. England, however, was not even supposed to be in Tier 1A at night. She slipped over there so she could be with Graner. "It wasn't my job to keep track of her," said her roommate, Felicia Nazelrod, at England's August 2004 military hearing in Fort Bragg, North Carolina, when asked about England's frequent absences from her bunk.[11]

Joyner is a broad-shouldered man who weighed 230-"ish," as he puts it, pounds while he was stationed at Abu Ghraib, and he has thin eyebrows, heavy hands, and an enormous chest. He is originally from

Smithfield, North Carolina, and was raised in Arlington, Virginia, and Landover, Maryland, and he had enlisted in the army in September 1999. Four years later, he left three children—ages eleven, eight, and seven—at home with their mother in Maryland and went to Iraq. "I personally didn't know what Abu Ghraib was," he says. "It sounded like something you catch on your feet."

The night he arrived at the prison, Joyner recalls, he was instructed not to take a shower after 8:00 PM. Insurgents prefer to attack in darkness. A few weeks later, a mortar hit a fuel tank roughly fifty yards from him. He could feel the explosion in his bones. "At that point, I really started to evaluate my desire to go into the army," he says.

"I felt like I was walking into the KKK," he explains. "You can't run or attempt to run. You don't know where you are. You don't know where you're going to run to." The whole setup at Abu Ghraib made him angry, especially the threats from the unseen enemy. "If it is my time to go I at least want to face the enemy head-on. Mortars. That's a punk way."

Joyner lived with seven soldiers in a room in an administrative building where he had a coffeemaker and a cot. ("If you closed your eyes real tight," he says, "you could think it was a bed.") The walls were decorated with posters of linebackers, cars, and beer. His area of the room was cluttered with photos of his children as well as CARE packages, drawings, and letters from participants in an "adopt-a-soldier" program in a Maryland elementary school. In their letters, children called him a "Hometown Hero," adding, "Thank you for fighting for our freedom." One letter said: "Thank you for being a G.I. Joe." He wrote letters back to the children and sent them Polaroid pictures.

He used to to get to work early at Tier 1A so he could talk to the soldier on the night shift, and he stayed late to debrief the next person who came on duty. Like Frederick, Joyner worked twelve- to sixteen-hour days, with little time for meals or breaks. Joyner took care of administrative tasks in a makeshift office on the upper floor, checking on the cell numbers and vital statistics of detainees, scribbled on a white board in the room. Then at 6:00 AM, two hours after his shift started, he would blow a whistle and wake up the prisoners.

"Good morning!" Joyner would call out.

"They'd say, 'Good morning, sir!' in English," he recalls. He would walk from cell to cell, visiting many of the one hundred men, women, and children who were living in the prison wing. "Anybody need a doctor?" he would ask. The detainees told him about their problems, and he relied on English-speaking prisoners to act as his interpreters: "my trustees, I called them." In a good-natured voice, he told the prisoners he wanted things expressed in clear, simple English. "I'd say, 'Break it down for me in Big-Bird terms,'" he recalls. He tried to pronounce the names of the detainees, but he stumbled over the Arabic sounds and so relied instead on nicknames that he gave them.

One of the detainees, was known as Thumbie, as Joyner recalls. I asked Joyner how Thumbie had gotten his nickname and what Joyner knew about him. "I know he don't know how to throw a grenade," explains Joyner. Thumbie was missing four fingers. Another detainee was Trap-jaw. "If you saw his grill," says Joyner, "you'd understand." Another prisoner, known as Spiderman, was suspected of having tuberculosis and had to wear a surgical mask. Another prisoner did not like being naked in his cell, Joyner explains, and had made a loincloth out of a Meals Ready to Eat (MRE) bag and placed it over his private parts, and so became Tarzan.[12] The nicknames may sound crude and offensive. In reality, Joyner has a gentle, teasing manner and was well-liked by the prisoners. He treated them with respect and dignity. It was not long, though, before he was told to treat them otherwise.

THE "GITMO-IZATION" OF ABU GHRAIB

Joyner, Graner, and Frederick all had the same problem. The prison was understaffed, and they worked long shifts and felt exhausted. The supervisor of one unit of the 320th MP Battalion was authorized to have 148 soldiers to oversee a group of approximately five hundred prisoners, for example. In fact, the unit had only 112 soldiers; the other twenty were reservists who had gone home on emergency leave and were granted "hardship discharges" because of family problems. Yet they were still listed as soldiers in Iraq, and their supervising officer at Abu Ghraib was not provided with other soldiers to replace the ones who were gone. The staffing situation during that time created a "tremendous, outrageous, criminal amount of soldier safety risks," according to a February 9, 2004, sworn statement from a 320th MP Battalion major in the Taguba Report.[13] On December 8, 2003, Colonel Pappas wrote a memo marked "SECRET RELEASE USA" on Department of the Army letterhead and requested one hundred and sixty three additional troops to protect the prison. "The security situation is precarious and the available forces are inadequate to remedy the problem," he wrote. "Recent HUMINT [human intelligence] reporting indicates pending attacks on the facility in the immediate future."[14] Officers were also short on interpreters, said Karpinski, explaining that she had complained for weeks that they didn't have enough linguists at the prison.[15]

Throughout the prison compound, officers were trying to cope with an inadequate number of soldiers, interpreters, and guards. The standard ratio of prisoners of war to military police is eight to one, according to General Paul J. Kern, who spoke about detainee operations at a September 9, 2004, hearing of the House Armed Services Committee.[16] The average ratio of prisoners to guards in U.S. prisons is four to one. At Guantanamo, where terrorism suspects are held and interrogated, the ratio is one to one, according to the Schlesinger Report, an investigation into detainee operations that was headed by former defense secretary James R. Schlesinger.[17] The ratio at Abu Ghraib, said Lieutenant General Anthony R. Jones at the congressional hearing, was seventy-five to one.[18] It was difficult under those conditions to maintain even the most basic level of services.

Yet on October 12, 2003, Lieutenant General Sanchez said that harsh interrogation methods such as sleep deprivation would be introduced at the prison. The methods are challenging tools to employ for interrogations under the most favorable of circumstances (and are severely criticized by human-rights advocates).

They were used at Guantanamo in a highly controlled environment. These techniques were now intended for prisoners at Abu Ghraib, despite the fact that the prison had minimal resources for the handling of detainees.

In October, a group of civilian interpreters and interrogators arrived to help mitigate the staffing shortage. Initially, it seemed as though they were there to resolve a problem at the prison that the army had been unable to rectify. However, some critics of the administration believe civilian contractors were not chosen simply because there were not enough military police and Military Intelligence; instead, they were chosen for roles at the prison specifically because they worked for the private sector and not for the military.

Human-rights lawyer Scott Horton has analyzed the subject of civilian workers employed by private military contractors in Iraq from his Avenue of the Americas office in New York City. (The room has a Russian Orthodox icon and a poster of the 1975 Nobel Peace Prize acceptance speech by his client, Andrei Sakharov. Glancing at the poster, Horton says, "I never thought I'd end up spending my time with torture cases in the U.S.") Horton believes the civilian contractors at Abu Ghraib may have been hired to assist with harsh interrogation techniques because they were not subject to the same legal standards as military personnel. As civilians, they could not be prosecuted under the Uniform Code of Military Justice or brought before a court-martial. In addition, neither soldiers nor contractors could be held liable under Iraqi law for anything they did to the prisoners. Members of the Coalition Provisional Authority had determined that they would be immune from prosecution in local courts. Soldiers could be prosecuted in the U.S. for crimes committed overseas under the military code. But the status of wayward contractors was murky. They were private citizens and there did not seem to be a clear-cut method for prosecuting civilians guilty of crimes against individuals in Iraq. That was the environment in which contractors—as well as soldiers and military officers—were operating at the prison.

"It's very, very clear that the Office of the Secretary of Defense thought it would be advantageous to bring people into the intelligence-gathering process—the contractors—who are outside the chain of command," Horton says. "One of the things they had was a back-door form of communications with the DoD." Provance and two other soldiers who were at Abu Ghraib told him Defense Department officials spoke directly with interrogators through secured telephone lines, ostensibly to provide "logistical support," explains Horton. In fact, he says, "They were involved in intelligence gathering."[19]

Many of the newly arrived interrogators and interpreters did not wear identification badges. It was often hard to tell whom they worked for, whether they were contractors, CIA, or Special Forces (all of which had sent personnel to Abu Ghraib). One group of interrogators took over a room, the Top Secret Controlled Intelligence Facility, in the fall of 2003 that had direct linkups to U.S. military bases. "I'd walk in the room and they'd get real quiet," Provance recalls. Other times, the stereo system in the top-secret facility was cranked up to make it hard for people to eavesdrop. White Stripes' "Seven Nation Army," for example, was blasted over the speakers when classified information was being discussed.[20]

Defense Secretary Donald H. Rumsfeld had a keen interest in the interrogations. A board with interrogation guidelines hung on the wall in the Joint Interrogation and Debriefing Center, according to Provance's congressional testimony.[21] A list of "approved approaches for All detainees," including "Emotional Love/Hate," "Repetition," "Rapid Fire," and "Silence," were listed on one side of the board. Methods that "require CGs [commanding general] approval," including "Dietary Manip," "Sleep Management (72 hours max)," and "Stress Positions (no longer than 45 mins)," appear on the other side of the board.[22]

A one-page memo also hung on a pole outside of the small corner office on the upper level where Joyner, Frederick, Graner, and others worked in Tier 1A, according to sworn testimony provided by Karpinski. The one-page memo, she said, was signed by Rumsfeld. "There was also a handwritten note out to the side in the same ink and in the same script as the signature of the secretary of defense," she said: "'MAKE SURE THIS HAPPENS.'"[23]

Pappas's executive assistant often told Major Michael Thompson, who was stationed there at the time, that "Mr. Donald Rumsfeld and Mr. Paul Wolfowitz" had called and were waiting for reports, according to testimony provided in the court-martial of an army dog handler, Sergeant Santos A. Cardona, as described by Hina Shamsi, deputy director for the Law and Security Program of Human Rights First, a nonprofit organization based in New York. (She attended the May 2006 Fort Meade, Maryland, trial.) Rumsfeld and Wolfowitz (according to a civilian interrogator, Steven J. Pescatori) and Thompson, received "nightly briefings."[24]

By mid-October, "Tiger Team University" classes were underway at Abu Ghraib: "Next class 11 October with JTF GTMO [Guantanamo] teams," according to Colonel Pappas's testimony in the Taguba Report.[25] In addition, an October 2003 Joint Interrogation and Debriefing Center PowerPoint report on interrogations was shown at Abu Ghraib. One of the slides shows a crudely drawn illustration of several interrogators and a sock puppet. The caption reads: "I realize this sounds rather cliché, but we have ways of making you talk."[26] It was a joke, of course. Yet the interrogation techniques, and the other methods recommended for handling detainees, were anything but whimsical.

THE PATH TO TORTURE

"You take those techniques and those ideas and those plans and you put those in the hands of relatively—comparatively, not relatively—inexperienced interrogation teams under far less supervision than what General Miller would have at Guantanamo Bay, and it's like a powder keg," Karpinski said in a deposition included in the Fay-Jones Report.[27]

The situation was difficult. But not everybody felt like they had to bow to the pressure from superior officers, or to apply techniques that seemed inappropriate. Joyner recalls the moment when a military intelligence officer announced that Joyner would be in charge of a sleep-management program designed to wear down the detainees so they would be more forthcoming during interrogations. "I said, 'Hold fast,'" Joyner says. "'I'm not just going to be doing this.'" He demanded to see the orders in writing. The orders were, indeed, passed down through the chain of command.[28] As he discovered, it was part of the military process that was in place at the time for the management of the interrogations.

A military intelligence officer drew up an interrogation plan that could include, for example, "a sleep plan," said Pappas in a sworn statement that appears in the Taguba Report. In theory, medics then reviewed each plan—as they did at Guantanamo—but there were not enough medical personnel. A deputy prison director was also sup- posed to sign the form, and, a Military Intelligence officer would take a copy to Tier 1A "to work out the specifics of implementation," Pappas explained. The soldiers in Tier 1A were then left to their own devices.

"Nobody came back to me saying, 'We had problems imple- menting the plan,'" Pappas said. "Nor were there any questions about the plan. The only time that occurred were when the MP [military police] came back to me saying that they saw some interrogators come down and they did inappropriate things to the detainees," he explained. "I looked into it, and I asked CID to come in, and I sus- pended those interrogators from further operation."[29] (There was a reported incident of detainee-related misconduct in the fall of 2003 when interrogators forced a prisoner to walk naked through a cell- block.) The system, Pappas claimed, worked. The soldiers who were instructed to implement the interrogation plans did carry out the orders, on most occasions. After all, says Joyner, the orders came from "the secret squirrels," as he calls the Military Intelligence officers who worked in the Joint Interrogation and Debriefing Center.[30]

In addition, the harsh interrogation techniques seemed to be common in other detention facilities in Iraq as well. The sleep plans, for example, were apparently used widely. "Sleep deprivation was a really big thing," a sergeant with the U.S. Army's 82nd Airborne Division who served in Iraq from August 2003 through April 2004 told a Human Rights Watch researcher. "Someone from [Military Intelligence] told us these guys don't get no sleep. They were directed to get intel [intelligence] from them so we had to set the conditions by banging on their cages, crashing them into the cages, kicking them, kicking dirt, yelling. All that shit."[31]

Like other soldiers, Joyner followed the orders to implement a sleep-modification plan: he set up a boom box in the cell block in Tier 1A and blasted everything from heavy metal to New Edition and R&B to keep prisoners awake. "Every now and then, I went old school and played some Temptations," he recalls. "I figure it might as well be something I like." According to several accounts, the *Barney & Friends* theme song got a lot of play. Not while Joyner was in charge, though. "That might have been on the night shift," he explains. "We don't play no *Barney* on the day shift."

Regardless of the genre, the boom box was played constantly—for weeks. The only time Joyner turned the volume down was when he took a detainee to the shower area. "We went through a lot of batteries," he tells me. The prisoners were tormented. "How much would you pay for a good night's sleep?" Joyner says and looks off into the distance. One day, he was sitting in his office as the music blared, he tells me. He felt his blood boil. "I thought, *Good Lord. Please turn this garbage off.*"

"I said, 'That's it,'" he says, showing me how he slammed his hand on the table in the prison office. "I thought, *If I'm going to get in trouble for turning the music off, so what.*"

He stopped the program. "You're not going to give me an order to have me hurt someone when they haven't done anything," Joyner says, explaining that he would refuse to follow a command if he found it immoral or wrong. "I'll stomp you in the ground instead."[32] He had finally decided that forcing the prisoners to stay awake was not right—and so he stopped doing it. Nothing happened. He was not even reprimanded. It raises the question of whether or not other soldiers were forced into mistreating the detainees—as many of them claimed after they were accused of detainee-related abuse. It is also possible, however, that Joyner was more confident than the other soldiers and felt strong enough to refuse to follow orders when he felt they were wrong.

"I think it has to something to do with me being so dog gone intimidating," he says, "Not everybody has that gift."

"JUST DON'T KILL HIM."

It was October 25, 2003. Four American soldiers had been killed and their bodies were missing. An army intelligence officer believed a detainee identified as Saad in government documents, or "Gilligan," as some American soldiers called him, knew where the bodies were and possibly who had killed the soldiers. The sergeant was planning to interrogate Saad and find out the vital information. First, though, Saad needed to be "stressed out," the sergeant said.

"What do you want us to do with him?" Frederick asked, according to his sworn statement. "I don't give a fuck what you do to him," said the sergeant, according to Frederick. "Just don't kill him."

The sergeant never told Frederick to put electrical wires on Saad's hand. The sergeant never said that Saad should be forced to stand on a box and then be told he would be electrocuted if he moved. Still, Frederick said, "I put the wires on his fingers. I believe it was his left hand. Well, there was some wires in the shower dangling, so I grabbed them and touched them together to make sure they weren't live wires." "I just wanted to scare the guy and I took it to another level with the wires but I had no intention of hurting the guy; that's why I touched them together to make sure they were not live wires. To me, [the sergeant] was like an authority figure, and when he said he needed the detainee stressed out, I wanted to make sure the detainee was stressed out."[33]

In addition, there were methods used on detainees that did not appear in any interrogation plans or notes, according to testimony in the Fay-Jones Report. For example, Frederick explained that he once walked into an interrogation booth where a detainee had been refusing to answer questions posed by interrogators, and so Frederick jammed a bag over his head. "Come with me, Piggy," Frederick said, as he later recalled. He placed the prisoner, stripped of his clothing, in solitary confinement. Thirty minutes later, Frederick returned and found the prisoner whimpering on the floor.

"You've been moving, Little Piggy," Frederick shouted. "You know you shouldn't move." He yanked the hood off his head. Eventually, the detainee was allowed to put his clothes back on and was released. Frederick spoke about the incident afterward with other soldiers, recalling a time in the recent past when he had been reluctant to treat the detainees in a harsh manner. "I want to thank you guys," he said, "because up until a week or two ago, I was a good Christian." [34]

HAPPY BIRTHDAY, LYNNDIE

Lynndie England worked in the in/out processing office near Camp Ganci, [35] and she delivered paperwork to the office in Tier 1A, according to attorney Hardy. [36] And almost every night at around ten, she headed over there to see Graner.

"In situations like Iraq, the first thing some young female soldiers look for is a protector—a senior male, let's say, who's sitting in a vehicle with her," Karpinski tells me. "She says, 'I'm really afraid.' And he says, 'Don't worry.' A closeness develops. It's intentional on his part. And naïve on hers. Graner is a big, hunky guy. He can probably put his arms around England and still touch his shoulders. Does she feel safe with him? Yes. And all she has to do is be sexually wild with him." [37]

In a supply room at the prison, England and Graner re-created a Virginia Beach photo shoot: she performs oral sex on Graner, and Frederick takes a picture. This time, England adds a flourish: she makes a thumbs-up sign.

"She was laughing and having a good time," said Frederick. "She didn't show any signs that she wasn't enjoying it or wanted to leave or anything at all."

"She posed for the photographs, one behind the detainees with Graner and then the one where she was pointing at the detainee's dick and giving the thumbs up," he said. "She would talk about them [genitalia], laugh about the size, getting hard, stuff like that." [38]

In one of the Abu Ghraib photographs, England is standing near a thirty-four-year-old detainee whose name appears as Hayder

Sabbar Abd in government records. She laughs as he pretends to jerk himself off. Again, she is making a thumbs-up sign.

Yet when I ask her about the photos, she says she was not enthusiastic about them. It was Graner, she says, who took the lead.

England seems to recall things differently than Frederick does. She says she wasn't enthusiastic about the photo-taking sessions. "I didn't want him to take the pictures," she says. "But he took pictures of everything. He kept a camera is his cargo pocket. He was always taking his camera out. Sometimes he took the pictures for himself. Sometimes he took them for documentation."[39]

"Graner was a picture person; he loved taking pictures," said Frederick later. "He always talked about being in Desert Storm and the things he saw and did and he had no way to prove these things happened, so this time around, he said he was going to take pictures to take back home as proof."[40]

One night, Graner walked into the cell of the detainee whose name appears as Hai Ismale Abdul Hamid in government documents. He was a "small man weighing approximately 100 pounds," according to government documents.[41] "[He] didn't like Americans," England recalls.[42] He had smeared his own feces on his body and had threatened to kill the guards. That night, though, he was peaceful. Graner put a strap around Hamid's neck, led him out of the cell, and handed the strap to England. She grabbed it. Graner took a picture. He sent the jpeg to his family in Pennsylvania.

"Look what I made Lynndie do," Graner wrote in an e-mail.[43]

On the night of November 7, 2003, a group of prisoners were stripped and forced to masturbate while standing next to each other in a hallway. "Corporal Graner jokingly told Private First Class England that the line of masturbating detainees were a gift for her birthday," according to a statement made at Frederick's court-martial.[44] The abuse continued until the early morning hours. Another prisoner, Hussein Mohssein Mata Al-Zayiadi (as his name appears in court documents), testified he was beaten during this time and placed on top of the human pyramid.[45]

"Yeah, I thought it was weird," England says. She was describing the human pyramid that was built in the hallway of Abu Ghraib and then photographed. As she talks, she watches Carter play with a picture book in the brig's visiting room. "We were told we were supposed to do those things. They said, 'Good job. Keep it up.'"

Who came up with the idea? I ask.

"It wasn't us. It was his daddy," England says, nodding at Carter. She reaches over and kisses him on the forehead.

Where did Graner get the idea? I ask.

"He said it was because it was a narrow corridor, and it would be better to put them all together and that it would keep them busy. He didn't tell us what he was going to do before he did it. He just told us as we were doing it."[46]

"[Graner] said it was very degrading for them to be seen by another male naked," Frederick testified. "There were a few detainees that were wearing women's underwear, on their head, and he said this was also degrading."[47]

Not only had Graner forced his subjects into grotesque poses, he also had trophy shots, hundreds, if not thousands, of photos of Iraqi men and women in pornographic acts. He passed them around. The man who appears at the top of the pyramid, al-Zayiadi, testified that he believed Americans were good when they removed Saddam from power in April 2003. However, the events of November 7 and 8, the night of the human pyramid, changed his view.

"What occurred that night has humiliated [al-Zayiadi] so much so that he has wanted to kill himself," according to a transcript of a military hearing for England. "But he does not have the means to do so because he is still in Abu Ghraib."[48]

Detainees like Zayiadi were despondent and suicidal. Many of the soldiers in charge of the prisoners were feeling the effects of the grim surroundings, too. Exhusted and stressed out, the soldiers turned to their supervisors and asked to be relieved of one of their duties: escorting the prisoners from their cells to the interrogation sites. As a result, a special band of soldiers was assigned to the task. The Robo-tripping partiers.

CHAPTER EIGHT

THE INTERROGATOR

Colonel Pappas assigned the task of escorting prisoners to Provance's friends, the Robotripping soldiers, and made them members of a guard force. In Pappas's sworn testimony, he said he made it clear that the soldiers must treat the detainees humanely. "The guard force needs to get to the same level of requirements, training and understanding of the Geneva Convention," Pappas said. "They do something outside of the standard, they know they do so at their own peril."[1] The soldiers seemed to have a different understanding of their role, especially since they were apparently provided with more lenient guidelines regarding the treatment of detainees while they were working in the field.

"They were taken on a tour of the isolation area [where some interrogations were conducted]. When they were down there, the MP's [military police] would tell them that they could do whatever they wanted to the detainees," explained Provance in a sworn statement.[2] In addition, the soldiers were working under a civilian interrogator who "was very aggressive and confident in his skills," according to Frederick. "He yelled and screamed a lot. He walked around like he was the man, and he would tell detainees how good he was and things like that. To me, he was a little bit on the side that he didn't care—and would pull all the stops if he had to."[3]

Unlike at Guantanamo, there were few medics to check on the blood pressure and pre-existing medical conditions of detainees while they were in U.S. custody or to assist them if they had a medical emergency. Human-rights advocates challenge the army's decision to include medical practitioners in harsh interrogations, saying that people in healing professions should not be placed in roles that help facilitate the mistreatment of detainees. Nevertheless, the interrogators at Guantanamo were supervised during their work and guided by the advice of medics. The system was set up partly to protect detainees from serious harm. There seemed to be little supervision of many of the civilian interrogators' work, however, or of the conduct of many other people who were handling detainees at the prison.

"WHO SHOULD BE IN CHARGE?" Pappas apparently posed the question in a presentation about interrogations at Abu Ghraib in the fall. He was referring to the chain of command within the interrogation units at the prison.[4] The question could have been asked of the entire Baghdad Central Correctional Facility.

"WE NEED THE DOGS."

One of the supervising officers at Abu Ghraib in the fall of 2003 was Lieutenant Colonel Jerry L. Phillabaum. He had a military record that indicated he may not have been the ideal candidate for the job. He had encountered problems earlier in the year as a battalion commander at another U.S.-run detention facility, Camp Bucca. An investigation into alleged detainee abuse at that facility was being conducted in November while Phillabaum was a supervisor at Abu Ghraib. One of the soldiers, Master Sergeant Lisa M. Girman, under his previous command at Camp Bucca, had allegedly assaulted an Iraqi prisoner who was accused of rape, according to a transcript from her court-martial.[5] Charges against her were eventually dropped. But in the fall Phillabaum was under a cloud of suspicion.

Taguba later described him as "an extremely ineffective commander and leader."[6]

Taguba also questioned Pappas's judgment and criticized Pappas for "failing to ensure that soldiers under his direct command were properly trained" in the international laws protecting detainees. Pappas had also supervised a controversial military exercise at the prison. On December 25, 2003, he organized a mock assault on the prison that was supposedly designed to frighten the detainees. Two helicopters hovered over the prison compound, blowing tents off the ground. Yards of fabric—gowns and other clothes worn by the prisoners—flew into the air, as they scrambled and pulled their clothes out of the sand and mud.[7] "You talk about waste, fraud and abuse," says Provance, sitting in the Hartley Inn. He snaps his silver wristband. "It's incredible that he could've authorized that."[8] Pappas was eventually given a General Officer Memorandum of Reprimand for his failures in leadership.[9]

By some accounts, Karpinski was not much better. In late October 2003, she granted Phillabaum a two-week leave at Camp Arifjan in Kuwait, according to the Taguba Report.[10] Another officer was supposed to watch over Abu Ghraib during that period. Karpinski apparently told almost no one about her decision. "Temporarily removing one commander and replacing him with another serving Battalion Commander without an order and without notifying superior or subordinate commands is without precedent in my military career," wrote Taguba.[11]

While Phillabaum was on leave, things reached a crisis point: the local contractors who provided meals were inefficient and disorganized, and many of the prisoners at Camp Ganci were forced to go hungry. "Have you ever experienced about 80 prisoners standing in line at 2130hrs at night, cold, and being told that the vendors do not have any more food?" wrote David DiNenna, an officer who was in charge of day-to-day operations at the camp, in an e-mail to a superior officer on November 2, 2003. The prisoners were threatening the guards and officers. As a result, DiNenna requested military dogs to help look for explosives that prisoners might have in their possession and to watch over the detainees so they would not start a riot against U.S. troops. "We need the dogs," he wrote. "I cannot emphasize enough how critical this is now."[12]

The dogs arrived on November 20. Four days later, a weapon was smuggled into the prison, and the place descended into "chaos," according to the Fay-Jones Report: "No one really appeared to be in charge."[13] One of the detainees had gotten hold of a pistol that had apparently been brought into the prison by an Iraqi police officer. An American soldier tried to confiscate the gun and was shot in the scuffle.[14] Eleven Iraqi police officers were detained as suspects. Rules governing how to handle suspects and to conduct interrogations had been difficult to pin down for contractors and soldiers who were working at the prison before the incident. That night, Sanchez apparently told the soldiers they could do whatever they wanted to restore order—or at least that is what the soldiers believed at the time. There was no mention of the Geneva Conventions. Instead, black Belgian shepherds were put to work.

Impromptu interrogations were being held at the prison in an effort to find out who had smuggled in the weapon and whether or not there were additional firearms or explosives hidden in the prison cells. A dog handler, Navy Chief Petty Officer William Kimbro, led one of the animals to Tier 1A and let the dog sniff the premises for explosives. The dog did not find any contraband, and they left the area. Not long afterward, Kimbro was asked to visit a prison cell in Tier 1B. He thought he had been called to look for explosives in that wing of the prison. After he arrived, though, he was less certain. People were yelling and screaming. His dog began barking wildly.[15]

Inside one of the cells, a civilian contractor was interrogating an Iraqi policeman named Salad Dawod, a man with a big belly and chest who stood five foot, eight inches tall and weighed 180 pounds. He was apparently the main suspect in the gun-smuggling incident.[16] Dawod was crouched in a corner of the cell. A civilian female interpreter[17] was also in the room.[18] "You see that dog over there," the civilian interrogator shouted. "If you don't tell me what I want to know, I'm going to get that dog on you!"[19] The interrogator and the interpreter left the cell. The corridor and pathway outside the room were narrow, though, and they crowded against each other. Kimbro's dog lunged. It grabbed the interpreter's forearm. Kimbro regained control of his dog, left the cell, and headed down a flight of stairs. Someone called to him, asking him to bring the dog back, but he refused.

It was a chilly night, possibly the same evening of the smuggling incident or several days later. The civilian interrogator and Frederick took Dawod out of Cell 4B and brought him outside. Dawod was stripped down to his boxer shorts, his flesh spilling over the elastic.[20]

"Make him crawl through the mud," the civilian interrogator said, as Frederick claimed in his statement. Frederick forced Dawod down on his belly. He slid about ten feet through the mud, first in one direction and then in the other, for ten minutes. Graner, who was standing nearby, made another prisoner known as Shitboy do the same thing. (Frederick only made Dawod crawl, as he explained later, not roll.) Then there were the interrogations.

Provance claims that the civilian interrogator used soldiers to threaten and assault detainees during interrogations. The interrogator seemed to expect Frederick to fulfill a similar task. When Dawod refused to answer a question, the civilian interrogator called for Frederick. "He told the Iraqi Police to answer his questions or he would bring SSG Frederick back into the cell," according to the Fay-Jones Report. "He encouraged SSG Frederick to abuse Iraqi Police detained following a shooting incident."[21]

The interrogation of Dawod took place in a room with a bed. Frederick said that initially he stomped into the room and stood close to Dawod. Later, Frederick slapped his hand against a wall to scare him. Sometimes Frederick hit the bed. This continued for a couple nights. Dawod still refused to provide any useful information. So Frederick began forcing him to do push-ups, the ritual known as "smoking" a detainee. (Yoo described this technique in his book.) A couple of days later, on either November 26 or 27, Frederick came in the room and put his hand on Dawod's shoulder in a casual manner—as if he were a friend, Frederick explained. Dawod started to say something.

"Shut up," the civilian interrogator said.

Dawod kept talking. A moment later, Frederick covered his mouth with one hand and pinched his nose, cutting off his air supply for five to ten seconds. Then Frederick let him breathe. Frederick said the civilian interrogator was initially surprised by the gesture. But by the third time Frederick reached for Dawod's mouth, the civilian interrogator knew what was going on. "He failed to prevent SSG Frederick from covering the detainee's mouth and nose restricting the detainee from breathing," according to the Fay-Jones Report.[22] Frederick later cut off Dawod's air supply and applied a "pressure point." It is possible to apply pressure on certain areas of the body, such as the head or neck, and control the movement of an individual without inflicting serious harm. Prison guards, marines, and police officers are taught how to use these methods, which are also known as "pressure point control tactics," in order to subdue a prisoner or a violent suspect. The use of pressure points is similar to the brandishing of a firearm or the use of a crowd-control baton. Like these weapons, pressure points can be used in a responsible manner—or maliciously.

When Frederick applied the pressure point, Dawod grimaced in pain and tried to pull away. Frederick backed off. The civilian interrogator applied the pressure point, as Frederick recalled. Again, Dawod flinched in pain. The interrogator did not relent. Instead, he held the pressure point longer.[23]

On November 24, soldiers and contractors at Abu Ghraib suspected that many weapons, not just the pistol that had been found, might have been smuggled into the prison. Many of the soldiers and contractors seemed to believe they were looking for information about concealed weapons that could save their lives and those of other individuals at the prison. Many also believed that Sanchez had officially suspended the military rules for them, allowing them to do whatever they wanted to the detainees. In fact, there was no such memo that suspended the rules of conduct. "The perception was that Lieutenant General Sanchez had removed all restrictions that night because of the situation; however, that was not true," according to the Fay-Jones Report. "No one is able to pin down how that perception was created."[24]

Many people who support the use of harsh interrogation methods on terrorism suspects believe that these techniques are necessary for the security of our nation. Some of the individuals at Abu Ghraib who treated prisoners in a harsh manner during those hours of chaos at the prison seemed to think they, too, were doing the right thing under the circumstances in order to protect the safety of U.S. troops. In addition, the incidents of abuse described in the Fay-Jones Report during this time seem to have occurred partly because of the lack of supervision and leadership at the prison. These two factors—a sense of righteousness and little or no oversight—seemed to lead to acts of cruelty at the prison.

Just outside the prison walls, American troops were trying to hunt down insurgents and prevent future attacks. But they did not always hit their targets.

CHAPTER NINE

THE SWEET SHOP OF ABU GHRAIB

Ali Haddad is sitting in a room on the sixth floor of the Hotel Regency in Amman, Jordan, on March 13, 2006. (His name and those of his family have been changed.) He has come to Amman this week to meet with Burke and the other lawyers about the lawsuit *Saleh v. Titan*. A fifty-five-year-old farmer and storekeeper, Haddad has a bushy mustache, and his face is tough and weather-beaten. His hands are huge, with pinkish nails, and covered in thick, dark veins; his white hair is swept off his face. It is warm in the hotel room, and he holds a string of prayer beads. The room has two single beds and a green lamp, and the sound of traffic can be heard from the street below. He pulls an Abu Ghraib prisoner ID bracelet from his pocket and sets the bracelet on a table in front of him. He looks at me suspiciously. "I don't want you to write anything light," he admonishes me. "Not a novel or anything like that."

Then he says, "I will start from the beginning."[1]

It was Thursday, November 13, 2003, during the Muslim holy month of Ramadan, Haddad recalls, and he was having dinner at his home in Al Baaisa, a village located just outside Abu Ghraib. (Abu

Ghraib is a prison, of course, but it is also a city of approximately 500,000 people.) He raises wheat and vegetables, along with cows and sheep, and he manages two stores. The stores are housed in two small buildings, each eight to ten feet across, and they are located sixty feet from his house. One store is filled with shelves of tea, cookies, and coolers of Pepsi. The other store is a bakery, Issawe Sweets, stocked with baklava and pastries.

At about eight that evening, the lights went out in the neighborhood. There was nothing particularly alarming about the power shortage. It happened all the time. The electrical grid in cities like Abu Ghraib and nearby Baghdad had been shaky for decades, and the war had made things worse. Not long after the house went dark, Haddad's son, Tareef, twenty-three, and several friends came inside. "Tareef said the neighbors wanted some sweets and something to drink," Haddad says. "He asked me if he and his friends could open the store."

Tareef carried a chair outside the house so his father could sit in a sandy patch of earth. It was more pleasant to be outside—even when the air was chilly and foggy as it was that evening—when the electricity was out. Then Tareef headed for the store. Not long after that, Haddad's other sons, nineteen-year-old Tamim, seventeen-year-old Amar, and his youngest boy, Asad, age nine, met Tareef at the bakery. Their cousin, sixteen-year-old Sinan Hakim al-Fulani, was there, too.

A shy, quiet teenager with heavy eyelids and thick eyebrows, Fulani had come to Amman with Haddad so he, too, could speak with the American lawyers about the lawsuit. Fulani sits in a chair in the hotel room near his uncle and tells his version of what happened at the bakery. Fulani and his friends were eating baklava and drinking Pepsi that evening as they sat on wooden and plastic chairs. They talked about games they had been playing in the park that day and about the Iraqi soccer team. They all loved soccer, especially Asad, a pale-skinned boy who liked to play marbles with his friends from school and was always running to keep up with Fulani and the older children.

That evening, as Haddad explains, one of their relatives, a man named Ali Wahed, stopped by the store to pick up some Pepsi. They had no reason to think Wahed was involved in anything criminal or dangerous. Yet Wahed was a suspect in terrorist activities, and that evening American troops had been tracking his battered 1982 Toyota pickup truck as he drove along the road. Wahed parked the truck in front of the bakery on Khawaled Street. "As I was sitting outside, I saw a helicopter," says Haddad. "It circled around my house."

IRON HAMMER

American troops had recently started a military campaign known as "Operation Iron Hammer" in the area. It was launched on November 12, 2003, the day before the helicopter hovered above Haddad's stores. Brigadier General Martin E. Dempsey, commander of the First Armored Division, described it at a press briefing in Baghdad on November 20 as an "intelligence-based, precise combat operation."[2] On that day, Dempsey explained, a group of insurgents had fired off mortars in Baghdad and headed for Abu Ghraib. A van carrying five suspects sped along the road after the attack. A helicopter, piloted by troops with the First Armored Division, followed it. Soldiers fired on the van, killing two men and injuring three others. Five suspected insurgents were captured. Lieutenant Colonel George Krivo, a military spokesman, told reporters that an 83-millimeter mortar tube was found in the rubble. Military officials believed the mortar tube was used in the attacks on Americans.[3]

One hundred fifty-three American troops had already been killed in Iraq by this time. The campaign to win the hearts and minds of Iraqis was not exactly abandoned on November 12. But Operation Iron Hammer marked a new development in the war. Colonel Russ Gold, the commander of the First Armored Division's Third Brigade, helped lead an assortment of Iraqi soldiers, Estonian troops, and Americans in the assaults on Abu Ghraib, according to Brigadier General Mark Kimmitt.[4] With the Abu Ghraib assault, and other U.S.-led attacks, the U.S. military became more aggressive in rooting out suspected insurgents. American troops began pursuing insurgents on the ground through more frequent house raids and with an increased number of neighborhood patrols. "How do we make sure we've got the people we really think we have?" said Dempsey. "If we have accumulated our intelligence well, then we should expect that about seventy-five percent of those we capture remain captured. And so we are very careful about that. We don't simply sweep a bunch of people up and throw them into Abu Ghraib prison and hope for the best. The enemy is neither ten feet tall nor is he everywhere," he explained. "What we're trying to do is figure out who he is, what he is, and how he operates."[5]

Previously, Apache and Warrior helicopters had been used exclusively for reconnaissance missions, according to military officials. With the start of Operation Iron Hammer, U.S. troops began hunting down and shooting the enemy from the air.

SEARCHING FOR ALI BABA

Nine-year-old Asad stared at the sky. So did Fulani and the other boys. The helicopter hovered above them. "It was still," Fulani recalls. As he described the helicopter, he shifts his weight in the chair next to me in the hotel room and scrapes his cuticles. He blinks nervously. "We just stood there, watching how it was hanging in the air."

"I wondered, *Why would a helicopter stop for no reason?*" he says.

The helicopter circled twice, flipped, and turned around. It was approximately 150 feet, or about fifteen stories, above them. Suddenly, there was an explosion. Troops shot three rounds of ammunition. They aimed at Wahed's pickup truck parked in front of the store, and shrapnel sprayed in all directions. Fulani's lower bicep and upper arm were torn apart by the blast. His clothes were in shreds, and his chest was covered in blood. He blacked out.

He rolls up his shirt in the hotel room and shows me the gashed, puffy scar tissue on his bicep that he got from the shrapnel. He holds out his fingers, but he can't move them.

"The nerves are dead," I say.

"Yeah," he says.

Haddad stood up that night and watched in shock. "When they started shooting, I screamed, 'Tareef! Tamim!' The names of my sons," he says. "No one answered."

Haddad ran toward the store. Wahed's truck—the one that had been parked on Khawaled Street—was shot to pieces. The sand, the chairs, and the stores were full of holes. The ground was soaked in blood. Tareef came out of one of the stores. He had been wearing white. His tunic was now dark red, and the fabric was covered in blood. Haddad called out for his other sons. "Tamim said, 'I am here. But I am hurt,'" Haddad recalls.

Other men slowly emerged from the store. They were stumbling and crying out in pain. The helicopter remained in one position above them. Haddad wandered through the area and found the bodies of two of his sons, Alim and Asad, piled on top of each other. Alim's head was missing. Asad had fallen over him. Haddad held Asad's body against his chest. As Haddad describes the blood that covered the corpse, his own body begins to shake. As he held Asad, he explains, the troops were planning to fire another round from the air.

"I lifted Asad to show the pilot that the little boy was dead," he says. "I pointed to Asad and myself, trying to tell him that this was my son."

He leans forward to demonstrate how he pointed slowly to his son's body and then to himself. He presses his finger hard against his chest. Then he shows how he lifted Asad's body up higher in the air. "The helicopter was so close that I was able to point out to the pilot and show him, 'This is my house, and this is my son,'" he explains.

He stared at the helicopter. The American forces decided not to fire their weapons. Haddad noticed that, as the helicopter descended, it was heading near electrical wires that were strung over one of the stores. He gestured to the pilot, trying to show there were wires that could entangle the propellers because he thought the helicopter might pitch to the earth if it hit them. The pilot flew higher, circled around two more times, and finally swerved away from the wires.

A moment later, the helicopter landed. A soldier jumped out. He swung his rifle through the air.

"There was a light on his rifle," says Haddad. "He was looking around."

Haddad stands up from his chair in the hotel room and shows how the soldier crept across the sand. "He picked something off the ground," he says. "It was the head of my dead son. He put the head on the ground between me and my other children. I screamed, 'We need a translator!'"

Nobody answered.

The soldier forced Haddad to lie down with his face pressed into the sand. Hummers arrived. The soldiers carried the wounded men and children to the helicopter and searched the stores. Suddenly, the electricity came back on, Haddad recalls. The soldiers opened the coolers and the refrigerators. Then they carried Pepsi cartons to the Hummers. There was money in the stores. They took the money, too. An Arabic-speaking man, an interpreter, with an Egyptian accent appeared before Haddad.

"What do you want?" the interpreter asked.

"I said, 'You can see the situation we're in,'" Haddad tells me. "'One of my sons is wounded. Two others are dead. We are very cold. My house is close. I want to get some blankets to cover the people who are still alive.'"

"The interpreter said, 'Do you have Ali Baba?'" Haddad recalls, using a term the American troops used to describe insurgents.

"I said, 'Who is Ali Baba?'" Haddad tells me.

The soldiers eventually agreed to let Haddad return to his house. They escorted him, walking beside him, in front of him, and behind him, on the way. He got the blankets and covered his children. The soldiers made him lie down again on the ground. They got nylon bags from a military vehicle and put the bodies of Alim and Asad in them. They shackled Haddad's hands behind his back and put him in the same vehicle with his dead sons. They left the bodies at a nearby hospital and took Haddad to Abu Ghraib.[6] Fulani was taken to Ibn Sina

Hospital in Baghdad. In a November 18, 2003, photograph, taken shortly after he left the hospital, he is shown with slumped shoulders, wild, matted hair and a battered, childlike face, and he was clearly still in pain from shrapnel wounds. He was taken that day to Abu Ghraib and eventually placed with other teenage boys in a confinement area at the prison compound. Several weeks after he arrived, Fulani says, he turned to an interpreter, a chubby, Lebanese American man.

"I said, 'Why was I brought here?'" Fulani says.

"He said, 'You're here because you were part of the resistance against the Americans and the British,'" Fulani says.

"I said, 'Does anybody ever protest or complain about being there?'"

"Sometimes people do," said the interpreter. "But we just close the door and leave."

Two months later, the interpreter appeared in the boys' ward with slips of paper in his hand. The documents explained what the boys had been charged with. Fulani noticed two of the pages of his document were blank.

"I said, 'I haven't been accused of anything,'" he says.

The interpreter snatched the pages out of his hand and scribbled a few words on the sheet of paper. "Shooting off a rocket-propelled grenade at coalition forces," read the charges written by the interpreter. Several weeks later, Fulani and the other boys, along with adult prisoners, staged a demonstration against their living conditions. The guards came with black military dogs. Some dogs were muzzled, says Fulani. Some were not. The snarling animals forced the children into a corner. Fulani screamed. He could feel the breath of the dogs on his skin and, he says, "their aggressiveness." After thirty minutes, the guards took the dogs out of the area. The protests stopped.

He was released from prison not long after that, without ever being formally charged with a crime. Issawe Sweets has been rebuilt, and he lives near the store. But he doesn't go there anymore.[7]

SYMPATHY PAYMENT

Under the Foreign Claims Act, Iraqi civilians who are injured or whose property is destroyed during wartime may be eligible for compensation from the U.S. government. The claims can also be filed by former prisoners for injuries they received while in U.S. custody or for damage to their homes or property during their arrests. In addition, civilians are eligible to receive $2,500 in a condolence payment when a loved one has been killed. The system for filing claims and receiving payment in the restitution program, however, has been problematic.

"There is a process, and everyone knows how it works except me, to be honest," explained Dempsey at the press briefing in Baghdad. "I just know it's out there. And I know that because [one of the officers] gives me a report every day about property-damage claims and how much money we've paid to try to redress wrongs that we may have committed."[8]

No wonder he was fuzzy on the details. "There are no guidelines," Sarah Holewinski, executive director of a Washington-based human-rights organization, CIVIC, tells me. "And if the program is not implemented effectively, you're going to create resentment. There's going to be one family that gets payments and one that doesn't, and you can't tell why."[9]

The soldiers make it a practice, however, to visit the houses of people who have suffered damages during arrests and raids. "Now, you know, I'm not running for mayor. So I'm not trying to convince you that I have the popular support of the people of Baghdad every time I shoot an Apache helicopter," Dempsey told reporters. "What I am telling you is that after we do that, one hundred percent of the time we go back. And one hundred percent of the time we try to make sure that people understand what we're doing."[10]

After Haddad was released from prison (he was never formally charged with a crime) in spring 2004, U.S. troops visited his house. He offered them cans of Pepsi and described the assault on his property and the deaths of Alim and Asad. Members of his family had taken photographs of the damaged property. He handed the soldiers the photographs and told them he had film footage of the wreckage that had been shot by an Iraqi television channel, al-Sharqiya. He and the American troops walked around the yard, and he showed them the traces of the bullets and shrapnel on the property. The soldiers spent more than an hour taking pictures and scribbling notes. Three days later, they returned.

"They said, 'We want the file,'" Haddad recalls. "'We will come back tomorrow.'"

Haddad slaughtered a lamb and, the following day, fed dozens of soldiers. "This file is our responsibility," an officer told him. "We cannot promise one hundred percent we will get restitution, but we are going to see what we can do." Five days later, army officials contacted Haddad and told him the file had been submitted. "They said, 'Please be patient,'" he recalls. "I said, 'I am not in a hurry.'"

He waited for weeks. But he heard nothing. On May 27, 2004, he picked up the file and prepared for a trip to an office in the al-Mansour district of Baghdad. He didn't feel steady enough to drive, he says, so he took a taxi. "I went to look for my rights," he tells me. In the office, he filed Claim #16D for $10,000 for "death and shop damage." He received a reply from the Department of the U.S. Army, Headquarters, 2nd Brigade, Combat Team, 1st Cavalry Division, Baghdad, signed by Capt. Keith Petty, Command Judge Advocate: "Disapproved based on a lack of evidence showing negligence of US personnel."[11]

I look at the documents and put them back on the table. It is clear that the army commander is not planning to compensate Haddad for the damages or to offer him a sympathy payment for the deaths of his sons. Haddad and I listen for a moment to the chanting of prayers from a nearby mosque and then are startled by a knock on the door. Haddad's relative, Ali, comes inside and asks if I have seen his favorite pen, a black one. I can't find it so I offer him another one. Haddad asks if he can have a pen, too. "As a souvenir," Haddad explains. I give him a blue felt-tip. As he gathers up his documents, I remember how nervous he had been earlier in the day in my hotel room. Now he has had a chance to tell his story and seems somehow relieved. I wish I could give him something that would acknowledge his loss and the fact there would be no official restitution, and I feel a bit thrown off balance by my own feelings of sadness and regret. I find myself grabbing a Polaroid picture of my boyfriend's cat—an orange tom called Bruno—that I keep on my bedside table and giving it to him. I do it without thinking, knowing only that I want to make a gesture to Haddad. In retrospect it seems embarrassing, but it was a response, however inadequate, to the tragedy of his story. He puts it in an envelope. I ask him if he thinks he will ever receive some form of restitution, through the civil suit or some other avenue.

He shakes his head.

"Even if President Bush were to call me and ask me to come to him and explain my case. Even if you asked me to go to America, and you assured me that you are going to give me compensation, I would not have any hope," he says. "Now we want to go to dinner. I am sorry I gave you a hard time."

Four months after our meeting, I call Haddad on the telephone to talk with him about the military claims. The lines between Abu Ghraib and Washington are scratchy, and we keep losing the connection. With the help of an interpreter, I manage to pose my question: why did you ask for a specific amount—$10,000—from the U.S. government?

"He says it was a number they told him to put on the form," the interpreter explains. "He says it doesn't mean anything to him. Nothing could compensate for the loss of his sons."

I had known that before I asked him. But I still felt disappointed. I somehow hoped he would receive restitution and that it would be a step toward making amends. But there was, quite simply, nothing I could do. I ask Haddad if he still has the Polaroid of Bruno, and I can hear him laugh on the telephone.

"Yes," says the interpreter. "He says he keeps it in a special place."

Haddad never even told me what things were like at Abu Ghraib. I heard that story from another man who came to Amman, a former Baath Party member and a "ghost detainee" who was held in CIA custody at the prison.

CHAPTER TEN

THE TRANSLATOR

I CAN'T GO THE BATHROOM WITHOUT AN NCO SNIFFING UP MY
ASS AND ASKING ME WHAT THE HELL I AM DOING, THEY'RE
GOING TO NOTICE IF AN IRAQI IS GETTING SHIT SMEARED ON
HIM OR ELECTROCUTED OR WALKED DOWN THE HALL WITH A
LEASH AROUND HIS NECK.

—Garett Reppenhagen, cavalry scout/sniper, 2-63 Armor Battalion,
1st Infantry Division, February 2004–February 2005. Baquba.
"What Was Asked of Us" by Trish Wood[1]

Adel L. Nakhla, a chunky, broad-shouldered Egyptian-American
interpreter with a soft, feminine voice, stood in front of Cell 43 in
Tier 1A. Graner stood next to him. Abdul-Hakim al-Mayah, a former
Baath Party member, was lying on a mattress behind the bars. (His
name and those of his family have been changed.) Mayah had been
classified as a "high-value target," a term for prisoners who are suspected of terrorist activities or may have knowledge of Saddam Hussein and his followers.[2] For military-security reasons, Mayah was not
given an identification number when he arrived at Abu Ghraib the
month before. Instead, he was under the supervision of the OGA, an

acronym that stands for Other Government Agencies, and means in most cases the CIA. Officially, Mayah, a "ghost detainee," did not exist.

"Get up, you criminal. You're pretending to be asleep," Nakhla said, as Mayah recalled. "Walk backwards—toward me."

Mayah, forty, is sitting in a green-striped, low-slung chair in Room 705 at the Regency Palace Hotel on a crisp March 2006 morning, nearly three years after he was held at Abu Ghraib. He is wearing a silver-buckled belt and has a high forehead and short hair. The room is warm, almost stifling, with frosted silver curtains and a gilded-frame mirror, but he is wearing a shirt with the sleeves rolled down. His wife, Qamar, forty-three, a woman in a pale-pink gown and glasses with inch-thick lenses, is sitting near him on a bed. She has been having problems with her vision (Mayah says she was hurt during the raid on their house when he was arrested), and they have come to Amman so she can speak with a physician about eye surgery.

This week, Mayah is also meeting with the American lawyers about the lawsuit *Saleh v. Titan*. U.S. government officials have not admitted that "ghost detainees" like Mayah existed in Iraq and elsewhere, and he is one of the few held at Abu Ghraib who has spoken with an American journalist about his experiences.

Formerly a high-level administrator in Saddam Hussein's Ministry of Industry and Military Industrialization, Mayah is funny, articulate, and arrogant. He also holds disturbing views. Over a cup of tea, he tells me he was arrested on November 19, 2003, less than three weeks after he had gone to a dinner party with a friend in Baghdad. At the time, it had been seven months since the fall of Saddam, and troops had cordoned off an area of the city, now known as the Green Zone, where Mayah had previously worked in a building next to Saddam's palace. He says he still admires Saddam, describing him as an "idol for the Iraqi people." And he goes on enthusiastically about the now-deposed Baath Party. "By law, the Baath Party still exists because the invasion was illegal and does not dissolve the party at all," he tells me. It occurs to me that his rhetoric probably did not endear him to the Americans he met at Abu Ghraib. Sometimes, it is better to be quiet, isn't it? I say.

"This was my problem with the interrogators," he says, laughing.

The night of the dinner party, he says, he had complained long and loud about the presence of U.S. troops in Baghdad. One of the guests, the host later told Mayah, was an informant for U.S. intelligence agents. The informant had apparently reported Mayah to U.S. forces and described his truculent views. Yet Mayah said he had no ties to the insurgency and knew nothing about the attacks on coalition forces.

That December evening in Abu Ghraib, Mayah says, he encountered Nakhla, who had been sent to Iraq by a private military contractor to work as an interpreter. Mayah says he later recognized Nakhla in the Abu Ghraib photographs. That night, Nakhla told him to step on a platform in the doorway of the cell. He climbed up. His hands were shackled behind his back.

"You son of a bitch," Nakhla said. "Move your legs away from the bar."

Mayah was infuriated by Nakhla's commands, but the other prisoners had told him he would be punished or perhaps killed if he didn't follow them. He took his feet off the platform and stepped into the air. This is known as a "Palestinian hanging," a form of abuse that Israeli troops have reportedly used on prisoners in their custody.

Mayah's feet swung in the air. He is five foot, eight inches tall, and at the time he weighed 156 pounds. With his weight supported by his arms, pinned behind his back, he found the pressure on his shoulders tremendously painful. He tried to put his hands out to stop himself and to put his feet back on the bar. As he hung in the air, he thought about Qamar and his four children. His youngest child was eleven.

"Don't," said Nakhla, who was known as Abu Hamid among the prisoners, and told Mayah not to place his feet on the bar. Nakhla was standing right behind Mayah. Mayah started to hear whistling in his head. He cried out for help.

"Abu Hamid, I am dying," he said. "Abu Hamid, I am going to die."

Mayah hoped Nakhla would talk to Graner and tell him to let him down from the cell door. He says he thought Nakhla would be more sympathetic toward him because they shared a common language and heritage. When Nakhla saw Mayah again reaching for the bar with his feet, though, Nakhla became angry and began to curse at him. Mayah eventually passed out. When he woke up, he was lying on the floor. He did not know who untied him or who put him on the floor. He never saw Nakhla or Graner again.

"WE HEARD THEM SCREAMING"

Palestinian hangings apparently occurred in various parts of Abu Ghraib, as well as in other U.S.-run detention facilities in Iraq, that fall. They can be lethal. Mayah's friend, Manadel al-Jamadi, died when he was placed in the position during a CIA interrogation in a shower stall at Abu Ghraib on November 4, 2003, and later became known as Ice Man. Soldiers posed next to his corpse for photographs. In one of the pictures taken, Sabrina Harman is kneeling beside the body and smiling broadly. Mayah says an American interrogator showed him a photo of Jamadi's corpse while they were asking Mayah questions about his involvement with the insurgency.

Graner did not participate in the CIA interrogation of Jamadi. Nor was Graner accused of mistreating Jamadi or contributing to his death. But, as I discovered during my reporting, Graner had received training in the use of stress positions from a Guantanamo interrogator and was familiar with Palestinian hangings. The use of stress positions has been cited frequently in the media. But until now there have been no detailed accounts of the technique or an examination of how widespread and damaging the use of stress positions, and especially the hangings, were at the prison. "Stress position" is somewhat benign-sounding term. It is a technique in which prisoners are forced to maintain a physical stance, such as a push-up or a squat, for a period of time. A prisoner who is suspended by his arms from the ceiling is sometimes described as being held in a stress position. On September 14, 2003, Lieutenant General Sanchez signed a memorandum approving the use of stress positions under certain conditions. "Use of physical postures (sitting, standing, kneeling) for no more than 1 hour per use," said the memorandum. "Use of technique(s) will not exceed 4 hours and adequate rest between use of each position will be provided."[3]

"There was a guy there one night from Gitmo and he was teaching Graner how to put them in stress positions to extract more information," explained Frederick in his November 2004 sworn statement. "The guy was an interrogator. I don't know who he was. He was short—about five foot, eight inches tall, 160 pounds, short brown hair, white male, and he had on DCU's [Desert Combat Uniform], but his top was off."[4]

"A stress position," says Guy Womack, a Houston-based civilian lawyer who represented Graner during his court-martial, "it wouldn't hurt–unless you moved."[5]

"That might happen during an interrogation," Womack adds, describing the use of Palestinian hangings. "But I've never heard of Graner being accused of that. He's never mentioned being asked to do it."

Graner knew how it was done, though. In October 2004, Womack and Graner rode in an MP vehicle on the dangerous road from Baghdad to Abu Ghraib. Graner drove. ("I was holding his rifle," Womack tells me. "It was awesome.") After they arrived, Graner took him on a two-hour tour of the prison and showed him the shower stall where Jamadi had been interrogated. "He said, 'Yeah, this is where it happened,'" Womack recalls. Graner pointed to a window, "three feet off the ground," Womack says, where Jamadi had hung from his arms.

A Texas sergeant described the stress-position technique to journalist Trish Wood. Graner had told the sergeant that the prisoners were "hanged by the handcuffs from bars above [with their feet] barely touching the floor. I heard this from different soldiers—not just Graner."[6]

One detainee, whose name appears in government documents as Amjed Isail Waleed (Prisoner Number 151365), was handcuffed and hung by his arms and left there, with his feet dangling in the air, for seven or eight hours in October 2003, according to a sworn statement he made on January 21, 2004, in the Taguba Report. "And that caused a rupture to my right hand and I had a cut that was bleeding and had pus coming from it," he said. Taguba said he found the account of Waleed and those of twelve other detainees "credible based on the clarity of their statements and supporting evidence provided by other witnesses."

One man who is identified as Mustafa Jassim Mustafa, Detainee Number 150542, said in a January 17, 2004, sworn statement in the Taguba Report, "Grainer [sic] used to hang the prisoners by hand to the doors and windows in a way that was very painful for several hours and we heard them screaming."

One night, Graner came to the cell of Ameen Sa'eed Al-Sheikh, Detainee Number 151362, according to a January 16, 2004, statement in the Taguba Report, and handcuffed his arms behind his back: "I told him, 'I have a broken shoulder, I'm afraid it will break again, because the doctor told me, 'Don't put your arms behind your back.' [Graner] said, 'I don't care.' Then he hung me to the door for more than eight hours. I was screaming from pain the whole night. Graner and others used to come to me and ask me, 'Does it hurt.' I said, 'Yes.' They said, 'Good.' And they [would] smack me on the back of the head."[7] Mayah says he remembers the night Sa'eed was hung from the door of his cell. Mayah could see him from his own cell across the hall. Mayah watched a physician come to his aid. "The doctor called for a medical team because he was shocked by what he had seen," says Mayah. "His shoulders were dislocated—separated from his body."[8]

MOONLIGHTING

Nakhla applied for a job as an interpreter with a private military contractor in the spring of 2003, according to court filings in the U.S. District Court for the District of Columbia. He had grown up in Egypt and had come to the U.S. in 1979 and was fluent in Arabic. He was offered a one-year assignment in Iraq.[9] He was a senior "terp," slang for "interpreter," explains Leonard Acho, a former assembly-line worker from Sterling Heights, Michigan, who worked with Nakhla at Abu Ghraib.[10] Like Acho and other civilian interpreters, Nakhla worked in a room, or in a makeshift space, with an interrogator, an analyst, and a prisoner. After Nakhla was finished with interrogations for the day, he often headed over to Tier 1A. He had no official responsibilities in that wing of the prison, according to Frederick. But Nakhla spent his free time there. It was common for interrogators to shift their schedules around, depending on the number and type of detainees who had arrived that day. Guards, contractors, and intelligence agents frequently wandered from one section of the prison to another.

There were few bilingual, Arabic-English speakers in the vicinity, and, apparently by default, Nakhla became the primary interpreter in Tier 1A and 1B. He lounged in the hallway, sitting on a white plastic lawn chair. Sometimes, he stayed till two in the morning. Graner used to tease him, said Frederick.

"You can't even speak Arabic!" Graner would tell Nakhla.[11]

Nakhla has thick fingers, broad shoulders, a double chin, and, on the day I saw him in May 2006 behind a counter in an eyeglasses store where he works in a Maryland shopping mall, he was wearing thick, black-framed glasses. His stomach stretched the fabric of his white jacket. "Fat Boy," says Hydrue Joyner, who knew him from Abu Ghraib's Tier 1A. "Got a lot of sugar in his tank."[12] Acho jokes about Nakhla's "boobs" and imitates the way Nakhla used to sway his body back and forth, undulating like a python, when he spoke with his friends. Acho demonstrates how Nakhla puts his palms together and places them on his chest, delicately, as if in prayer, when he talks. People said cruel things about Nakhla when he wasn't around. And sometimes when he was.

"A-a-a-ad-e-e-e! Aa-die!" Acho chants Nakhla's first name, Addie, in a high falsetto for me.[13] Several weeks later in the hotel room in Amman, I say Adel Nakhla's name in the same, sing-song voice Acho had used. Mayah looks up, and his face breaks into a smile. "Even the American soldiers made fun of him," Mayah says. "They would call him that—'Aaaa-deee.' We considered him a disgrace for Arabs. His voice was very feminine."[14]

TURF WARS

Before working as an interpreter in Iraq, according to court filings, Nakhla had previously been as a sales-support specialist for a large health-benefits company and for a health-insurance company. From 1998 to 1999, according to a resume posted on the Internet, he worked for a business communications company in Virginia.[15] The offices are located on the ground floor of a five-story building on a congested, seven-lane road across from a Woodburners Two restaurant and a Liberty Quality Inn.

"He was one of the nicest guys who's ever worked here," says Don Eckrod, a company vice president. "He's a big guy, size-wise. Just a lovable-bear kind of a guy. Almost too nice."[16]

On the street where Nakhla lives, he has a different reputation. He and his wife, Nadine, a quiet, dark-haired woman, and their two school-aged daughters live in a white row house with a black gate securing the front door on a cul-de-sac, where the Nakhlas have been since 1989. An American flag sticker with 9/11 imprinted on it is pasted in their front window. A dark blue Toyota Corolla with a cross and a keychain soccer ball dangling from the rearview window is parked in front of the house.

A next-door neighbor, David Sykes, an art director for a local television station, tells me there have been "some real shouting matches" between Nakhla and their neighbor, Steve Kerr, a systems analyst.[17] The exterior of the row houses on the block are almost identical. Inside, too, the floor plans and decorating styles of the Nakhlas and the Kerrs are similar. The Nakhla living room has a chandelier and muted blinds. The Kerr living room is comfortably cluttered with a *Good Housekeeping* magazine and a signed photo of President George W. Bush. Despite the things they have in common, including a shared property line, they are not on speaking terms.

Steve's wife, Nancy, says she still has "a rambling letter, telling me how horrible my children are" that Nakhla wrote 11 years ago. After receiving the letter, she called the police. She recalls how, another time, she had watched Nakhla kick her Glad trash bag across the yard to move it to another spot. The expression on his face, she said, "was like, 'Oh, I hate this.' Oh, my gosh. Anger, just anger."[18]

THE ACCUSATIONS

Nakhla is standing near three naked male prisoners in a hallway of Tier 1A in a time- and date-stamped photo: 11:06 PM, 25 October 2003. A white fan, suspended from a bar, is spinning above them. At least six other soldiers and one officer are standing in the hallway, too. The prisoners had been accused of the rape of a fifteen-year-old boy. Nakhla is wearing desert-camouflage pants and a short-sleeved shirt. His hand is on or near the neck of one of the prisoners.

11:13 PM, 25 October 2003: Nakhla is standing in a hallway of Tier 1A near two prisoners who are lying on the floor. A white plastic lawn chair is pushed against the side of the wall. His hands are on his hips, and he is staring down at the men.

11:16 PM: Nakhla is sitting on the lawn chair. He is roughly three feet from the prisoners lying on the floor.[19] Some of the soldiers thought Nakhla had positioned the group of prisoners and was "quarterbacking" the event, says attorney Womack.[20] As Nakhla sits in the chair and looks at the prisoners, a soldier goes to retrieve a Nerf-style football that had apparently been flung at the prisoners and had then rolled down the hall. Nakhla tugged and pulled at the legs of the prisoners at some point, placing them on or near each other, said Frederick.[21] The prisoners were forced to touch each other in sexual ways. They were also piled on top of each other and handcuffed together so that their genitals were pushed together. If their bodies fell to the side or were no longer touching, Nakhla, Graner, or another soldier would push their buttocks back toward the floor so that they would rub against each other.

11:17 PM, 25 October 2003: Nakhla is crouched on the ground next to three naked male prisoners. Two of the doors to prison cells are partly open. Nakhla's hands are placed on or near the body of one of the detainees.

Nakhla later admitted in a sworn statement in the Taguba Report to holding prisoners down while they were nude and placed in sexual positions.[22] According to the Fay-Jones Report, an individual who is identified as "Civilian-17" and is most likely Nakhla is accused of hitting a detainee so hard his ear later had to be stitched up.[23] A contractor, "Civilian Translator, Titan Corp., Assigned to the 205th MI Brigade," is listed as a "Suspect" in detainee-related misconduct in the Taguba Report. He is widely believed to be Nakhla. In Nakhla's own sworn statement, he talks about three detainees who were "hand-cuffed and nude" and "on the floor." He said he held one of the detainees in place by grasping his foot—though "not in any powerful way." In addition, Nakhla said, he asked the detainees if they were gay or if they enjoyed what was being done to them.

"Did you realize at the time that you were saying these things to the detainees that it was wrong to tell them these things the soldiers wanted you to say?" Taguba asked.

"I do realize that it was wrong at that time to say those things," Nakhla said. "I even apologized to the detainees."

A detainee whose name appears in the Taguba Report as Hiadar Saber Abed Miktub-Aboodi saw Nakhla differently. Miktub-Aboodi said in a sworn statement that Nakhla was present for a ten-day period when soldiers put hoods on the prisoners, forced them to masturbate, to get on all fours and bark like dogs. He also stepped on their hands, according to Miktub-Aboodi, and beat them "with no mercy."

There were other accusations. The following account is based on the investigative summary of a report issued by a Baghdad-based office of the CID and a January 18, 2004, sworn statement from one of the prisoners whose name appears as Kasim Mehaddi Hilas in the Taguba Report. A boy "about 15 to 18 years" had been arrested on a simple assault charge on September 15, 2003, in Baghdad and placed in Cell 23. (He has a tribal name that is redacted.) Hilas said he saw Nakhla, whom he referred to as Abu Hamid, assault the boy sometime October 3 and October 23, 2003. Nakhla was "fucking a kid," said Hilas. "The kid was hurting very bad, and they covered all the doors with sheets. Then when I heard the screaming, I climbed to the door because on top it wasn't covered. And I saw Abu Hamid, who was wearing a military uniform, putting his dick in the little kid's ass. . . . And the female soldier was taking pictures."[24] The boy was transferred out of Abu Ghraib on October 23 and released to the Iraqi Ministry of Justice. The CID listed several statutes Nakhla could be charged with, including 18 U.S.C. 2241, Aggravated Sexual Abuse. If convicted, he could face up to life in prison.

England tells me she didn't take pictures of an incident like that. If there were any taken, they could have been done by Harman or Ambuhl, she says.[25] Keys to the cells were easy to obtain. Graner and Ambuhl often left them hanging in an office in Tier 1A.[26]

NIGHT MUSIC

Six boys, and possibly more, were held prisoner at Abu Ghraib in the fall of 2003.[27] They were housed in Tier 1B—adjacent to Tier 1A, which held terrorism suspects—because that wing of the prison offered more protection from mortar attacks as well as from the violent crime that occurred in the open-air tents with adult prisoners. (In U.S. prisons, juveniles are held separately from adults for their safety. The young Iraqi prisoners who were held in close proximity with adult detainees in U.S. custody were in danger of assault. In one case described in the army surgeon general's report, a young detainee at a detention facility in Balad in spring 2003 was allegedly "gang-raped twice in a holding facility—[the] second time after being returned to the same area." According to the report, "MPs had no guards assigned directly within the facility. Unclear if any actions taken."[28])

General Karpinski spoke with one child during a visit to the prison. He told her that he was twelve years old. But, she says, he looked like he was about eight. "My brother is here," he said. "But I really want to see my mother. Can I please see my mother?"[29] "He was very small, very slight," she tells me. "He could speak a little bit of English. He was crying. You can tell crocodile tears from real tears. He was afraid. I asked [Colonel] Pappas, 'Are you planning to interrogate him?' He said, 'Well, ma'am, if we have to.'"[30]

The children were fed meals that were prepared by a private contractor. They were also served apples, bananas, chocolate cake, and bread baked at the prison. As long as the bread was fresh, says Joyner, it tasted fine. Sometimes, though, you could barely bite into it.[31] And there never seemed to be enough food to go around. The children reached their hands out of the cells and begged for more to eat. One female detainee, Minnah Karam al-Kamil, fifty-one, a seamstress with seven children in Baghdad, says she would wait for a quiet moment when the guards were not paying attention (name changed for security reasons). Then she would toss pieces of fruit, cheese slices, and cake to the children in the prison cells.[32]

England says she used to wander the hallway in Tier 1B at night. She chatted with the boys. They never wanted to go to bed, "just like juveniles everywhere," she says. She would try to help them calm down so they could get some sleep.[33] Nakhla, too, walked the hallway. Sometimes, says England, he visited the boys. The doors of the cells were painted greenish-yellow, and they were secured with sturdy metal padlocks on the outside. The floors were made of cracked concrete. Sometimes, a sheet would be left hanging from a railing in the hallway. Or a mattress was turned over on its side, leaning against a wall. Mayah remembers how Nakhla would stop in front of a cell where a ten-year-old southern Iraqi boy was held.

"Abu Hamid would say to the boy, 'Sing,'" says Mayah. "'If you don't, you will be punished.'"

"He would sing with a lovely, lovely, but sad voice," says Mayah, recalling the lyrics. Mayah nods his head and then rests his chin against his hand. The boy was kept in a prison wing separate from his father. Through his songs, he told his father to take care of himself and not to worry about him. When his voice faded away at night, Mayah says, he and the other men in Tier 1A would find themselves in tears.[34]

OTHER GOVERNMENT AGENCY

People in other parts of the prison knew something strange was going on in Tier 1A. Specialist Luciana Spencer, a member of the 66th Military Intelligence Group, described a "screen saver for a computer that was up in the isolation area. The screen saver had detainees naked in a pyramid," according to the Taguba Report.[35] The men who were involved in the death of Jamadi tried to remove his body discretely from the premises. But England—and others—had memories of the night he died. "She said, 'You could hear him screaming throughout the prison,'" says Christy Hardy, a friend of England's and the wife of Roy Hardy, England's attorney. "She said she had nightmares for days."

In December 2003 England and her mother, Terrie, walked into Hardy's law office located across the street from the Keyser, West Virginia, courthouse. England wanted legal advice about filing for a divorce from Fike. Hardy is a tall, flirty, dark-haired Gulf War vet with an imposing gut and a military discount he offers clients, and he and his wife recalled watching England enter the room. "She was so skinny," Christy says. "She looked like the wind would blow her away."[36]

"Most people don't make up their excuse until after they're in trouble," says Roy Hardy. England told them that things weren't right at Abu Ghraib weeks before the initial military investigation into the abuse. She described how she and the other soldiers would "smoke" the detainees as well as make them wear women's underwear on their heads and comply with other unusual disciplinary measures. "She told me their job was to keep them awake: let them sleep a little bit and then wake them back up. I said, 'Are you allowed to do that?' and she said, 'Oh, yeah, that's what we're told to do,'" explains Roy Hardy. "She told me the officers were involved and knew what was going on. There were a lot of what she called 'OGAs.'"[37]

Officially, OGA stands for "other government agency." But Hardy, and everyone in the army, knows it meant the CIA. They will also tell you that it means don't ask questions.

"It's a different situation than just working at McDonald's," says Klinestiver, describing the predicament her sister faced in Iraq. "If you're told to do something by someone who's higher-ranking in the military, you do it. If you don't, you're going to be court-martialed. Lynndie basically found out you're damned if you do and damned if you don't. And being in love with Graner, that made it even harder."[38]

Military police and contractors in other parts of the compound talked about the harsh treatment of prisoners in Tier 1A. They knew what was happening in that building, but nobody did anything about it. In detention facilities in other parts of Iraq, things seemed to be the same.

CHAPTER ELEVEN

THE PLAYBOY

IT WAS VERY AMBIGUOUS TO ME WHAT I WAS ABLE TO DO WITH AN ENEMY PRISONER OF WAR. IF I KNOCKED HIM CLEAN OUT, I'M SURE NOT A SINGLE PERSON WOULD HAVE SAID A THING.

—Garett Reppenhagen, cavalry scout/sniper, 2-63 Armor Battalion, First Infantry Division, February 2004–February 2005. Baquba. "What Was Asked of Us" by Trish Wood[1]

At 7:00 AM on Tuesday, December 16, 2003, three days after the capture of Saddam Hussein in an underground lair in Ad Dwar, Iraq, Hisham L. Azzam Dilami, forty-five, left his house in Baghdad and headed for work. (His name and those of his family members have been changed.) He was an administrator in the Ministry of Culture and was overseeing the reconstruction of a small cultural center approximately thirty miles outside of Baghdad.

Work on the cultural center had been underway when American troops arrived in Iraq in March 2003. Then Dilami lost his job, which paid $120 a month, because of his Baathist affiliation. Two months later, he and many other former Baathists were rehired in their government jobs in order to help rebuild the country. He returned to the construction site only to find the windows broken and the building ransacked by looters. He hired a crew of twenty-seven full-time construction workers as well as two teenage boys to cook meals for the crew. For several weeks, Dilami had been driving to the cultural center every day so he could check on the workers' progress. He became suspicious at a certain point of the two cooks. He had heard from his workers that the teenagers were bringing drugs and alcohol to the site and that they were also visiting American soldiers stationed at a nearby U.S. military installation. The situation made him uneasy.

That day in December, a group of U.S. soldiers made a surprise visit to the construction site. Four Hummers and three heavily armored vehicles pulled up, and a helicopter hovered above the building. Dilami had been a tank commander in the Iraqi army, and he greeted the American troops in a professional manner. Then he checked his watch. It was 9:20 AM. At the time, Dilami thought the cooks had brought on the raid because of the rumors that they had been selling recreational drugs to U.S. troops. Yet the soldiers paid no attention to the teenagers. Instead, they handcuffed Dilami and several of the workers and made them sit on cold sand and gravel about five feet apart so they could not speak to each other. The soldiers inspected Dilami's toolbox and, for seventy minutes, searched the site for contraband and weapons. They did not seem to find anything. Two and a half hours after their arrival, the soldiers took Dilami and eleven other men to Camp Mercury. They left the cooks and the other workers alone.

Dilami was later escorted into a room in an olive-green building at the U.S. military installation. He heard a guard talking with someone outside the facility. "All the mice are in the trap," the guard said.[2]

LOOKING FOR INTELLIGENCE

March 10, 2006. It has been more than three years since Dilami was arrested and taken to the U.S. military installation. He approaches me in a conference room in the Regency Hotel in Amman, where he is meeting with American lawyers about the lawsuit *Saleh v. Titan*, and hands me a slip of paper that he has folded neatly into fourths. His name and hotel room number and two short sentences are printed in block letters: "I need help you. Thank you."

Several hours later, Dilami is sitting, with his back ramrod straight, in a chair in a chilly hotel room. Attorney Judith Chomsky, sixty-five, an interpreter, and I are sitting on the other side of the room. Chomsky has springy curls and impeccable taste. (She is fond of Arabic-style lamb chops and had stored a paperback novel and a Prada gift box under her seat on the flight from Paris to Amman.) She ferried draft dodgers across the Canadian border during the Vietnam War[3] and, decades later, an officemate's client was charged with conspiring to plant a bomb in the U.S. capital and was placed under supervision at Chomsky's house (and then fled, prompting Chomsky to call the FBI).[4] Her brother-in-law, Noam, is the well-known educator and author whose recent book, *9-11*, according to his Web site traces the attacks back to "the actions and power of the United States, which he calls 'a leading terrorist state.'"[5] Judith, too, has a penchant for sweeping statements. "We have blood on our hands all the time now," she told me at dinner in the hotel one evening.

Dilami has a thick, broad nose, a neatly trimmed mustache, long eyelashes, and velvety black, thinning hair. He chain-smokes Miami cigarettes and brushes away the ashes when they fall across his lap. He comes across as an elegant, thoughtful, and charming man—and a valuable resource for the attorneys working on the lawsuit. "Because he is so observant and detail-oriented," explains Chomsky, "he can help us identify who did what."[6]

Dilami says he was not planning attacks on U.S. forces in December 2003, despite the U.S. military's accusations to the contrary.

He says he was bewildered by the questions posed by the interrogators. He says (truthfully) he did not know the whereabouts of the weapons of mass destruction. He also says he did not have information about a Chinook helicopter that had recently crashed in Iraq. He was, however, a decades-long member of the Baath Party and an admirer of Saddam Hussein. "He has a strong personality," Dilami tells me. "He controlled the country with power and with an iron grip, but it was necessary. That was evident after Saddam Hussein was removed. Afterward, there was a great deal of corruption. Even those who once hated him were calling for his return and for the union of the Iraqi people."

Dilami's privileged position under Saddam indicates that he was likely more than just a Baath Party member. He had been a significant stakeholder in the old regime and had an incentive to support the undermining of the U.S. occupation and subsequent Iraqi government. The interrogators were aware of his past affiliations and of his current views. In addition, there may have been other reasons for the U.S. interrogators to be wary of him and want to question him aggressively. Yet these grounds for suspicion were perhaps unfounded.

Dilami says after he was released from U.S. custody he discovered the two cooks had been paid $25 apiece for providing information about him to U.S. intelligence officers.[7] It is difficult to determine with any certainty whether the teenagers knew about clandestine activities Dilami had been involved in (despite his claims of innocence)—or whether they just wanted to make a bit of cash, or they disliked him and therefore said things about him that were not true. If they had, they would not have been the only Iraqis peddling false information to American intelligence agents during that time.

On December 16, 2003, the day Dilami was arrested, American troops were in high spirits over the capture of Saddam Hussein. Their intelligence-gathering efforts—partly based on collecting information from former associates, friends of Saddam's family members, and Iraqis who lived in or near Ad Dwar—had paid off. It was a victory for the U.S. troops and for most people in Iraq. Yet not everybody was pleased. In Baghdad, Fallujah, and other cities where Saddam had a loyal following, the insurgency was growing in strength and numbers. American military leaders seemed uncertain how to proceed through such terrain. "We did not prepare our military forces for civil-military missions, to deal with terrorism and insurgency, to play the role of occupier in a nation with an alien religion, language, and culture, or to have the mix of [human intelligence] and weapons they needed for the 'war after the war,'" Anthony H. Cordesman, a scholar at the Center for Strategic and International Studies, said at a Senate Foreign Relations Committee hearing on February 1, 2005.[8]

"In an insurgency, of course, intelligence is the key," said General Richard B. Myers, chairman of the Joint Chiefs of Staff, at a Senate Armed Services Committee hearing on Iraq on June 30, 2005. "And indigenous intelligence is even more of a key."[9]

Placing an undercover agent in the midst of enemy forces is one way to collect intelligence. But there were few Arabic-speaking U.S. agents who could have infiltrated the Iraqi insurgency groups and survived long enough to report back to the army on their plans. That meant U.S. troops and intelligence agents had to rely in part on informants. This method of intelligence gathering was done partly through a "tips" program. A senior U.S. military official speaking on background at a January 7, 2004, press conference explained why people in Iraq had been providing information to U.S. forces. "The motivation for how that intelligence came into our hands is probably hard to find," said the military official. "Some may have been motivated by the money; some may have been motivated by patriotism. There may have been a number of motivations. All we know is that those people who provided direct intelligence that led to the killing or capture of the high-value targets are certainly much wealthier today than they were the day before."

The military official touted the success of the tips program, explaining that it had led the U.S. military and intelligence agents to forty-two out of the fifty-five Iraqis on the Pentagon's most-wanted list—the famous deck of cards that featured former members of the Saddam Hussein regime. "We want to focus like a laser beam on the diehard insurgents and the most violent individuals," he explained.[10]

Tips programs are familiar to anyone who has watched an episode of *America's Most Wanted*. There were no Iraqi TV programs about fugitives from justice in 2003, though, encouraging people to turn in suspected terrorists. (Those programs appeared on television later.) Instead, American soldiers tried to dress casually and canvas neighborhoods and ask locals if they had any information about insurgents, explains Dave DeBatto, a former army counterintelligence agent who served in Iraq in 2003 and has spoken about intelligence issues on Fox News and National Public Radio.

U.S. agents started out paying Iraqi men and women "a dollar a day and a jug of water and an MRE," DeBatto says, for information. By the fall of 2003, informants were paid ten to twenty dollars. ("That's inflation," he adds.) If someone provided intelligence about a high-value detainee, he or she could be paid a sizable sum of money. Sometimes, Iraqis would wander into local police stations on their own initiative and tell American soldiers about insurgent activity in the area. Later, when things got more dangerous, Iraqis might pull aside soldiers while they were on armed patrols and whisper things to them. The problem was that, as time went on, insurgents seemed to be everywhere and it became more difficult for U.S. officers to speak freely with Iraqis. Besides that, the informants had different agendas. Some wanted to rat out a neighbor, get back at a difficult boss, or make some cash so they could feed their family that night.

The decision on whether or not to act on information provided by local informants was not always easy. DeBatto says he and other intelligence officers tried to verify the information with at least two sources. But sometimes U.S. troops would charge into an apartment or a house after receiving a tip from only one informant.[11] Or they would arrest people based on information they believed was true but was likely embellished. Or the informant was simply wrong. Regardless of the circumstances of his arrest, Dilami did not provide answers the interrogators wanted to hear. Yet, at least according to his account, the interrogators went to great lengths to convince him to talk.

BAGHDAD ROMANCE

Dilami grew up in a neighborhood, Al Mansour, "the Class-A area in Baghdad," as he tells me. He attended Al Mansour Preparatory School, located about a half mile from his house, and studied engineering at the Ministry of Higher Education Technical Institute Russfa. He joined the Baath Party in 1975 at age seventeen. After he completed his engineering degree in 1981, he became a captain in the tanks unit of the Iraqi military's Armored Weapons division. He started as a commander of three tanks and ended as a commander of eleven. He served eleven years and eight months in the military.

On August 2, 1990, Iraqi forces entered Kuwait. United Nations resolution 687 lambasted "the unlawful invasion and occupation" and American troops went to battle in the region. After their defeat, Iraq began to downsize its military. Dilami says he left the Armored Weapons division at that time and submitted an application for employment to the Ministry of Finance in Baghdad. He was eventually hired to work in the engineering department of the Ministry of Information and Culture. As a thirty-one-year-old bachelor working at the Culture Ministry, he enjoyed going to the theater. His favorite play was Shakespeare's *Merchant of Venice*. "It shows the nature of humans," he explains, "and how they can be deceitful." He also hung out in nightclubs and chatted up Filipino waitresses, sometimes taking them on a tour of Baghdad.

In 1992, shortly after Dilami started his job at the Culture Ministry, he met and fell in love with a twenty-year-old schoolteacher, Rasha Khalaf, who lived near his house. They went to the theater together and took walks through Baghdad's Al Zawraa Park. He and Khalaf now have two sons, Saad, ten, and Mustafi, nine, and, with the young boys at home, they watch a lot of action and comedy DVDs, especially *Mr. Bean*. In one of Dilami's favorite movies, Mr. Bean tries to paint an apartment by placing a bomb in a paint bucket and letting it explode in a room. "Sometimes he does things but he doesn't know what he's doing," says Dilami. "He walks next to a magnetic pole and gets static in his hands. Then he goes up to a girl and makes her skirt fly up. But he does it with innocence."

It is easy to see why Dilami likes Mr. Bean. "Although I am forty-eight years old, people say I don't look it," Dilami says. "They say I seem like a young person." He is flirty, addressing an interpreter as "my dear," as well as fun, curious, and gregarious—a playboy, in every sense.

THE INTERROGATION

On the day he arrived at the U.S. military installation, Dilami was—like most prisoners—placed in a holding cell. Detainees were usually held there for three days, interrogated, and then taken to Abu Ghraib, according to a September 2005 Human Rights Watch report about a U.S. military installation in the area that was partly based on an account provided by Capt. Ian Fishback. The detainees' stay at the military camp was often trying. Members of the U.S. Army's 82nd Airborne Division routinely mistreated detainees at the military installation in 2003 and 2004, beating them and breaking their bones, withholding food and medication, and piling them in human pyramids, according to the report. "[The soldiers] said that they had [taken] pictures that were similar to what happened at Abu Ghraib, and because they were so similar to what happened at Abu Ghraib the soldiers destroyed the pictures," Fishback said. In addition, personnel apparently working for the CIA brought detainees into private rooms at the military installation and conducted their own interrogations.[12]

Dilami was stripped of his clothing not long after he arrived at the military camp and was taken to a fifteen-by-fifteen-foot room smelling of tobacco, off a hallway lined with office doors. Three American men and an interpreter were there. Dilami saw a clock on the wall, a white plastic board with his name and several words scribbled in English in red and blue ink, and a table and two chairs. There was also an electronic device in the room. It was a square-shaped contraption the size of a desktop computer with an antenna, wires, and clips.

"Put your hands in the air," the interrogator told him.

Dilami held up his hands and, as instructed, stated his name and occupation. Then the soldiers and an interpreter told him to sit down. Dilami says he remembers that the chair's metal frame felt cold on his bare skin. His hands were fastened behind his back, and his legs were shackled to the chair. The interpreter held him by his hair and pulled his head back.

"Tell us about the weapons of mass destruction," said the interpreter, who spoke with a Lebanese accent. "Tell us what you know about the place where Saddam Hussein had been hiding."

"I'm just an average citizen," Dilami said. "I don't know."

"Cooperate with us or we'll use this on you," said the interpreter, gesturing toward the electrical device in the room.

The interrogator took the shackles off Dilami's wrists. His hands fell loose by his sides. Then the interrogator shackled Dilami's hands in front of him. The interrogator then slipped on a pair of rubber gloves and took four vials of blue, red, and multicolored liquid from his cargo pocket. He put them on the table. Then he held out a syringe and started shaking it.

"Are you going to talk?" the interrogator asked. "Or are we going to have to use this?"

He wrapped a rubber cord around Dilami's left bicep. Then he tapped and rubbed Dilami's skin, looking for a vein. "Will you talk?" the interpreter asked.

"I don't know what to talk about," Dilami said.

"You need to cooperate," the interpreter said. "If you don't, we will give you a shot. You will be paralyzed."

Sitting in the hotel room in Amman, Dilami shows me how the interrogator tapped his arm and looked for a vein. Dilami demonstrates how he held out his arm at the time and was then injected with a hypodermic needle. "The interpreter said, 'Now see what's going to happen to you,'" Dilami recalls.

The interpreter and the interrogator left the room. Dilami's head started to hurt, and he felt chilled. After a while, the interpreter returned with a blond man in jeans and T-shirt. Silently, the blond-haired man poured water on Dilami. Then Dilami was taken to a cold, dark, three-by-one-and-a-half-yard cell. His head was pounding. And he saw water on the floor. "I was naked. The floor was wet," he says, holding a set of red, plastic prayer beads attached to a worn tassel. (The beads were given to him, he says, by a farmer who was shot and killed at Abu Ghraib by a guard in April 2004.) His legs are jiggling up and down. "I felt hatred. Mostly, I felt disbelief. I had heard that Americans fight for human rights. I was wondering if it was true that the shot was going to paralyze me. I just gave up and thought, *If I'm going to die, there's nothing I can do about it*," he says, describing how he curled up in a corner of the cell that night and tried to sleep. When he woke up, his arm was numb. He could not move his fingers.

Monday, December 22, 2003. The interrogator had a wooden baton in his hand. A yellow dragon, spitting fire, was painted on it. Dilami was sitting in a chair in an interrogation room. His hands and legs were shackled.

"You have to talk," the interpreter said. He asked again about Saddam's weapons of mass destruction. "I don't know anything about them," Dilami said.

The interrogator struck Dilami on his back with the baton. The interrogator and the other men in the room gave him four bottles of water and told him to drink all of them. Dilami drank half the water in one bottle. "The interrogator was wearing gloves. I always knew they were going to hit me or torture me because they were wearing gloves," he says. The interrogator stood behind him. Dilami thought the interrogator was going to choke him. Instead, the interrogator took out a string, bent over Dilami and tied the string around his penis. Then he pulled the string As Dilami talks, he wraps the string of the prayer beads around a roller-ball pen and puts the pen between his legs and shows what the interrogator did to his penis. Dilami pulls the strand of prayer beads around the pen as tight as he can.

On the day of the interrogation, Dilami had screamed in pain, he recalls. He leaned back in the chair during the abuse. Every time he tried to move back to ease his discomfort, the interrogator shoved him forward. "The translator said 'You talk, or we'll cut it off,'" he recalls. "It was very painful. I still have marks where the string was."

Then the interpreter fetched a container of hot water and poured it over his penis. "It wasn't burning hot," Dilami says. "It was coffee-hot—a bit hotter than the water in a shower." After a while, he was taken back to his cell.

Two days later, the interrogator brought him back to the same room.

"I will help you," the interrogator said, calmly. "And you help us."

"Help you with what?" Dilami asked.

"Tell us about the Chinook that went down," the interrogator said.

"I heard that it was a technical error," said Dilami.

"No, it was the Iraqis," said the interrogator.

Dilami laughed.

"How can I bring down a helicopter?" he asked.

"You know nothing about the WMDs," said the interpreter. "You know nothing about the Chinook. What do you know?"

When Dilami was alone in his cell after the interrogations, he would tear up scraps of paper he had gotten from an Iraqi janitor. He wrote notes to Khalaf, telling her not to worry about him. "I would say, 'I'm in prison, but I don't know where. Take care of the house and children.' Or, 'I miss you,' or, 'I've been abused,'" he recalls. "But I wouldn't give her details."

He asked Khalaf to contact his colleagues at the Ministry of Culture so they could help get him released from the detention facility. After scratching out messages on slips of paper, he folded them into tiny, one-fourth-inch squares and gave them to the janitor. As Dilami describes the notes he wrote to his wife, he wads up a slip of notebook paper with his hands. The crumpled-up note looks like the slip of paper he had handed to me in the morning in the hotel conference room, and I wondered how he thought I could help him. He was no longer imprisoned, of course, but he was still suffering. At the military installation, the janitor stuffed Dilami's handwritten notes in his nostrils or tucked them underneath his tongue, smuggling them out of the detention center, and then delivered them to Khalaf.

On Thursday, December 25, 2003, more than a week after

Dilami's arrival at the military installation, he was taken to a room with an emblem of the International Committee of the Red Cross fastened on the door. The medical office was located approximately five yards from the interrogation room. Inside, an American physician in army fatigues greeted him. Dilami was covered in bruises. His arm was numb from the injection, and his penis was swollen from the beatings. The physician gave him two tablets to ease the pain, and an interpreter, an elderly woman, assisted the physician during the medical exam.

"Did you tell the doctor you had been beaten?" I ask.

"The bruises on me were very obvious," says Dilami. "I didn't have to tell him what had happened."

The physician and the interpreter did not ask Dilami how he had been injured or whether the marks on his body had been inflicted before he arrived at the camp or during his stay, Dilami says. In fact, the injuries seemed to be a common occurrence at the camp, at least according to soldiers who were stationed there at the time. "The torture of detainees reportedly was so widespread and accepted that it became a means of stress relief for soldiers," according to the Human Rights Watch report.

The interrogator was standing outside the door of the medical office during Dilami's exam and watched him through a window in the hallway. Every time Dilami looked up, the interrogator gave him the finger. On December 28, 2003, Dilami was taken to Abu Ghraib.[13] (The dates of his detention, as well as his prisoner-identification number, were confirmed by an army spokesman.)[14]

SHOCK TREATMENT

Few accounts of the application of electricity, or the threat of its use, during interrogations in Iraq have been reported in detail in the U.S. media. Yet descriptions of the technique were provided by Dilami, as well as by other detainees I met in Amman, and accounts appear as well in government documents. On April 13, 2004, for example, Sergeant Matthew K. Travis of Camp Pendleton, California, First

Marine Division, suggested using electrical shock on a prisoner at a detention facility at Al-Mahmudiya, Iraq, according to a transcript of his general court martial. He was tried in Fallujah, Iraq, on August 19, 2004. Travis had previously worked a twelve-dollar-an-hour factory job in Jacksonville, North Carolina. He had prepared for battle in Iraq during his army training. Instead of fighting in combat, though, he was put in charge of detainees at a facility in Mahmudiya. As a guard, he had become increasingly frustrated with one prisoner, a five-foot-ten-inch man in his mid-twenties, for petty offenses like tossing trash out of his cell. One day Travis told a soldier, Private First Class Andrew J. Sting, about his idea of shocking the detainee with electricity as a way of disciplining him for the infractions.

"Look what I found," Travis said, holding out a set of wires, as Sting recalled. Travis explained how the electricity would be transmitted through three-and-a-half feet Romex wires, or basic household wiring, that would be plugged into a converter box. Sting is the son of an electrician. He agreed to hold the wires and the converter and to assist in the disciplinary procedure. The prisoner was escorted out of his cell. His hands were secured in flexicuffs, and his head was covered in a sandbag.

"Let's get him," Sting recalled Travis saying.

Sting walked behind the prisoner and put the wires on the detainee's shoulder. Nothing happened. Sting fiddled with the converter box and tried again, placing the wires against the prisoner's forearm until 110 volts of electricity were transmitted into his body. Travis and Sting were found guilty of detainee-related misconduct. Travis was sentenced to fifteen months of confinement, and Sting to one year.[15]

Like many (perhaps most) tools of torture and abuse, electricity is an instrument that is easily accessible and serves a duel purpose. People who have been tortured say that ordinary household objects, such as a chair or table leg, are used often during abusive interrogations. Electrical devices and wires are easy to find at a military camp. And the use of electrical shock inflicts an added layer of torment that a piece of furniture cannot impose. It is worth noting the case above because it was apparently not the only time a detainee was subjected to electrical shock while being held in U.S. custody in Iraq. Other prisoners also accused their captors of applying electricity to their bodies.

One detainee, a thirty-four-year-old Iraqi man who was on a Most Wanted list issued by the U.S. military, was captured on April 27, 2004, at his home in Tikrit. He was taken to a nearby interrogation site in a building called Kheirolla Tolfah, which had previously been occupied by one of Saddam Hussein's uncles (and was subsequently taken over by American personnel). The detainee claimed that a Kurdish interpreter beat, slashed, and shocked him with "a tazer type device" in the presence of a "white male" in American uniform.

Twenty-eight days later, the detainee was taken to Abu Ghraib and underwent a routine medical screening "to determine if he was medically fit to undergo interrogation," said a medic in a May 30, 2004, sworn statement made in the Joint Interrogation Debriefing Center at Abu Ghraib during an investigation into allegations of detainee abuse. "During the course of the evaluation, the patient reported 28 days prior experiencing physical abuse while in the 'Kheirolla Tolfah' house." The detainee "stated that he was hit with 'power' on different parts of his body. He indicated this was a device of some kind that produced electric shocks. He also stated that he was cut in his left arm area with a knife. His exam showed a linear scar in the left arm that was consistent with a knife injury. He also had multiple circular scars on his extremities consistent with the electric burn injuries the patient described," said the medic. In addition, the medic said, "Pictures were taken of all visible injuries."

"Were the injuries consistent with his allegations of abuse?" someone asked the medic.

"Yes," the medic said. "Everything he described he had on his body."

Another detainee was captured at the same time and also held in Kheirolla Tolfah house. He said that a Kurdish interpreter had mistreated him in the presence of Americans. "One of them shock my feet with electricity," he said, according to a translation of a sworn statement that was obtained by the CID. The Kurdish linguist, according to the detainee's account, "was wearing [a] black mask with two holes for his eyes and a hole for his mouth—he was hitting me and pulling me.

"I was naked and they were laughing and stepping on my body with their boots, and rubbing my skin with their boots," the detainee said. "All of them start hitting me on my head.

"They took me to another room—they hanged me about one meter from the floor but the handcuffs opened and I fell on my head and one of them shocked my feet with electricity. They took me to a different room. The Kurdish linguist was carrying pliers and he told me to open my mouth. 'Dog,' [he said]. He put [the pliers] inside my mouth and tried to pull my teeth, and he wanted to pull my teeth but he suddenly stopped. I don't know why."

The army medic's statement had corroborated one of the detainee's accounts and had also said photographic evidence of the abuse had been obtained. Yet military personnel determined on October 1, 2004, "There was insufficient evidence to prove or disprove the allegations of Aggravated Assault, Cruelty and Maltreatment, and Conspiracy occurred as originally reported," according to an Agent's Investigative Report. And in a November 2004 report about this incident, as well as other allegations of detainee abuse, Brigadier General Formica concluded the "allegations of abuse and maltreatment to be incredible and unsubstantiated." The investigation was closed.

It is possible that the claims of the detainees were unfounded or untrue. Nevertheless, it is unfortunate that further investigation was not conducted to find out whether or not the allegations of abuse were accurate. It was apparently difficult, if not impossible, to conduct a thorough investigation of the events at Kheirolla Tolfah interrogation site. Army investigators said they were not able to speak with many individuals involved in the alleged incidents at the site. A March 26, 2005, memo from the 48th Military Police Detachment CID under the subject heading "CID Report of Investigation" explains the reason: "DUE TO OPERATIONAL AND NATIONAL SECURITY INTERESTS, THE DETAINEE ABUSE TASK FORCE IS UNABLE TO OBTAIN ACCESS TO THE INFORMATION

AND PERSONNEL NECESSARY TO COMPLETE THIS
INVESTIGATION." The problem was simple. As CID documents
explained, "This center belonged to the CIA."[16]

The case remains a mystery, with unanswered questions about the
alleged use of electrical shock on detainees. In his report, Brigadier
General Formica wrote that he had found "a stick and wires" in an
interrogation room at the site that the detainees had described in
their accounts of electrical shock and abuse. Formica said only that
the items were covered in dust and cobwebs and took no further
notice of them in his investigation.[17]

A TAZER-LIKE DEVICE

In the first week of January, shortly after Dilami arrived at Abu
Ghraib, he was taken to an interrogation at the prison compound. He
had not eaten in two days, and he felt weak with hunger. (He weighs
about 170 pounds today; he says he dropped down to 135 pounds
while he was held at Abu Ghraib.) He was escorted to a small, chilly
room that was lit only by an orange glow that came from the hallway.
An interpreter was sitting in a chair in the corner. Dilami caught a
glimpse of a device, a Tazer-like, rod-shaped machine that was the size
of a water bottle and had a handle and two wires, positive and negative, that jutted out of the top. Two interrogators dressed in jeans and
T-shirts walked into the room. Both men were tall and muscular and
had short hair, and one of the interrogators had a goatee. Dilami was
told to stand next to a wall and face the cement. The interrogators
shackled his right hand. They noticed that his left arm—the one
where he had received an injection—was limp and allowed it to
dangle free.

"Tell us who the freedom fighters are," one interrogator said.

Dilami did not answer.

"Spread your legs," an interrogator told him. "As far as you can."

"In any interrogation, anywhere in the world, they have some
proof of what the people have been accused of," Dilami tells me.[18]
His lips form a tight line, and he stares out the hotel window. He

tightens his hand into a fist and holds a cigarette in the air like a smoldering torch. "They had nothing on us."

Someone—he is not sure whether it was an interrogator, an interpreter, or another individual—poured a bottle of water over him as he stood next to the wall in the room. He was dimly aware of what the interrogators were planning. "I'm an electrical engineer," he explains. "I know that if someone were to get his hand wet and touch an electrical socket, it will be painful. Water is a good conductor of electricity. And since my whole body was wet, it would carry electricity all over my body regardless of where they applied the electrical device. If my body were dry, the only place the electricity would affect is that particular part of the body."

Someone pressed the device against his underarms, under his ears, behind his knees, on his throat, and on his penis. "These are the most sensitive parts of the body," he explains. "They transmitted the electrical shocks all over. My whole body began shaking."

The device made a buzzing, ripping noise. "It would go, 'Zzzzzz,'" he explains.

His nerves were soon paralyzed, and his limbs became numb.

"I felt confused," he says. "I thought they were going to kill me. If they had applied the device to my mouth, they would have. I thought it was over for me."

His legs buckled. As he fell toward the floor, he wondered what would happen to him. He knew he would not survive the electrical shocks much longer. His heart would stop. Yet after some time—he is not sure how long—he realized he was being returned to his cell. Three months later, he was informed of the accusations against him: "Planning and executing resistance against American forces." He was released from Abu Ghraib on May 21, and was never formally charged with a crime.

An Iraqi physician examined him after he left the prison, he says, and told him that his sexual organs were damaged. "Due to the torture that I underwent, I cannot have more children," he says, adding. "I cannot have a daughter."

"It must be very hard not to have more children," says Chomsky.

"Yes, of course," he says, curtly, briefly departing from the polite tone he had maintained throughout the afternoon. He rubs his nose and coughs. Then he picks up his ID card and wraps the cord around his fingers. It is difficult for him to imagine a democratic society in Iraq, he says, after the damage inflicted by U.S. troops. Now, he says, he is hoping for something else, regardless of the political system in Iraq. "I want peace," he explains.

Dilami talked about the way he was subjected to electrical shock and brutal interrogation techniques. Another Iraqi man, a sound engineer, was taken to a secret facility at Baghdad International Airport. He told me about a different kind of abuse.

CHAPTER TWELVE

BLACKOUT

WE REMAIN HORRIFIED BY THE IDEA OF USING PHYSICAL OR
MENTAL PRESSURE TO ELICIT INFORMATION, BUT WE CANNOT
RULE IT OUT IN ALL CASES.

—John C. Yoo, "Interrogation," War by Other Means: An Insider's Account
of the War on Terror[1]

December 29, 2003. Mohammed Rahman and his seventy-year-old father stood next to an electric generator in a shed across the street from their house in Adhamiya, a neighborhood of Baghdad built around a shrine more than a thousand years ago. (His name and those of his family have been changed.) For months they had tinkered with the generator until it was running smoothly. Now it was able to provide backup power for their house and more than 100 other families during the frequent blackouts in the area. Rahman, a graduate of Baghdad University's College of Arts, had an entrepreneurial streak and hoped someday to make money from the operation by charging for access to the electricity.

The Sunni Muslim neighborhood of Adhamiya had been facing

a slow descent into poverty, power outages, and lawlessness for months. There was almost no cooking oil available in stores, no access to clean water, no trash pickup. Drivers waited in line for hours, sometimes days, to tank up their cars at gas pumps, if they were lucky enough to have a car that worked. It was a bitter time for the residents of Adhamiya. The chaos was even harder to accept because they lived only several hundred yards away—across the Tigris River—from a more prosperous Shiite area known as al-Kadhim, which was full of bustling stores, street vendors, tidy houses, and somewhat more reliable municipal services.

The name of Adhamiya comes from an Arabic word "al-Adham," which means "one who is greatest." The name of the nearby al-Kadhim district comes from a word that means "one who suppresses his anger." Under Saddam, the Sunnis in Adhamiya had been all-powerful while their Shiite neighbors across the river were subjected to misery under the tyrannical ruler. Now things had changed. Shiites were moving into positions of power in the post-Saddam government while the Sunni Muslims watched their authority and livelihoods disappear. Now it was the Sunnis, not the Shiites, who seethed with resentment.

Luckily, Rahman had the generator. The heap of scrap metal in the shed might have looked unimpressive, but to Rahman, the contraption represented, quite literally, light, both for his home and as a way out of the darkness he and his neighbors had faced since the American troops had arrived. That night of December 29, 2003, Rahman stubbed out his cigarette and went inside the house to get something to eat, leaving his father to watch over the precious generator.

At 11:30 PM, Rahman heard an explosion. He was standing in his house, a three-bedroom structure made of reinforced concrete, with a fence that surrounded the property. His wife, a physician who worked in the ob/gyn department of a city hospital, raced upstairs to check on their three daughters, Manar, seven, Johara, four, and Dahab, who was six months old. At first, Rahman thought the generator had blown up. Then he thought the noise might have been from a political demonstration gone awry.

Baghdad is divided into eighty-eight sections, each with its own advisory council, and Adhamiya was one of the most violent. Many of Rahman's neighbors had been Baathists who had worked for the Saddam Hussein regime, and his own father had been an official in the agricultural ministry until he retired in 1988. Saddam was last seen as a free man on the streets of Adhamiya on April 9, 2003, waving to a crowd from the top of a car in front of the Abu Hanifa shrine. In the months that followed, Adhamiya was filled with insurgents and guerilla fighters who spoke out in favor of Saddam. Local residents hung chicken wire over the street to trip up American soldiers. Thieves broke into shops and donated money to the insurgency. Thirteen- and fourteen-year-old boys roamed the streets with AK-47s, rifles, and handguns and stared menacingly at the soldiers.

In November 2003 American soldiers struck back at the insurgents in Adhamiya with a raid on a cell of guerilla fighters that had yielded several prisoners and weapons seizures. Yet the number of attacks on coalition forces continued to climb, jumping from twelve a day in late summer to roughly thirty a day by November. The day after Saddam was captured, people in Adhamiya took to the streets. Covering their faces with scarves, they marched down a wide avenue and proclaimed their loyalty to the deposed leader. Coalition Provisional Authority officials had outlawed pro-Saddam marches, and it wasn't long before more than 300 American soldiers in Abrams tanks and Bradley fighting vehicles were exchanging fire with hundreds of Sunni Muslims brandishing AK-47s and rocket-propelled grenades. The Americans suffered no casualties, but seven Iraqis were killed. Afterward, buildings were covered with graffiti that said things like "Baghdad, patience, we will free you from your occupiers" and "Allah is great, and Saddam is brave."

CLEARING THE HOUSE

Sitting in a room at Le Royal Hotel in Amman on December 6, 2004, less than a year after his arrest, Rahman describes his detention from December 29, 2003, to January 6, 2004. As he speaks, he dabs his eyes with a tissue. He covers the damp tissue with a fresh one and places them both carefully on the table. A slender, dark-haired man with brown eyes and neatly-trimmed nails, he has fastidious manners and eats a cheese sandwich with a knife and fork at lunch. He has a ruptured ear drum (a soldier periodically blasted a horn in his ear) and a scarred wrist that looks as if it has been skinned (he was kept in flexicuffs for days).[2]

During the two weeks leading up to Rahman's arrest, a U.S. Army commander, Lieutenant Colonel Garry Bishop of Philadelphia, had been leading soldiers, some of whom were issued pamphlets titled "Iron Soldiers' Spiritual Fitness Nuggets," through Rahman's neighborhood in an effort to root out insurgents and to track down several of Saddam's deputies who were believed to be hiding in the area. Bishop and the soldiers were, understandably, skittish when they burst into houses and questioned local residents. In Bishop's division alone, two soldiers—a scout and the driver of a Humvee—had been killed by insurgents in recent months.[3] The work had begun to pay off, and slowly but surely Bishop's men began to disrupt the insurgency's network. Baath party principals remained top priority, and on December 29, 2003, American forces apparently received a tip that Saddam's top deputy, former vice president Izzat Ibrahim al-Douri, had been at Rahman's house in the afternoon.

Rahman had heard about the search for al-Douri on television. He watched al-Douri's face flicker across the screen, reminding him of the days under Saddam when al-Douri made frequent public statements on TV. During the days of the pro-Saddam marches, Rahman and his family had stayed in their house on al-Binook Street, watching the television news (when the power was on). His wife was studying to become an internist and hoped someday to set up a private practice. He spent his time tinkering with the generator.

That December night, the explosion was so loud it shook the foundations of the house. "When I opened the door, I saw ten soldiers," he says. "They were firing at the generator. Everyone was screaming and crying. I held my children very tight."

He could hear two helicopters circling above the shed. His father was still trapped behind its flimsy walls. Within minutes, a dozen U.S. troops burst into the shed and surrounded the generator, crouching down on their knees to pump bullets into its metal exterior. It sounded as though the might of an army platoon had been unleashed on the generator. The attack might have surprised even Joseph Heller's Captain John Yossarian, who knows a bit about the absurdity of war. But the soldiers had their reasons. They knew from a previous incident that a generator is not always what it seems.

On October 26, ten antipersonnel rockets had been fired at Baghdad's al-Rashid Hotel, killing a U.S. Army colonel and injuring seventeen people. (Two high-profile guests, Paul L. Wolfowitz and the *New York Times*'s Pentagon reporter, Thom Shanker, escaped unharmed.) The rockets had been hidden in a metal container designed to look like a generator, loaded onto the back of a two-wheeled trailer, and left near the hotel.

The night of December 29 was cold and clear in Adhamiya, with temperatures dropping below seventeen degrees Fahrenheit. With bullets pounding off the generator and the screams of Rahman's sister, mother, wife, and children, the noise was almost unbearable. Rahman ran back to the house and found his wife holding their baby, Dahab, while his mother was crouched near Manar, telling her everything would be okay. He picked up Johara, who was dressed in her pajamas and sobbing hysterically, and held her in his arms to stop her from shivering. Her tears seeped into his shirt, and she gripped his shoulders so tightly he could have let his arms drop to his sides and she would have remained there. After a few minutes, he sent them upstairs so they could hide in the bedroom.

Soldiers burst through the front door, racing past Koran passages displayed on the living-room wall. Rahman was knocked to the ground and professionally "ziplocked" into flexicuffs. "One of the soldiers put his foot on my face and pointed the rifle at my head. They kicked me in the face," he says. An interpreter with a Lebanese accent, and dressed in a helmet, a bulletproof vest, an ammunition belt and blue jeans, began shouting, "Where are the guns?"

"I don't have a gun," Rahman told them. He was lying on the ground and, he says, "The boot was still in my face."

In the hotel room, he stands up from the table and takes off his jacket. He takes a deep breath and lets it out, exhaling for several seconds.

That December night, he says, a soldier, spitting on the floor, threw an explosive device upstairs and stormed up to the bedroom. It was part of "clearing a house," a term used for the process of driving insurgents out of a building. The soldiers swore in English and began shooting above the heads of the children. Troops ransacked the dressers, seizing gold earrings and child-sized bracelets and stuffing them into their breast pockets. Within minutes, Manar's math book, as well as family photographs, medical research papers and identification documents were scattered on the floor. The rug was scorched and burned. Rahman was taken outside and, standing in the yard with his hands bound, watched his mother, sister, and wife, each carrying a child wrapped in a blanket, walk across the frozen earth in their nightgowns. One of the soldiers pushed his mother, and he watched helplessly as she fell to the ground.

At 2:30 AM, the shelling stopped. Silence hung over the street, and the neighborhood was enveloped in medieval darkness. The only light came from the fluorescent glow sticks brandished by the soldiers. The interpreter pushed Rahman toward a military vehicle parked on the side of the road.

Rahman says his heart felt ready to burst. His legs were shaking with fear and rage. "Is my father okay?" he said. "'There is nothing wrong with him," said the interpreter. "He is with the neighbors. Where's al-Douri? He was at your house at four today."

"All of this was because of al-Douri?" Rahman cried. "I have nothing to do with him!"

The interpreter punched him in the mouth and ripped open his lip. Blood poured down his chin. A soldier put a hood over his head, secured it tightly, and placed him into the vehicle. They drove away.[4]

THE BLACK ROOM

In the early morning of December 30, Rahman was taken to a secret, U.S.-run detention center, Camp Nama, run by a special military and CIA task force in facilities at Baghdad International Airport. Members of the task force in charge of the prison had apprehended Iraqi terrorists, Baathists, and war criminals and brought in Saddam Saddam and Abu Musab Al-Zarqawi. Operations were tightly controlled. The International Committee of the Red Cross was not allowed to visit the site.[5] When General Miller arrived at the site, "acting like he's Patton or something," recalls Karpinski, without getting prior clearance, a noncommissioned officer at the camp turned him away.[6]

That morning, shortly after Rahman had arrived, the military vehicle ground to a halt in front of a building. He was escorted to a room and stood before two American interrogators, a blond man in glasses and a crew cut in his midtwenties and a silver-haired man in his fifties, and a translator. The younger man stared hard at him and, through the translator, told him to explain his relationship with al-Douri.

"I don't know him at all. I've seen him on TV—that's it," Rahman said.

The interrogator looked angry.

"Tell us everything you know about al-Douri, or we will kill you," he said.

Rahman said again he had never met him.

"So you don't feel like telling us anything," the interrogator said. "I'm going to have to make you."

The interrogator walked behind Rahman and put his elbows on his shoulders. He jerked his head up, forcing him to sit straight in the chair. He banged his forearms down on his shoulders.

"He was very angry," says Rahman, as we sit at a small table cluttered with half-empty plastic bottles of water. His shoulders are tense, and he keeps his eyes cast toward the ground. "He lifted my head and started to choke me." He shows how the interrogator grabbed his chin and pushed his head back. That day in the interrogation site, he twisted violently against the chair. Finally, he says, he pushed the interrogator away. He sucked in mouthfuls of air and gripped his chest and then the interrogator punched him.

"We're taking you someplace else," the interpreter said.

Hooded and handcuffed, Rahman was escorted to another building. It was a wooden structure—he could tell by the sounds the floor made when he walked across it. According to the human-rights report, the building had at least four rooms: the black room, the blue room, the red room, and a medical screening room. The most brutal interrogations were conducted in the black room. There, the walls and ceiling of the twelve-by-twelve-foot room were painted black.[7]

"It had speakers in the corners, all four corners, up at the ceiling. It had a small table in one of the corners, and maybe some chairs," said an interrogator who worked at Camp Nama in 2004. "But usually in the black room nobody was sitting down. It was standing, stress positions, and so forth. The table would be for the boom box and the computer. We patched it into the speakers and made the noise and stuff. Most of the harsh interrogations were in that room. . . . Sleep deprivation, environmental controls, hot and cold, water . . . I never saw anybody who was hot, you know, but it was cold a lot of times or we used cold water, we poured cold water onto them. [Certain times interrogators would] take clothes from the prisoners and so forth . . . loud music, strobe lights—they were used as well. Some interrogators would beat detainees in the black room," he added, "hitting and kicking them during interrogations."

The interrogator explained the criteria for individuals taken there.

"It depends on what the [detainee's] status is coming in from their target reporting. O.K., when they come in, for whatever reason they were chosen to get rounded up in the first place—sometimes it's just the wrong guy or whatever, but that's neither here nor there," he said. "If it's the right guy, if we think it's the right guy, and it's kind of a higher-value type of target or somebody who can push us further into the circle, as they said—you have a circle, and [Abu Musab al-]Zarqawi's [a Qaeda leader] in the middle, and lieutenants and so forth, like it was an onion—and if he can push us further into the circle, and we didn't think that we couldn't get past through normal methods or a normal type of approach in interrogation—then they would want to go hard on them. . . . The senior interrogator—the interrogation leader usually wanted to go hard on people like that."[8]

During the time Rahman was there, a CD player blared acid rock. It was cold in the tiled space. Rahman, who had also studied film directing, said it seemed as though the Americans had arranged things like a movie production. The techniques, which had been originally discussed by Yoo, Flanigan, and others as a method of extracting information from high-level al Qaeda suspects, were now being used on a man who had maddeningly little to say.

One of the interrogators put Rahman's hood back on and secured it tightly. Sometime that day, or maybe it was the following day, he and another hooded detainee were forced to run back and forth in the room. The ordeal lasted for hours. When Rahman and the other detainee bumped into each other, a husky American in a T-shirt and camouflage pants would grab the loose cloth on the back of their hoods and crack their skulls together. "Bang," says Rahman. "He kept doing that for a while."

Exhausted, disoriented, and too weak to move or to respond, Rahman lay on the ground. Three of the interrogators surrounded his limp body and began to shove it back and forth across the slick tiles, dribbling it like a soccer ball. As they kicked and pushed, they talked and laughed and made jokes, occasionally breaking the rhythm with a kick to the groin. Someone else joined them later, beating him with a wooden stick, as if it were a perverse kind of sport, striking the most painful of blows to his kidneys. Afterward, an interrogator took his hood off. Rahman looked around, blinking at the men standing in front of him. Within seconds, they put another kind of hood on him, a thick cloth that soaked up water like a sponge. Rahman felt someone yank the wet material on the back of the hood so hard he nearly choked to death. A damp seal covered his lips and nostrils.[9]

The former Camp Nama interrogator explained harsh techniques required approval from superior officers. Like at Abu Ghraib, interrogators submitted plans that included sleep deprivation and other requests. "There was an authorization template on a computer, a sheet that you would print out, or actually just type it in," the former interrogator said. "And it was a checklist. And it was all already typed out for you, environmental controls, hot and cold, you know, strobe lights, music, so forth. Working dogs, which, when I was there, wasn't being used. But you would just check what you want to use off, and if you planned on using a harsh interrogation you'd just get it signed off. I never saw a sheet that wasn't signed. It would be signed off by the commander, whoever that was, whether it was 03 [captain] or 06 [colonel], whoever was in charge at the time. . . . When the 06 was there, yeah, he would sign off on that. . . . He would sign off on that every time it was done. Some interrogators would go and use these techniques without typing up one of those things just because it was a hassle, or he didn't want to do it and knew it was going to be approved anyway, and you're not going to get in that much trouble if you get caught doing one of these things without a signature."[10]

That day in the black room, Rahman says, he felt himself suffocating inside the hood. Panicked, he tried to tear away the damp cotton that covered his face. He fell on the floor and then managed to pull his hands in front of his body. The flexicuffs cut into his skin, and his wrists bled. His lungs felt as if they were torn apart, and he pulled the hood up over his mouth so he could breathe. An interrogator hit him with the wooden stick. His vision became blurry. His legs, arms, chest and hands became numb. Finally, he passed out.

The interrogators worked in shifts, he tells me. It is a different philosophy from the one embodied in the interrogation method known as monstering, in which a skilled interrogator sets up a sleep and dietary regimen for an individual and follows it himself until either the interrogator or the suspect breaks down, wrote Mackey in *The Interrogators*. It was an interrogation technique used at a detention facility in Afghanistan.[11] At this U.S. facility in Iraq, interrogations were based on a Henry Ford model. Each interrogator had a specialization and operated as if he were on an assembly line. This technique is more complex (it involves several individuals) and brutal (interrogators take turns, allowing the abuse to continue unabated) than Mackey's method. It is an evolved, mechanized Monstering, in which (as the philosopher Nietzsche once warned) interrogators may behave as monstrously, if not more so, than the individuals they are questioning.

"Every few hours, they would change the music," Rahman says. "It was slightly different. That's how you'd know there was a new shift."

Rahman recognizes the interrogators by their techniques. *Oh, there's the guy who works with cold water,* he would think. The Cold Water Interrogator poured water on his skin while he was dehydrated and watched him lick off the drops. Another interrogator beat him with the metal folding chair (until it broke into pieces). A female interrogator used sexual tricks. She exposed her breasts and simulated sex while someone else held him down. It was a live porn video, only it was used not to titillate him but to humiliate and to remind him of his helplessness.

"DADDY, HELP ME"

One interrogator had a CD on which a child cried over and over again, "Daddy, help me. Save me!" When Rahman heard the recording in the interrogation room, he thought about Manar, Yohara, and Dahab shivering in their pajamas in the yard.

"This baby—this child—was crying on the CD," he says. He covers his face with his hand in the hotel room and begins to cry. His shoulders are shaking.

As he heard the recorded children's voices, he says, he remembered seeing Manar's tears on the night their home was raided. He collapsed and fell on the floor of the interrogation room. The interrogators hit him and poured water on him, telling him to stand up. Still, he couldn't get on his feet. They grabbed the material of his hood and used it to pull him along the floor, shoving him in front of the CD player. The lights were still turned off in the room, except for flashes that pulsed from a mirrored light that hung from the ceiling. They moved the CD player still closer to his face, as the screams from the speakers filled his head. They stretched him across the floor, lifting his head to prop his chin up on the CD player. The interrogators, still looking for a man named al-Douri, proceeded to kick and beat Rahman as he laid there prostrate in the black room under a twirling disco ball, surrounded by the sounds of a child screeching for its father.

"So how do you feel now?" the silver-haired interrogator said. "Are you sure you don't want to tell us anything?"

LAST RITES

In Baghdad, there is no record of Rahman's detention. Detainees who were held for fewer than fourteen days were not processed, and Rahman was detained for only eight. But there are photos of his houseshot by Al-Jazeera and described by the BBC that show a bloody floor and smashed gates following the "raid-and-search campaign" by U.S. troops on December 29, 2003. Rahman was released without charge on January 6, 2004.

After his release, Rahman was taken to a nondescript location near the airport and left on the side of the road. He took a taxi home. As the cab pulled up to his house, he saw a black banner. His father had been killed in the raid. An autopsy listed the cause of his father's death as gunshot wounds, including three bullets fired at short range into the back of his head.

Several days later, an army colonel came to Rahman's house. He filled the street with Hummers and then got out of his military vehicle. His name was embroidered on his right breast pocket, and on his left pocket, "U.S. Army." Officers like him had worked hard to win the trust of the Sunni Arabs in Adhamiya. Troops had rebuilt a school and repaired a soccer field for Iraqi children. After months of living in Baghdad, though, fatigue was etched across the officer's face.

"We're sorry for what happened," said the officer. "We got some bad information."

The two men stood looking at each other for a moment. Rahman's family members pulled Rahman aside.

"Show him what they did," one of his relatives said.

At his family's urging, Rahman pushed aside the material on his pants. The officer looked at his leg. It was covered in blue and purplish bruises and swollen almost beyond recognition. The officer sucked in his breath.

"I think the colonel was affected by what he saw," Rahman tells me.[12]

PART III

INVESTIGATION

CHAPTER THIRTEEN

BRASS TACKS

I SAID, "SIR, MILITARY INTELLIGENCE IS DOING SOME PRETTY
WEIRD THINGS TO NAKED DETAINEES." HE SAID, "JUST STAY
OUT OF THEIR WAY." I SAID, "WELL, SIR, DON'T EVER ORDER
ME OVER THERE." AND HE SAID, "YOU'LL DO WHATEVER
YOU'RE ORDERED TO DO, SERGEANT."

—Ken Davis, 372nd Military Police Company, Abu Ghraib Prison.
"What Was Asked of Us" by Trish Wood[1]

Charles Graner gave Joseph Darby a CD filled with snapshots. When Darby clicked through the images, he expected to see snapshots of their friends in Hilla. Instead, Darby realized that Graner had stored thousands of photographs on the CD—and that many of them did not look at all what Darby had anticipated. The photographs included the now-infamous ones from Tier 1A. "To be honest, at first I thought they were pretty funny," Darby said in an article, "Prison of Conscience," in GQ magazine (September 2006). "I'm sorry, people can get mad at me if they want, but I'm not a Boy Scout. To me, that pyramid of naked Iraqis, when you first see it, is hilarious. When it came up out of nowhere like that, I just laughed. I was like, "What the fuck?! I'm looking at a pyramid of asses!"[2]

Darby and Graner were not friends, England tells me. Still, an affinity for pranks and an *espirit de corps* among them and other Military Police was strong both because of the danger the soldiers faced from insurgents and because of the prison setting. The solidarity felt among prison guards—and their reluctance to complain about prisoner abuse when inflicted by another guard—is well documented. Michael G. Santos, author of *Inside: Life Behind Bars in America,* said that, for guards, "the only thing lower than an inmate is an 'inmate lover,' a 'hug-a-thug.'"[3] Moreover, the prisoners at Abu Ghraib were seen as the enemy during wartime.

Provance says the situation at Abu Ghraib was similar to the one faced by soldiers in Brian DePalma's film *Casualties of War.* In the film, Provance says, soldiers rape and kill a female villager. "They said, 'Oh, she's Vietcong,'" explains Provance. "They armed themselves with that perspective. Michael J. Fox [a soldier] reports it. The commander basically says, 'If it gets out, this is going to make us look really bad.'"[4]

Nevertheless, Darby gave the CD to a military investigator.[5] It was a surprising move. Even Hydrue Joyner, who says he was appalled by the Abu Ghraib photographs when they were released, was unhappy when Darby reported the abuses to the CID. "I like to think that me and Darby—we were cool. We were boys," Joyner says, sitting in a Starbucks in Washington. He throws out his arms in a display of affection. "He could have brought them to me. But he slipped them under the door of the CID. A whole lot of careers and lives have been flushed down the toilet because Darby didn't follow the chain of command."

Why did he turn the pictures over to the military investigators instead of to his superior officer? I ask.

"For the attention?" says Joyner. "I don't know. Maybe he didn't get enough hugs as a kid."

Or maybe Darby thought nobody would do anything if he reported the abuses to an officer in his unit, I say.

"That's B.S.," says Joyner. "I guarantee if it got to me, I would have gone to somebody stomping and thumping my chest and somebody would have heard me."

Darby chose to turn over the evidence of detainee abuse to the army's CID, however, and prompted a full-scale military investigation of the incidents. At 11:30 on January 12, 2004, Karpinski came home from a meeting at a detention facility she supervised, logged on to her computer, and saw an e-mail from Colonel Mark Marcello, a CID commander. She felt anxious as she scrolled down to read his message. "His e-mail said, 'Ma'am, I just want you to know I'm going in to brief [Lieutenant] General Sanchez on the progress of the investigation out at Abu Ghraib,'" she tells me. "This is regarding the investigation of allegations of prisoner abuse. And the photographs."

She stared at her screen. After a moment, she recalls, she composed a one-line e-mail. "I don't know what to say," she wrote. She hit "Send."[6]

"I'M IN A LITTLE BIT OF TROUBLE"

On the day in January when England called her mother from Iraq and told her the bad news about the military investigation, icicles had formed on the corrugated metal that surrounded their trailer in Fort Ashby. A rusted laundry bar in the yard was frozen, and the earth was hard. Terrie strained to hear her daughter's voice on the scratchy line. Klinestiver says the conversation was brief.

"She was like, 'I just want you to know that I'm in a little bit of trouble but not to worry,'" Klinestiver says. Terrie spoke with officials from England's army unit in Maryland, and she tried to call Baghdad. "Nobody would say anything," says Klinestiver. "They'd started the investigation."

Lynndie England lost her military rank as an army specialist and became Private, First Class. She requested a lawyer, but she was not allowed to retain one at that time. Terrie cried and smoked cigarettes. Klinestiver was worried about Lynndie, and about Terrie, too. "I love my mom," says Klinestiver. "But I'm like, 'Mom, breathe!'" She pretends to look at her mother—as if her mother were sitting in a chair across from her—and then claps her hands four times.[7]

ACCOUNTABILITY LAPSES

On Friday, January 16, Lieutenant General Sanchez said in a statement released by the army's public affairs office that investigators had started looking into allegations of detainee abuse at Abu Ghraib. "A senior Pentagon official said authorities had been alerted to the possible abuse of detainees in the past few days and were taking the allegations 'very seriously,'" wrote Eric Schmitt on the following day in a brief *New York Times* article, "Inquiry Ordered into Reports of Detainee Abuse."[8]

On January 19, Lieutenant General Sanchez formally requested a report on the conduct of the 800th Military Police Brigade at Abu Ghraib. Sanchez was concerned, according to the inquiry, entitled "Article 15-6, Investigation of the 800th Military Police Brigade," about "recent reports of detainee abuse, escapes [from confinement facilities], and accountability lapses." The investigation was headed by Major General Antonio M. Taguba.[9]

Provance and a group of soldiers heard the news on American Forces Network Europe, displayed on a twenty-inch television set in a large room in the Joint Interrogation and Debriefing Center. (The program was available through satellite decoders in Iraq.) "There was kind of a hushed whisper because Sanchez was saying there was an investigation," says Provance. "I was like, 'I told you people this was exactly what was going to happen.' Then there was complete silence in the room."[10]

Now that Lieutenant General Sanchez had announced a formal

investigation, Provance was ready to talk. At 3:20 PM Tuesday, January 21, Provance sat across from an army investigator, Special Agent Ryan D. Bostain of the 323rd Military Police Detachment, in a small room at the prison compound. Provance spoke about the detainee abuse and mentioned the names of his friends. He described the officers in charge at the prison who he believed had been complicit in the abuse. "Every time I said something about how I was worried about the treatment of the detainees, they would either say, 'They are the enemy,' and 'If I was out there they would kill me,' so they didn't care," Provance told the investigator. "I'm glad that something is finally being done; it's kind of shameful what's been going on."[11]

THIRTY-TWO BOOTS

Army investigator Marcello carried a briefcase into the Tactical Operations Center office at Camp Victory on the night of January 23. Karpinski was sitting at her desk. "He said, 'Can I have a little time?'" she recalls. "'I'd like to show you the pictures.'"

He opened up the briefcase and handed her a manila folder with a stack of photos. The first thing she saw was a picture of a human pyramid. "There was little Lynndie England, looking like some two-bit prison marm with that cigarette dangling out of her throat and her thumbs up," Karpinski says. She felt sick to her stomach and, for a moment, she says, it seemed as if the world were caving in on her. Her arms and hands felt cold. "I never, ever, ever imagined what I saw in those photographs. It was not in my brain to even think that way," she tells me.

"Why would they do those things and take pictures of themselves?" she wondered out loud on that night. "Are they out of their minds?"

She turned away, but Marcello insisted she look at the photos again. One image showed a group of men gathered around several naked prisoners lying on the floor. The prisoners were barefoot or in sandals. The other men were wearing boots. The colonel had counted the number of boots—thirty-two—in the photograph. "I said, 'Thirty-two boots means we have sixteen U.S. people in this picture,'" she recalls. She recognized Graner and Nakhla.

"What are the translators doing in the cellblock?" she asked, referring to Nakhla.

"Ma'am, those aren't translators," Colonel Marcello told her, glancing at the other men shown in the photograph who were wearing the clothes of civilian workers. "They're contractors. They're working for Colonel Pappas."

"He said, 'This one's an interrogator. So is this one,'" she says.

"Who are these *other* people?" she asked.[12]

Marcello turned in his report, and the Taguba Report was complete in February. It includes graphic descriptions of sexual abuse, humiliation, and other incidents that were depicted in the photographs that Darby had given to investigators as well as accounts of American military personnel and civilian contractors who were shown in the photographs and implicated in the detainee abuse. The report featured a psychological assessment of the soldiers stationed at Abu Ghraib and their "conspiracy of silence," an indictment of the civilian contract personnel, saying they lacked proper supervision and may have contributed to the difficulties "in the accountability process."[13]

The Taguba Report is, according to legal experts who have studied the issue of detainees and U.S. policy, the most thorough official account of the Abu Ghraib events. It was completed before the release of the Abu Ghraib photographs and the glare of negative publicity, and, since that time, the military has conducted no comparable investigation into the abuse scandal. The stream of reports that followed, according to legal experts, did more to obfuscate the subject of detainee abuse than to shed light on the events at that prison and in other U.S.-run detention facilities.

PARTY TIME

Provance's friends left Iraq on Friday, February 13, 2004. Some of them found "a loaf of bread in a small bag of groceries" in their room in the barracks, wrote Jon R. Anderson in the European edition of *Stars and Stripes* on February 20. "Outside in the hallway, a party had already erupted"—with one of the soldiers "cracking open beers for his buddies." "With rucksacks and gear still splayed next to doors, the soldiers were already telling war stories and remember-whens," Anderson wrote. "'It'll be a pretty good party tonight, I imagine,'" said one of the soldiers. "'There's a lot of steam to let off.'"[14]

CHAPTER FOURTEEN

PHOTOGRAPHIC EVIDENCE

MY LIEUTENANT WAS A CLERK IN A CONVENIENCE STORE AND
LIVED AT HOME WITH HIS PARENTS, SHARING A ROOM WITH HIS
BROTHER. HE WAS IN HIS THIRTIES. OUR COMMANDER WAS A
SALESMAN FOR WINDOW BLINDS. OUR FIRST SERGEANT
WORKS IN A CHICKEN FACTORY. I HAVE TO ASK MYSELF, WHAT
IS MORE EMBARRASSING— ADMITTING WE MADE A MISTAKE OR
SAYING AN E-4 BROUGHT THE ARMY TO ITS KNEES? I DON'T
BELIEVE IT WAS JUST A FEW BAD APPLES. I AM NOT GOING TO
BE LIED TO BY A GOVERNMENT THAT I WOULD HAVE GIVEN MY
LIFE FOR IN IRAQ.

—Ken Davis, 372nd Military Police Company,
September to December 2003, Abu Ghraib Prison.
"What Was Asked of Us" by Trish Wood[1]

On Wednesday, April 28, 2004, *60 Minutes II* broadcast the images of
Abu Ghraib. Two days later, the photos appeared on the Web site of
the *New Yorker*. The pictures showed a man with a sandbag covering
his head and standing on a cardboard box with electrical wires dangling from his fingers (he became known as the Hooded Man); naked

men stacked in a human pyramid in a prison hallway; and England leading a prisoner named Hamid on a leash. Over a six-month period in 2004, the networks devoted more time to the Abu Ghraib scandal than to anything else in Iraq, including the Fallujah insurgency in which the bodies of four American contractors were hung from a bridge.[2] The Abu Ghraib photos changed the way Americans saw themselves, and changed the way many people in the world saw America.

"You saw the pictures," says Nabil, the lawyer who told me about his brutal interrogations. "Wasn't this a sign of having power over others and at the same time having an inferiority complex?"[3] The U.S. had once been a beacon of democracy and freedom for many people in Central Europe and the Middle East. Now it was a symbol of hypocrisy. The image of the hooded man became known in Iraq as the Statue of Liberty.[4]

"Ask any soldier in Iraq when the general population really turned against the United States and he will say, 'Abu Ghraib,'" wrote Fareed Zakaria in Newsweek on November 14, 2005. "Polls showed that 71 percent of Iraqis were surprised by the revelations. Most telling of all, 61 percent of Iraqis believed no one would be punished for the torture at Abu Ghraib. Of the 29 percent who said they believed someone would be punished, 52 percent said that such punishment would extend only to 'the little people.'"[5]

"I knew the insurgency was going to escalate. It recruited tons more people to fight against us and I knew that there'd be an increase in violence and that I'd have to deal with that," Garett Reppenhagen, a cavalry scout/sniper, told journalist Trish Wood. "The Iraqis that were on the fence pretty much jumped over on the side of the insurgency when news of what was happening at Abu Ghraib got out."[6]

Meanwhile, administration officials expressed their own outrage. On May 7, ten days after the Abu Ghraib story broke, Defense Secretary Rumsfeld and Acting Secretary of the Army Les Brownlee appeared before the Senate Armed Services Committee. Brownlee said they would make sure that the individuals "responsible for the shameful and illegal acts of abuse are held accountable."[7]

Officials tried to dismiss accusations that General Miller, who had once talked about "softening up" prisoners at Abu Ghraib, set conditions at the prison that led to the abuse. At a House Armed Services Committee hearing on May 7, 2003, Rumsfeld said Miller had made suggestions for the interrogation of detainees at Abu Ghraib, but, as Lieutenant General Lance Smith, deputy commander of U.S. Central Command explained, that "is a very different thing from 'softening up.'"

"The idea of softening up was in no sense intended to do the sorts of things that we were talking about here or that we saw in the pictures," Smith said, "but simply a matter of being part of the whole solution."[8]

Full-scale military investigations were promised. Lieutenant General Sanchez appointed an officer, Major General Fay, to examine allegations that the 205th Military Intelligence Brigade had been involved in detainee abuse. CID agents studied scenes of the alleged crimes. At the same time, U.S. Justice Department agents began investigating civilian contractors who had been accused of abuse. There were other allegations of mistreatment at U.S.-run detention facilities. But the work of the army's top-notch investigative agents, the collection of forensic evidence, the interviewing of witnesses and suspects, had a singular focus: the photos of Abu Ghraib.

AMERICAN IDOL

Two Frankfort High School seniors, Heather Helmsetter and Matt Sampson, were honored as the students Most Likely to Become Famous in the West Virginia school's Class of 2001 yearbook. Their classmate, Lynndie England, who has short, brown hair and sleepy eyes in her photo in the same yearbook, had only a modest record of achievements. (She had, for example, served as a member of the yearbook staff for one year.) Yet England, four and a half months pregnant with Graner's child, suddenly became known around the world.[9]

"We turned on CNN, and my mouth dropped," says Klinestiver. She leans forward and opens her mouth in mock surprise. ""I was like, 'Why would Lynndie be on TV?' It was an actual shock. Me and my mom sat down on the couch. We were just like glued to the TV. Then reporters started showing up."[10]

Attorney Hardy stationed himself at the door to the Englands' trailer. He folded his arms across his chest and fended off journalists. One Boston newspaper reporter managed to speak with Klinestiver, who was at home in a nearby trailer. Hardy confronted the reporter, who said she was trying to find out more about Graner and England. "She said, 'I want to do the "lust-in-the-dust" story,'" Hardy recalls. The reporter was turned out of the trailer park. Another time, a network producer showed up at the Englands' doorstep in the middle of the night. The Englands posted a No Trespassing sign in their yard and went on a turkey-hunting trip.[11]

"SCRATCH THAT FROM THE RECORD."

On May 1, Provance met with Fay in a room in an army building in Darmstadt, Germany. A reservist and former executive vice president of Chubb Group of Insurance Companies, Fay was an unusual choice as the head of an investigation into detainee abuse at Abu Ghraib. As attorney Horton and other critics of the administration have pointed out, Fay was also a financial supporter of the New Jersey Republican Party. Horton and others believe he was chosen for that reason.[12]

In Darmstadt, Fay spoke with Provance about his background in military intelligence. Provance tried to tell him about the abuse at Abu Ghraib. "I kept bringing back up to him that I'd heard a lot of things," says Provance. But Fay did not seem interested. "He was sighing, like a frustrated sigh." Finally, says Provance, "He said, 'Okay, fine. Tell me what you heard.'" Fay put his hands on the table, as Provance recalls, and he had a stern expression on his face. Provance described the incidents at the prison.

"He said, 'Well, I don't know,'" says Provance. He recalls how Fay picked up a manila folder from the table and took out Provance's statement about detainee abuse that had appeared in the Taguba Report. Fay held up the sheet of paper. "He said, 'You should have said something earlier,'" Provance says. "'You could have busted this thing wide open.'"

There was "a certain dramatic pause," Provance says, "as if he were giving me an opportunity to say, "Okay, just scratch that from the record.' And I would have walked out like everybody else. And everything would be back to normal. My state of mind was: *If I keep this up, my career in the army is over.* It was kind of like an impasse or a crossroad. Either I keep going, or I stop. I kept going."

At the end of the three-hour interview, claims Provance, Fay told him he planned to recommend administrative action against him since he had failed to report the incidents in the fall. Provance hitched a ride back to Heidelberg that evening with a soldier who drove at breakneck speed along the autobahn, saying she did not want to be late for a punk-rock concert. No one, thought Provance, was taking the investigation seriously.[13]

Attorney Scott Horton says Fay's report is "whitewashing." "During the interviews, [Fay] would say, 'Now if anyone saw anything and failed to intervene, they can be charged with a crime. Did anyone see anything and fail to intervene?'" says Horton. "They'd all say, 'No, sir!'"[14]

Provance tells me again about the film *Casualties of War* in an e-mail from Heidelberg, citing the similarities between his own experiences and those of a character in the film, , which depicts a military culture that makes it difficult to report crimes committed by other soldiers. After one soldier turns in other soldiers, wrote Provance, "He was confronted by his sergeant who was in charge of the crimes. And then he had this to say to that sergeant; "Nobody cares. I told everybody. I told them. So you don't have to worry. You don't have to try to kill me, man. I told them, and THEY DON'T CARE!'"[15]

"TRYING TO SAVE FACE."

For seventeen months, Fishback had approached superior officers and told them about the abuse at the military camp. He also asked superior officers and others for help in sorting out international laws that protect detainees. He got nowhere. Finally, the September 2005 Human Rights Watch Report, based partly on his account of the detainee abuse, was released. It led to a military investigation, congressional hearings, and an amendment to clarify rules on interrogations.

"We're proud to say to our donors, 'Look what we've done,'" says John Sifton, a researcher with Human Rights Watch. "But we wish we didn't have to do this."[16]

And even so, it has not been an easy road. Two Democratic congressional officials who met Fishback have praised his integrity. "He's a very powerful person," says one congressional official. "The most honorbound individual I've ever encountered in my life," says another, both speaking on background because they are not authorized to talk to a reporter about him. That is not, apparently, how CID agents saw him.

"What did they investigate first?" says Kenneth Roth, the executive director of Human Rights Watch. "What they wanted from Captain Fishback was the names of the two sergeants who had spoken to us and what his relationship was with us."[17]

Gary D. Solis, an adjunct professor of law at United States Military Academy at West Point, has similar concerns. Fishback is a West Point graduate who cited Solis's work (though not by name) in congressional testimony. After Fishback spoke publicly about detainee abuse, Solis was interviewed by a CID agent and another military investigator. "Perhaps somebody else is looking into Fishback's allegations," says Solis. "But the questions asked of me were ones that looked into his actions."[18]

Elizabeth L. Hillman, a professor at Rutgers Law School—Camden and author of *Defending America: Military Culture and the Cold War Court-Martial*, told me she thought the Fay-Jones Report and other military investigations were inherently flawed. "There is a quagmire of different interests in the pantheon of abusers—interrogators, commanders, reserve forces, contractors. That complicates the nature of the criminal investigations," she explains. "The army is trying to save face even as it's trying to investigate wrongdoers."[19]

Or, as one fifty-two-year-old former CID agent who asked not to be identified ("I have enough going on in my life right now") says, agents have become increasingly aligned with the army. "It's useful not to be too chummy with the people you have to investigate," he says.

William V. Gallo, a U.S. assistant attorney in San Diego, says he also believes that the conflict of responsibilities is compromising the investigations. He acted as an investigating officer in December 2003 and January 2004, and he knows it can be hard to get people to testify against each other during wartime. "All the potential witnesses were comrades-in-arms with the accused and to get any evidence is difficult," he says. "It's hard to get someone to say, 'My best friend killed this guy'—particularly when he's believed to be an insurgent."[20]

CASE CLOSED

On June 3, 2003, two months after Pfc. Jessica Lynch was taken prisoner in Iraq, a suspect in the attack on her convoy, a detainee who is identified in government documents as Nagem Sadoon Hatab, fifty-two, was detained by U.S. forces. He was taken to a detention facility near Nasiriyah, where he was beaten and strangled to death. Two Marines, Sergeant Gary Pittman, forty, and Major Clarke Paulus, thirty-six, eventually faced criminal charges at high-profile courts-martial in Camp Pendleton, California, in 2004.[21]

It seemed like an easy case to prosecute—complete with witnesses to the brutal beatings. Ultimately, though, the most serious charges were dropped. Pittman was eventually convicted of dereliction of duty and assault and sentenced to sixty days of hard labor. Paulus was found guilty of dereliction of duty and maltreatment and dismissed from the marines.

Ultimately, pathologist Lieutenant Colonel Kathleen M. Ingwersen ruled Hatab's death a homicide and placed blood, urine, and tissue samples in a cooler to be shipped back to Armed Forces Medical Examiner's Forensic Toxicology Laboratory in Washington, D.C. But the cooler got left on a tarmac in 100-plus-degree heat, explains assistant U.S. attorney Gallo.

"The cooler exploded," he says.[22]

Hatab's fractured hyoid bone, a key piece of evidence, was shipped to Landstuhl, Germany, and his rib cage was sent to Washington. Or maybe it was the other way around. Attorneys and human-rights researchers who have investigated the case are still not certain how the mistake happened or where the body parts ended up. In the end, the evidence was irrevocably damaged.[23] "You send one body part to one country and another to another country, and of course you can't prosecute," says Deborah Pearlstein, formerly director of Human Rights First's U.S. Law and Security Program and currently a Princeton University associate research scholar. "The evidence is destroyed through what looks like incompetence."[24]

Despite the lapses in the proceedings, some people think justice was served in the Hatab case.

"The investigation was conducted in a combat zone and understandably mistakes are going to be made," says Gallo. "Had there not been mistakes—if the cooler not exploded on the tarmac, for example—maybe the outcome would have been different. But, yes, I think justice was done because the system worked despite the mistakes."[25]

No one doubts, though, the evidence in the Hatab case had been compromised. There has been a pattern of disregard for the niceties of evidence collection, storage, and processing, as well as the handling of witnesses, in dozens of cases in which detainees have died in U.S. custody. And those are just the on-the-ground investigations.

A U.S. Department of Defense spokesman, Lieutenant Colonel Mark Ballesteros, told me that all credible allegations of detainee abuse are investigated. "We have first-class investigators—experienced, knowledgeable about the latest investigative techniques in criminology, forensic science, and crime-scene analysis. And the CID has one of the highest solve rates in the nation for a federal law enforcement agency," he explains.

Ballesteros says he and his colleagues are proud of the investigations, especially considering the working conditions in Baghdad. "The investigations are done in austere and sometimes dangerous environments," he explains. "Some of the agents have literally been shot at during the course of the investigations."[26]

Given these conditions, it is not surprising record-keeping has been, at times, subpar. Files at Abu Ghraib have been lost, says an army officer stationed in Baghdad who doesn't have authority to speak on the subject and so requested anonymity. File cabinets were in short supply when detainees first arrived at Abu Ghraib, he says, and background information was kept in cardboard boxes and on a dry-erase board, with predictable results. "Some interrogation-related information was recorded on a whiteboard which was periodically erased," according to the Fay-Jones Report.[27]

Rahman never filed a formal complaint. Nor did sixteen-year-old Fulani. It was not clear whether they were even aware of the opportunity to file a complaint while they were in U.S. custody or following their release. As a result, chances are their cases will never be fully investigated. If complaints are not filed by the detainees, or the acts of abuse are not photographed or described in articles that appear in the U.S. media, it is less likely that agents will look into the alleged abuses. Therefore, the identity of the men who beat Rahman will probably never be known, nor will the identity of the Lebanese American interpreter and the dog handlers who terrified Fulani and the other boys at Abu Ghraib.

"When the Army CID set out to really investigate, they can," says researcher Sifton. "They have the tools to look at forensic evidence and so on. But what we see are inconsistencies. Sometimes they push hard. Sometimes they don't."[28]

According to a source familiar with CID operations in Iraq, if a CID agent can't find the file on a detainee with an abuse complaint, the case is closed. To make matters worse, the military is notoriously understaffed. The army officer who requested anonymity told me that in 2005 there were no pathologists authorized to do autopsies on detainees who died in U.S.-run detention facilities in Iraq. So military officers learned to adjust. "They'd hold remains until they had enough for a medical examiner to come over," he explains. "It might take a few weeks or a month."

The investigators, too, are overworked. Ballesteros won't say how many CID agents are tasked to Iraq—"for security reasons," he says. But two sources familiar with CID operations says there are only three agents who go into Iraq or are working in the country, with more than 100 abuse cases to investigate.

They do their best, at times employing a technique known as a "CID hold," which, according to sources familiar with CID operations, means agents keep someone in detention so they can ask questions about an abuse allegation rather than letting them go and then having to track them down later in war-torn Iraq. "Somebody can be kept in prison merely because they witnessed somebody else being tortured," explains one individual who knows about CID operations. "It's shocking."

It is also not allowed—at least officially.

"They [detainees] aren't held past any routine or regular release date unless they're suspected of criminal wrongdoing," says Ballesteros.[29] The practice of holding detainees who file complaints about their treatment makes it easier to see why prisoners like Fulani would be reluctant to report the incident to a military investigator.

Whether it is because of missing files, lack of evidence, or simple inertia, most complaints end up like the one filed on July 12, 2004, at Abu Ghraib. In the statement, a detainee describes how, on the night of April 27, 2004, he was pulled from his home, hooded, and placed in the back of a Stryker vehicle. At that point, he said, an officer "put his hands around my neck [for] one minute and he pressed hard and I felt like I was dying from choking." He also describes three days and nights in Mosul when he was forced to hold his hands high for six hours or more and repeatedly doused with icy water.

"Do you wish to add anything to this statement?" an investigator asked.

"Yes," the detainee replied. "I need justice and my rights. ///End of Statement///"[30]

Case closed.

REMAINING LEADS

Within weeks after of the appearance of the Abu Ghraib photographs on television, things began to crumble at the Nakhla household. On May 20, 2004, Department of Defense officials referred the case of an unnamed civilian contractor to the U.S. Department of Justice. The following day, a Justice Department spokesman made an announcement: "The Department of Justice received a referral from the Department of Defense regarding a civilian contractor in Iraq and opened an investigation into the matter."[31] That same day, a Titan representative announced a civilian interpreter working in Iraq had been fired.[32]

Afterward, the media showed up at the Nakhlas. A *Washington Post* reporter and two Associated Press reporters were there. One journalist repeatedly rang the doorbell. (Nadine filed a complaint about a "suspicious person," says Lieutenant John J. Fitzgerald, a deputy commander in one of Maryland's Sixth District police stations.)[33] Meanwhile, a *Baltimore Sun* reporter contacted Nancy Kerr. Kerr called her husband, Steve, at work and told him Nakhla had been implicated in the Abu Ghraib scandal. "I said, 'We are vindicated. We are not the only ones who think this guy is a big, fat bully.'"[34]

During much of the "Operation Iraqi Freedom investigation," as the official inquiry was known, Nakhla stayed inside his house.[35] In August, says Kerr, he finally came outside to mow the lawn. "The best thing that ever happened to this street was Abu Ghraib," she says. "I didn't see him for three months. It was absolute nirvana."[36]

Two years later, the Nakhla household has settled back into a routine. Nakhla still doesn't talk to the Kerrs. (But he had not for years.) Members of the family do the household shopping, leaving a case of mineral water next to the front door one afternoon. And Nakhla takes care of the yard, a scrubby patch of grass filled with pink flamingoes, a stone cherub, and wisteria. He—like many of the eighteen other civilians who were referred to the Justice Department for investigation of detainee-related abuses—can at this point safely assume he will not be prosecuted for any crimes.

Human-rights researcher John Sifton has met with Justice Department officials and spoken with them about Nakhla and the other civilian contractors under investigation. Sifton tells me he does not think much has been done on the cases. "Maybe they're about to indict everybody tomorrow, but I doubt it," he says. "My feeling is they're just running up the clock and nothing will ever happen."[37]

On December 19, 2006, *New York Times* reporter David Johnston seemed to confirm Sifton's view in an article ("U.S. Inquiry Falters on Civilians Accused of Abuse"). "Lawyers who have been briefed on the work of the Justice Department unit, initially made up of six federal prosecutors, said problems with evidence and the fragmentary nature of some of the accusations had proved so daunting that prosecutors never even reached the point of grappling with difficult legal issues involving permissive interrogation guidelines," wrote Johnston.[38]

An analysis of the documents regarding the inquiry into Nakhla by this author reveals a series of missed opportunities, despite the gravity of the accusations and the statute (aggravated sexual assault) under which Nakhla could have been prosecuted as well as the high-level officials who had shown an interest in the case.

The case was under scrutiny for a period of time by Justice Department officials, FBI officers, and administration officials. Between May 14 and August 18, 2004, for example, twenty special agents, attorneys, operations officers, coordinators, and others working for the Defense Department, the army's CID, the CIA, the FBI, and the Justice Department were involved in "strategy sessions," meetings, e-mail correspondence, and telephone calls about the case.[39] In a July 15, 2004, e-mail, an unnamed CIA officer said, "The AG [attorney general] may have something to say about this as well. . . ." Yet, despite the amount of attention the case received, it was not, at least judging from the records kept by special agents assigned, a particularly efficient inquiry.

Under a heading, "Offense: Forcible Sodomy," dated May 28, 2004, a CID special agent records the steps that needed to be taken in the investigation, including the following: "obtain listings of juvenile detainees," "determine identity of female soldiers working at AGPC during incident," and "obtain list of guards on duty at incident location."

None of those efforts seemed to get far. According to a July 1, 2004, memo, the CID investigation was terminated: "The delay in the initiation of the investigation negated the potential value of any physical evidence." The CID agent also notes there are "Remaining Leads": the alleged victim, the witness, and the female soldier who apparently recorded the incident were listed. None of them were interviewed.[40] Indeed, it is hard to imagine how prosecutors could go forward successfully with a case based on such scant evidence. It is not clear why the investigation was delayed or ended up yielding so few clues about the alleged crime—though some critics of the administration believe the investigation did not have enough support among government officials to proceed in a forceful manner.

"From the start, there were doubts among some Democrats in Congress that the Justice Department could mount a serious prosecutorial effort against intelligence officers and other civilians accused of violence against terror suspects," wrote Johnston in the *New York Times*. "It was the Justice Department, through a series of legal opinions and memoranda, that played a crucial role in erecting the legal framework intended to give C.I.A. officers the widest possible latitude in interrogating terror suspects and virtually indemnify them from legal liability."[41]

In the early afternoon of April 13, 2006, almost two years after the Abu Ghraib scandal, I walk up to the front door of Nakhla's house. Over a period of several weeks, I had submitted a request for an interview by writing Nakhla a letter, sending him an e-mail, and calling him on the telephone. He did not respond to any of my queries. His attorney, Adam L. Rosman, told me on the telephone neither he nor his client would answer my questions about the allegations or the case.[42]

Nadine Nakhla greets me at the door. One of their daughters, a girl around twelve years old, hovers behind her mother. I introduce myself as a journalist and remind Nadine that we had spoken briefly on the telephone. She compliments me on my beaded purse. I admire the rose bushes in their yard. "My husband knows everything about flowers," says Nadine. "He takes care of them." She says she will speak with her husband about granting me an interview with him. As I leave her house, I wonder if she's lonely.

Two days later, I go back to their house. The air is heavy with the scent of flowers and wood chips. Nadine opens the door. Her dark hair is pushed back behind her ears. Her shoulders are hunched up. I can barely hear her when she talks. Her soft voice is drowned out by a lawn worker, blowing away leaves and grass from a nearby yard.

"We are not interested," she says. "My husband does not want to talk with you."

Not long after that, I visit the shopping mall where Nakhla works. I sit on a bench in the mall and watch him amble down the hall and pick up a pizza. Judge Robertson of the U.S. District Court in the District of Columbia decided in June 2006 that his court could not exercise jurisdiction over Nakhla. In other words, Nakhla could not be held liable for damages in the civil case, *Saleh v. Titan*, because he does not live in the District of Columbia. Lawyers and human rights advocates say Nakhla will probably never have to explain what happened at Abu Ghraib in a court of law.

"It's certainly fair to say he hasn't been brought to justice," says attorney Burke. "For him, it's over."[43]

CHAPTER FIFTEEN

COLLATERAL DAMAGE

Marla Ruzicka, a twenty-eight-year-old human-rights worker, calls me from New York one afternoon in February 2005. She tells me she had read my article about female detainees ("Abu Ghraib's Forgotten Prisoners") that month in *The American Prospect*. She says she wants to meet the Iraqi women who appear in my article and help them file military claims with the U.S. government so they can receive payments for the injuries they received while in detention facilities. I know that filing restitution claims will not necessarily lead to payments being made to the victims. But I also know it may be the only chance that Selwa, Kamil, and the other women I had interviewed will receive restitution for their injuries. Still. I tell Ruzicka the women will be nervous if an American, even a well-intentioned one, contacts them. I can't just hand over their phone numbers.

Ruzicka calls me again a couple days later and says she is going to Baghdad.[1] She had received a $5,000 travel grant from the Ford Foundation, a New York–based philanthropic organization, so she could find out about female prisoners who had been abused at Abu Ghraib and in other U.S.-run detention centers in Iraq.[2] She explains she has worked with Bobby Muller, the head of Vietnam Veterans of America, and Tim Rieser, chief of staff for U.S. Senator Patrick Leahy of Vermont and others on the Senate Appropriations Committee, to raise awareness of the problems faced by civilians in war-torn Afghanistan and Iraq.[3] Eventually, they won appropriations totaling approximately $30 million for programs assisting civilians affected by the wars in Iraq and Afghanistan.

On the telephone, Ruzicka asks me again if I can help her get in touch with the female detainees. I tell her it is a controversial subject and she should stay away from it. "You'll end up in an orange jumpsuit," I say, joking with her.

Or worse, I thought. I suggest that she meet the detainees in Amman, as I had done, instead of going to Baghdad. Other people she knew, including author David Rieff and Sam Zia-Zarifi, Asia research director for Human Rights Watch, told her the same thing, I later found out. As Zia-Zarifi explained to Jennifer Abrahamson, who wrote a book, *Sweet Relief: The Marla Ruzicka Story*, he had suggested "the sources travel to Jordan to meet with Marla, rather than her going into Iraq. But she couldn't resist."[4] Ruzicka was determined to meet the Iraqi women in Baghdad. "I'm going to have a hotel room, and the women will come and see me," she tells me. "I won't leave the hotel."

I tell her she should speak with a Pentagon spokesman I know, Lieutenant Colonel Barry Johnson, who was based in Baghdad, about her trip to help ensure that she was safe in Iraq. I also put her in touch with my Amman-based interpreter and, within days, basically handed everything over to Ruzicka: my electronic files, documents, and contacts in Damascus, Amman, and Baghdad. She thanks me for helping her, and in one of our telephone calls says she wants to know about the background of my sources in Iraq.

"Are they clean?" she asks.

I tell her I'm not sure about all of my sources. Some might have been involved in the insurgency. But I don't have proof. Ruzicka and I talk on the phone frequently and e-mail, sorting out details of her upcoming trip and gossiping about people we know in Washington and New York.

"I am getting some good things set up with ministries, etc.," she emails me. "But the visa stuff is going to be a nightmare! X, marla."[5]

Ruzicka had blond hair and a sweet laugh. She was also the fastest e-mailer I'd ever met; she'd shoot me the transcript of a Senate hearing as we talked on the phone, fire off a CNN corrrespondent's e-mail to me, or send me the phone number of a claims processor at the Defense Department. She was always telling me about people I should get in touch with. She took to heart E. M. Forster's dictate, "Only connect."

"A human switchboard," one journalist said about her.

She is so charming, I tell my friends and colleagues that spring. Watch out.

A native of Lakeport, California, Ruzicka wore knotted hair extensions. She also gave back rubs that "could leave bruises," according to her friend, Catherine ("Cat") Philp, a *Times* of London reporter, Ruzicka got up every morning and made a list, recording how many calories, alcoholic drinks, and cigarettes she could have that day. "Today, I will be a better Marla," she would say, standing in front of a mirror, Philp recalled. By nighttime, Ruzicka usually forgot about the list. She was a fixture, if not the instigator, of expat parties in Baghdad, Kabul, and other cities and was the Holly Golightly of the foreign-press corps, flirting and playing the reporters she met. She never heard a compliment she didn't pass on. In her e-mails to me, she'd write, "You are a sister!" In different ways, big and small, she made people feel good about themselves and showed them how they could reach out to others. She started traveling on a regular basis to Iraq in April 2003 to speak with men, women, and children who had been affected by the war. She tallied up the number of civilian casualties and, in many cases, helped survivors fill out military-claims forms for the U.S. government.

In March 2005, shortly before her last trip to Baghdad, I get a call from her in New York. She says she has found a woman who had been held at Abu Ghraib and was willing to speak openly about the abuse she had suffered. I ask Ruzicka if she can help me get an exclusive interview with the former prisoner. Like all journalists, I want to be the first one to publish the story.

"I don't do exclusives with human-rights stories," she tells me.

How admirable, I thought, not to care about who gets the story first. And how annoying. A few days later, Ruzicka is on the phone with me again, saying she had gotten a call from a *60 Minutes* producer. She has agreed to give them an exclusive on the story. I knew that *60 Minutes* would bring the issue to millions of Americans, a bigger audience, to put it mildly, than I could offer. Holding the phone receiver in my hand, I am both peeved that Ruzicka is working with CBS and in awe of her. On March 23 she flew to Baghdad.

She got a room at the Hamra Hotel, Philp tells me. After Ruzicka arrived at the hotel, she gave Philp a copy of my *American Prospect* article. "She simply said, 'Read this,'" Philp tells me.[6] My interpreter helped Ruzicka set up appointments with the women I had interviewed. Ruzicka and her colleague, Faiz Ali Salim, forty-three, who helped run their organization, CIVIC, began asking fixers and journalists for leads. "A local journalist had lined up a string of other sources who had information about the abuse claims, but Marla wasn't sure if she trusted them," wrote Abrahamson. "During her first few days in Baghdad, many characters, some unseemly, streamed in and out of Marla's hotel room."[7]

One of the visitors was Victoria Dirbash, a fifty-four-year-old bank director who had told me in an interview that an American interrogator had put his hand on her cheek and threatened to send her to Guantanamo. "Victoria is very angry," Ruzicka wrote in an e-mail.[8] Another former detainee, Houda al-Azawy, the manager of a Baghdad-based trading company, also came to the Hamra Hotel to meet with Ruzicka.[9] Azawy had spoken publicly about grisly details of the murder of her brother in a prison cell while being held in U.S. custody. I had considered including Azawy in my article, but I finally decided against it because I had no way of verifying the story about her brother's death or the other accounts she had provided about imprisonment and could not find any material in government documents that supported them. I was told Ruzicka felt the same way.

"She wasn't entirely certain Houda was a good source," Philp tells me.[10]

Getting the story about female detainees for *60 Minutes* turned out to be much harder than Ruzicka had anticipated. Philp tells me how she and Ruzicka used to hang out on a balcony and talk about the interviews she was doing at the hotel. Ruzicka was frustrated with her progress. "I am fine, just not finding that much about women!" Ruzicka wrote to me in an e-mail that month.[11] She and Salim were used to tough assignments; they had traveled to some of the most dangerous regions in Iraq to help civilians file restitution claims. But the people Ruzicka and Salim met at the Hamra Hotel posed a special set of problems. They talked about the torture they had experienced in U.S. custody. And some of them seemed threatening and dangerous. One afternoon, Ruzicka and Salim burst into Philp's hotel room, "racked with nervous giggles," wrote Abrahamson. "Faiz joked that he needed a drink. 'What's going on with you two?' Cat asked. 'We just interviewed one of the famous torture victims,' [Ruzicka] said, referring to one of the Iraqi prisoners whom U.S. soldiers had photographed at Abu Ghraib. 'Cat, he was really freaking me out. He kept saying how much he hates America. What am I doing to do? Oh, my God, Cat, this scary dude was in my room and knows where I *live*.' Cat calmed them down, helping them laugh off the harrowing experience. After Faiz left, Cat took a more serious tone," continued Abrahamson. "She was worried, and so was Marla."[12] Yet Ruzicka had gone to Baghdad and recorded the man's story— and those of other former detainees. She told me not to worry about the danger she faced while traveling and interviewing people in Iraq.

"She didn't sit behind a desk," her father, Cliff, of Lakeport, California, tells me on the telephone later that spring. "She went out into the field and documented the damage done to the families in Iraq. In order to do that, you have to go to the dangerous places in dangerous times."[13]

On Monday, April 18, 2005, I sat in a café in Clarendon, Virginia, and opened up the *New York Times* and found out she was dead.[14] By the time I got back to my car in the parking lot, I had a cell phone message from Burke. Her voice was shaky from crying. Congressional aide Rieser left a teary message on my machine at work. After a memorial service at an Adams Morgan restaurant in Washington in May 2005, Lieutenant Colonel Johnson drank a gin and tonic. "Her death really affected me," he says. "It was the first time since the start of the war that I cried."[15]

On April 16 Ruzicka was riding in a car with Salim on the road to the Baghdad International Airport when a suicide bomber exploded in a nearby vehicle and killed both of them. Their car was covered in flames, and she had burns on 90 percent of her body. A medic who treated her on the scene heard her last words: "I'm alive."

It was just like her to say something hopeful. Today, her legacy is large. Under the Marla Ruzicka Iraqi War Victims Fund, according to Rieser, $35 million has been appropriated to programs assisting civilians affected by the war in Iraq since April 2003.[16] "Did you hear what the priest said at her funeral?" Senator Leahy tells me on the telephone that spring, describing a memorial service that had been held for her in California. "He said, 'Well, God's going to be busy now.' And everybody who knew her kind of looked at each other and said, 'Well, he got that one right.'"[17] In her last e-mail to me, eight days before her death, she wrote, "see you in dc in june x, marla."

CHAPTER SIXTEEN

STATE SECRETS

It is the photographs that give one the vivid realization of what actually took place. Words don't do it. The words that there were abuses, that it was cruel, that it was inhumane, that it was blatant; you read that and it's one thing. You see the photographs, and you get a sense of it, and you cannot help but be outraged.

—Defense Secretary Donald H. Rumsfeld,
Senate Armed Services Committee Hearing, May 7, 2004[1]

American Civil Liberties Union (ACLU) paralegal Catherine Itaya, who works in the ACLU's national-security program, steps into an elevator on an October 2005 afternoon in the lobby of the southern-most building in Manhattan and glances up at a Captivate Media television mounted in the corner. "At first everyone thought people were spying on us," she says. "There was no picture—just a screen."[2]

The deputy director of ACLU's National Security Program, Jameel Jaffer, greets her on the seventeenth floor. A thirty-four-year-old, Harvard Law–educated attorney who plays squash, Jaffer had been working in financial derivatives until he heard an ACLU spokesman talk about civil liberties in the fall of 2001. Then he joined the staff of the organization. He seems pleased when I tell him I will not record our interview. "Now I can be more open," he says.[3]

Itaya and Jaffer have more reason than most New Yorkers to act skittish around tape recorders. The ACLU has been around for decades. (So has its lobby, decorated with a photo of a boy walking past a police line, two dusty potted plants, and a stack of back copies of *The Nation*.) Over the past four years, Jaffer has sued the government at least six times: the suits include *Doe v. Ashcroft* and *MCA of Ann Arbor v. Ashcroft*, both of which challenge the USA Patriot Act; *ACLU v. Department of Defense*, a suit that demands the release of additional Abu Ghraib images and documents, and *ACLU v. National Security Agency*. The suit against the Defense Department may have the biggest impact, Jaffer says, explaining how he and other ACLU lawyers have demanded the release of eighty-seven photographs and four videotapes of alleged detainee abuse at Abu Ghraib, as well as tens of thousands of pages of classified documents from the government.

Administration officials had argued strenuously against the release of the material, citing national security concerns. But they did not convince the judge. On September 29, 2005, Judge Alvin K. Hellerstein, who was appointed to the federal bench in 1998 by President Bill Clinton, ruled that the Defense Department had to release the additional images and documents requested by the ACLU under the Freedom of Information Act (FOIA). In his decision, Hellerstein allowed for the disclosure of seventy-four of the eighty-seven photos and three of the four videos requested under FOIA. The images are collectively known as the "Darby Photos," as Darby had turned them over to an army investigator. Hellerstein sided with the ACLU lawyers, saying the Darby Photos should be released, despite the government's efforts to keep them hidden from view. But he had a provision. He said some of the images, including those of female detainees apparently being abused, should not be released under any circumstances.

The government's efforts to suppress the additional Darby Photos reflect a pattern of officials withholding sensitive material concerning prisoners held at Abu Ghraib and in other detention facilities. Some of the images and documents that are withheld depict the mistreatment of female prisoners or sexual misconduct among military personnel. On February 15, 2005, an Australian television program, *Dateline*, released many of the classified Darby Photos, including images of abuse at Abu Ghraib that Jaffer and other ACLU lawyers had been trying to pry from the government. Within weeks, nearly all the classified images were made public. The government dropped the case.

As a result, one aspect of the legal dispute has been resolved. But a close look at the case helps to shed light on two aspects of the government's handling of the Abu Ghraib scandal. First, government officials have shown a special sensitivity to issues relating to women or sexual behavior at the prison. Second, government lawyers may have resorted to a national security defense in order to suppress documents and images that could be embarrassing to the administration. In some cases, the decision to withhold the images was made to protect the privacy of the individuals involved, a group that includes both the victims and the suspects who have not yet been charged with a crime. In other cases, though, government officials have tried to suppress sensitive material about detainees apparently because it makes the administration look bad. "The Americans who are complicit in this are doing their best to make sure this doesn't get public attention," says attorney Burke. "It's kept away from the media."[4]

ACLU's Jaffer says that at least one of the photographs being withheld by the government includes the image of a woman. Physician and human rights expert Steven Miles, who has read extensively among the government documents relating to torture and abuse of detainees, has concluded that many descriptions of female detainees are missing. Pages about female prisoners, he says, tend to be heavily redacted.

"Why are the pictures of the degraded male prisoners at Abu Ghraib readily available," Miles wrote in an essay for *One of the Guys: Women as Aggressors and Torturers*, an anthology edited by this author.

"Why are the pictures of degraded women prisoners classified? Why has the Defense Department released the death certificates, autopsies, and investigations pertaining to male prisoners but a hand-scrawled note in a memo is the only hint of the death of a woman prisoner?"[5] He believes that government officials have withheld documents about the deaths of a woman and a child in U.S. custody for a reason: "There's been a move to depict the prisoners as al-Qaeda," he tells me, "and it's hard to do that if you're talking about women and kids."

WHAT THE GOVERNMENT
DOESN'T WANT YOU TO SEE

"We're talking about rape and murder here," U.S. senator Lindsey Graham, a Republican from South Carolina, said on May 7, 2004, outside a Senate Armed Services Committee hearing room. "We're not just talking about giving people a humiliating experience."[6]

"I have heard rumors that there are videotapes and pictures of detainee abuse," a navy dog handler said on February 1, 2004, in a sworn statement that appears in the Taguba Report, "and I heard rumors there was a videotape of a rape."[7] Seymour Hersh, the journalist who broke the My Lai story in Vietnam and wrote the groundbreaking *New Yorker* series about Abu Ghraib, has talked about a videotape depicting sexual assault at the prison. "Boys were sodomized with the cameras rolling," he said at an ACLU convention in San Francisco on July 7, 2004. "And the worst above all of that is the soundtrack of the boys shrieking that your government has. They are in total terror. It's going to come out."[8]

It is still not clear whether or not there is a "rape video." (Hersh has partially backed off from his statement.)[9] But the photographic images are disturbing. On May 14, 2004, select members of Congress—including U.S. representative Jim Moran, a Democrat from Virginia and a member of the Appropriations Committee's Defense Subcommittee, and U.S. senator Barbara Boxer, a Democrat from California and a member of the Senate Foreign Relations Committee—gathered behind closed doors on Capitol

Hill and looked at approximately one thousand unreleased Darby Photos.

"There was an upfront photo of sexual intercourse being performed," Moran tells me on January 30, 2006, at an event on "Torture and the Laws of War" cosponsored by NYU Law School's Center on Law and Security in Washington. "It was some perverted group of people who were probably sexually repressed or something."

I ask him if he saw any female detainees in the photos or videos.

"There was one that appeared to be a detainee. She was naked to the waist," he says. He is a broad-shouldered man who often speaks—even in small groups—as if he is holding a bullhorn. As he talks about the photographs, though, his voice trails off.[10] He shows me how the detainee lifted her shirt to expose her breasts, apparently describing a photograph that is mentioned in the Fay-Jones Report: "A criminal detainee housed in the Hard Site was shown lifting her shirt with both her breasts exposed. There is no evidence to confirm if [this was] consensual or coerced; however in either case sexual exploitation of a person in US custody constitutes abuse."[11]

At a Senate Foreign Relations Committee hearing, "Iraq: The Way Ahead," on May 18, 2004, Senator Boxer spoke about the photographs that were shown in the closed congressional briefing: "One of them that is haunting me is that of a beautiful Iraqi woman who is staring into the camera with dead eyes and then, in the next shot, she is lifting her blouse, and she is exposing her nudity to the camera, with the same dead eyes."

Paul Wolfowitz, then-deputy secretary of defense and a witness at the hearing, responded to her remarks, "I consider it very important to make restitution and to do it as quickly as we possibly can and as generously as we possibly can," he said.[12] He called Senator Boxer that evening and assured her he was looking into the issue of female detainees, according to Senator Boxer's chief counsel Charlotte Oldham-Moore. Yet apparently nothing was done to help the female detainee or to find out more from her about the incident.

"The woman in the photo, forced to expose her breasts, was released in November 2003," Oldham-Moore wrote me in an e-mail on September 29, 2004. "Neither DOD or Iraqi Governing Council ever located her or spoke with her about the incident."[13]

On February 16, 2005, Senator Leahy asked about the female prisoners at Abu Ghraib during a Senate Appropriations Committee hearing entitled "Fiscal Year 2005 Emergency Supplemental Budget Request." Marla Ruzicka had apparently brought Senator Leahy's attention to the issue, and she had e-mailed me a transcript of the hearing on February 22, 2005, several weeks before she was killed in Baghdad.

"My last question, though, is from the Taguba Report that talked about the abuse of Iraqi women in U.S. custody," said Senator Leahy. "It commented on the videotaping and photographing of naked male and female detainees. The Fay-Jones report describes similar incidents. Insurgents in Iraq have cited the abuse of female detainees as a motivation for their violent acts. Whether it's an excuse or not, they've cited it. Are you, Mr. Secretary, aware of reports that Iraqi women detainees in U.S. custody were assaulted or raped? And if so, who's investigating that?"

"There have been nine reports on detainee investigations," said Secretary Rumsfeld. "There have been over 15,000 pages. Plus another 16,000 pages delivered to Congress. Nine-hundred-and-fifty interviews have been completed. There have been thirty-three courts-martial, fifty-five nonjudicial punishments, seventeen reprimands."[14]

Congressional aide Oldham-Moore told me that Secretary Rumsfeld had simply "stonewalled" when he was pressed on the issue of the sexual abuse of women at Abu Ghraib. "Most, if not all, of the female detainees have never been questioned about whether or not they were sexually assaulted or raped at Abu Ghraib," she wrote to me in an e-mail. "Therefore, as the DOD spins it, no allegations 'surfaced' so no corrective measures are needed."

A LETTER ASKING FOR POISON

Low-slung, butter-colored houses of Amman, Jordan, shimmer in the cold sunlight outside the windows of a conference room in Le Royal Hotel on the afternoon of December 8, 2004. Inside the room, attorney Riva Khoshaba turns on a tape recorder. After being arrested in Samarra (an incident described in Chapter Six), former detainee Selwa was taken in flexicuffs to a detention facility in Tikrit, 100 miles northwest of Baghdad, where approximately 700 male Iraqi prisoners were living in desert tents. Soldiers and guards forced her and other prisoners to crouch on the ground with their arms above their heads in hundred-degree weather: "They told us, 'You are cowards. You are Saddam's children. You are fighting against the Americans.' If we complained, they said, 'Shut up. Put your face against the wall.'"

The next day, a stocky American officer in boots and a T-shirt told Selwa she was responsible for cleaning an outhouse known as a "burn shitter," a structure made out of a 55-gallon drum, filled with diesel fuel and waste. He lit the mixture of human feces and urine in the metal drum and gave Selwa a heavy club to stir it.

"The fire from the pot felt very strong on my face," says Selwa. She leans forward and sweeps her hands through the air to show how she stirred the excrement. "I became very tired," she says. "I told the sergeant I couldn't do it. There was another man close to us. The sergeant came up to me and whispered in my ear, 'If you don't, I will tell one of the soldiers to fuck you.'"

"It is a shame on them," says Khoshaba. She is sitting across the table and looking sympathetically at Selwa. "Not on you."

Selwa closes her eyes and nods her head, trying to show she is listening. But it is as though she were sitting at a table far away and can hear Khoshaba's words but can't make out their meaning. Selwa nods again and sinks back into her chair.

"I said, 'I will go on.' I stirred for two hours," Selwa says. "Then I fainted."

For Selwa, it was only the beginning of a nightmarish journey. In early October of 2003, she was strip-searched and given an ID bracelet and a prisoner number. She had arrived at Abu Ghraib. When Selwa talks about the prison, her voice is soft.

"Whenever I remember, it's like a fire goes out," she says. "Once I saw the guards hit a woman, probably thirty years old. They put her in an open area and said, 'Come out so you can see her.' They pulled her by the hair and poured ice water on her. She was screaming and shouting and crying as they poured water into her mouth. They left her there all night. There was another girl; the soldiers said she wasn't honest with them. They said she gave them wrong information. When I saw her, she had electric burns all over her body."

She and a group of women lived in Tier 1B. She had a small room with a toilet and access to a sink. The place was infested with maggots. She used to wash her slip and her robe and then put the damp clothes on and let them dry as she was wearing them. As she talks, I lean forward and ask her a difficult question: were you sexually assaulted?

"No," she says. "They respected me." She pushes her chair away from the table.

Did they ever make you take off your clothes? I ask.

She leans back and pulls her jacket over her chest and covers part of her face with her hand. She looks downward and bites her thumb. Her eyes are half-closed, and her shoulders are slumped.

"I don't remember," she says. She folds her arms across her chest and her eyes fill with tears. She stares at the ground. A few minutes later, she excuses herself and leaves the room.[15]

Neither Selwa nor any of the other Iraqi women I interviewed would say outright they had been raped or sexually assaulted, and for good reason. "You're asking this in a culture that kills you for being raped," says attorney Khoshaba.[16] A persistent rumor is that one of the prisoners, Noor, sent a letter to friends and family, asking for poison so she and the other female prisoners could commit suicide because they were distraught over the sexual violence. The letter was described in the Taguba Report.[17]

"I think many women who were held at Abu Ghraib were raped by Americans," says a human-rights worker, Nadia, who worked in the Baghdad-based office of Burke's legal team. (Her name has been changed for security reasons.) She is committed to her role in helping Iraqi women—despite the fact she has received death threats. Taking off her *hijab* and loosening her hair in a hotel room in Amman in December 2004, she says one man threatened to kill her if she spoke negatively about the insurgency. "He said, 'We will put you in the back seat of the car like Margaret Hassan,'" she tells me.[18] (On October 19, 2004, CARE International staffer Hassan was kidnapped in Baghdad, and a videotape of her calling for the release of female Iraqi prisoners was made. A videotape of Hassan's execution—she was shot in the head—was released that November.)[19]

Nadia has persisted with her work, but notes that it is difficult to get women to talk. "Selwa told me, 'I want to talk to you without my sister in the room,'" she recalls. "She said, 'They did everything bad to me and may God take them all to hell.' She began to weep bitterly. She didn't tell the truth to her family." Nadia keeps notes from interviews she has conducted in Baghdad in a file that she brought to Amman and shared with me. The files include the stories of more than a dozen former detainees, including a sixty-year-old woman and two girls under the age of eighteen, who say they were raped or sexually assaulted while being held in U.S. custody.

If a woman were to admit publicly she was sexually assaulted, her family members would not necessarily kill her. But her life would change. "First of all, she would lose her respect. She couldn't go to her job," says Nadia. "Her family would act as if they're disgusted with her." She made a face, as if there were a bad smell in the room.[20]

A seventy-year-old tribal sheik who wears a charcoal tunic and has a gray-speckled mustache tells me he met a female detainee on May 4, 2004, the day they were both released from Abu Ghraib, on a bus ride home. "She sat two rows away from me," he says. "She was wearing a hijab, and her face was completely dried up. It looked as though she hadn't seen the sun in a very long time. 'I've seen terrible things,' she said. 'We went through hell.' She was crying and saying women had been tortured and raped."[21]

"The windows in the building were broken, and they were covered with wooden panels," Iraqi attorney Nabil, who was held at Abu Ghraib, recalls. "Sometimes I could hear screams and shouts. Women were calling for mercy. There were also children between the ages of ten and twelve. The children became hysterical. I was told the women were tortured in front of their children. One day, a sheik came back from a medical clinic where he'd been treated. He was in tears. 'What happened?' we asked. He told us he had seen a young girl, fifteen years old, with internal bleeding. She had been raped over and over again by the soldiers, and she could no longer talk. He is a deeply religious man. But that night, he shouted at God. 'How is it possible that you are there and these things are happening?' he said."[22]

In December 2004 I spoke with a Pentagon spokesman on the telephone about the sexual abuse of women at Abu Ghraib. "There are no allegations of rape by any female detainees," he tells me.

I mention the stories I had heard and ask whether or not military investigators have tried to contact the women who have been released. "Well, we don't really have a mechanism for reaching out and finding former detainees," he says. "If we have allegations and they're brought to us, we would open the case."

It's hard for them to talk about this, I tell him.

"Certainly, there is a stigmatism in this culture when a female is detained or put in prison," he says. "It has been an education for us to understand this. And when I know there is someone who is talking to people like you, I try to remind you that there are people at the [Iraqi] Ministry of Human Rights—there are females there—and they deal with detainees on a daily basis."[23] (A U.S. State Department official, Sandra L. Hodgkinson, told me in March 2006 that as a senior advisor on human rights for the Coalition Provisional Authority in 2004 she helped set up the Iraqi human-rights ministry. The U.S. government has devoted $140 million to human rights and transitional-justice programs in Iraq.)[24]

What kinds of things have you heard from Iraqi women? I ask the Pentagon spokesman.

"Well, frankly, I just don't think there have been too many former detainees who have gone to them," he tells me.[25]

And regardless of the evidence, rape has become a potent symbol in Iraq of what many Iraqis feel has happened to their country. Photos purporting to show American soldiers sexually assaulting Iraqi women, for example, were posted on Abasrah.net and other Arabic-language Web sites as "proof" of American brutality at Abu Ghraib. Yet they have been traced back to a porn site, "Iraq Babes." In addition, some fake photos were apparently provided by a New York–based company, Extreme Traffic, and a Budapest company, Sex in War.[26] Besides the bootleg digital images, fake photos of detainee abuse appeared in May 2004 in a British newspaper, *The Daily Mirror*, causing a scandal that led to the firing of its editor.[27]

Meanwhile, in a Baghdad art gallery in the summer of 2004, artist Qasim Sabti displayed a figure of an Iraqi woman who had been raped—a metaphor for the anguish many Iraqis feel about how prisoners were treated at Abu Ghraib.[28] A *New York Times* reporter described a flier found at a Ramadi mosque in October 2004 that showed a woman in a black gown "being raped by men in sunglasses, presumably Americans." [29]

In some government documents that ACLU lawyers have obtained through the Freedom of Information Act, officials have crossed out sections about insurgents who demand the release of female detainees. Yet the information about the insurgents had already appeared in the *Washington Post* and the *New York Times*.

"Virtually every factual sentence redacted from the publicly filed submission recites facts that have been widely reported in the media," wrote the ACLU lawyers in an August 3, 2005, brief, demanding to know why the government has refused to release even the documents that present their argument to have the case dismissed: "The government's insistence that unclassified information that is already in the present domain should be suppressed is truly extraordinary."

As the ACLU lawyers pointed out in their brief, government officials redacted information about a kidnapping in Iraq that had already been reported on September 30, 2004, in the *New York Times*. The hostage takers had demanded the release of all Iraqi women held in American military prisons. Government officials, explains Jaffer, said that certain passages in the documents were a threat to national security. The passages concern the kidnapping of Hassan, and the fact that she had "called for the release of all female prisoners in Iraq" before she was murdered, and the fact that, according to a 2003 State Department report, "[under Saddam] women [were] often raped in order to blackmail their relatives."

These documents, as well as other Defense Department documents about the treatment of female prisoners, were redacted before being released under the Freedom of Information Act.[30]

BLACKMAIL

General Richard Myers, chairman of the Joint Chiefs of Staff said releasing the additional Darby Photos would "endanger the lives and physical safety" of U.S. troops. A judge advocate, Charles Gardner Mills, who works with the American Legion, a three-million-member organization of U.S. veterans, filed an amicus brief saying the photos should be withheld.

"There is a real, serious danger—almost a certainty—that if these photos are made public, people will get killed," he explains.[31]

Judge Hellerstein said in his decision that there were other things to consider.

"Our nation does not surrender to blackmail," he said. "With respect to the concerns expressed by General Myers, my task is not to defer to our worst fears but to interpret and apply the law, in this case, the Freedom of Information Act, which advances values important to our society, transparency, and accountability in government."[32]

No doubt the additional as yet unreleased images and information would provoke strong emotions, and certainly headlines. And that, says Thomas S. Blanton, director of the National Security Archive at George Washington University in Washington, D.C., is why it is necessary to declassify them.

"The Pentagon argues the images should be covered up because they would turn world opinion against the U.S.," says Blanton, who filed his first Freedom of Information Act request as a reporter in 1976 and now oversees an organization where staffers file roughly 2,000 requests each year. "It's one of the most creative arguments for covering up official misbehavior the government has ever come up with: 'Because the government's behavior is so reprehensible, it must be hidden.' It turns the whole argument for open government on its head."[33]

For some, the official response is hardly surprising.

"The administration has a propensity not to tell the whole truth," says Karpinski. "It's not that they're lying. It's that they're not telling everything they know."[34] In fact, the release of the photos on Australia's *Dateline*—the images the U.S. government had tried to keep from the public—did not set off an explosive reaction at all. It led the news that day in the U.S. and European media and then faded.

ACLU executive director Anthony Romero says they devoted five lawyers and considerable billable hours—"it's tens of thousands of dollars, easily"—to the Defense Department suit.[35] ACLU executives, Romero said, considered the lawsuit, as well as related cases, to be crucial efforts to shake the government out of its habit of keeping things secret, purportedly to protect the security of the United States, even when the documents or images that are being withheld (such as documents that include information that has already appeared in American newspapers) seem to pose no such threat.

A SECRET ARGUMENT—ABOUT SECRET PHOTOS

It is dark and rainy outside, and Jaffer sits behind his desk and holds up a twenty-three-page affidavit filed on July 28, 2005, in the U.S. District Court in Manhattan. In the affidavit, General Myers explained why releasing additional Abu Ghraib photos through the Freedom of Information Act is a bad idea. Yet there is little to be seen of Myers's argument on the page, regardless of the lighting in the room.

In fact, whole sections of the affidavit filed in the civil suit, *ACLU v. Department of Defense*, and in particular pages sixteen, seventeen, and eighteen, are blank except for ghostly, dotted lines and the words "Redacted" and "[SEALED]." Another affidavit, filed in the federal court on the same day and signed by a former State Department deputy assistant secretary got similar treatment: chunks of white space and "redacted" are found on twelve of the eighteen pages, with seven pages completely blank.

The affidavits include much of the government's argument for withholding the additional Abu Ghraib photos from public view, yet many passages are expunged. "This information is very sensitive and is not the type we would voluntarily disclose due to its national security and intelligence value," said General Myers in his affidavit. That is, basically, the same argument government lawyers are using to keep the Darby Photos classified, says Jaffer. Releasing the images could incite riots in Muslim countries and put U.S. troops in danger.

Still, why can't the *arguments* in the suit be seen by the public? I wonder.

"It's a kind of secrecy creep," says Jaffer. "Not only are the images secret, but the reasons for keeping the images that way are also secret—or were."

Jaffer and other ACLU lawyers demanded the release of the unredacted briefs. Judge Hellerstein partly agreed. The Defense Department refiled the affidavits in expanded form on August 29, 2005. The passages range from the banal to the "embarrassing," says Jaffer. He believes the blank spaces are part of a larger strategy.

"The redactions were made for political reasons," Jaffer continues. "The government did not want the arguments to be subjected to public scrutiny because many are indefensible generalizations about the Muslim and Arab world. I think the government has adopted this secrecy strategy over the last few years in the way officials have dealt with the Patriot Act, for instance, and after September 11 when the government rounded up hundreds of immigrants and refused to release even their names."

In one section of the sealed affidavit in the *ACLU v. Department of Defense* suit, General Myers said, "Our democratic idea of public accountability—the airing of misdeeds by government officials and employees in order to hold government to the highest standards of conduct—is an idea that is misunderstood in other parts of the world."

"They're saying: 'Other people in the world don't understand democratic accountability. We do,'" says Jaffer. "It's quite galling."[36]

Some passages in the legal briefs, explains Jaffer, were apparently expunged because they make the government look silly. In one section of a brief, for instance, the State Department official explains why photos of detainee abuse shouldn't be released. "The stigma associated with masturbation or public nudity can limit a man's prospects for marriage, limit his prospects for employment, diminish his role in the community and lead him to being cast out of the family," he wrote.[37]

Khaled Fahmy, an Egyptian-born, forty-one-year-old New York University associate professor who specializes in studying the relationship between the human body and the modern state, says the government's insistence that Muslims would experience this in a dramatically different fashion than people of other religions shows a cultural misunderstanding. For that reason, the disclosure of a State Department official's remark would be embarrassing to the government.

"These pictures are offensive to anyone, regardless of his or her religion. To assume this would be particularly offensive to Muslims is itself offensive," says Fahmy, who served as an expert witness in the case. Somehow, he explains, the State Department official has "unwittingly accepted the twisted and bizarre logic of the perpetrators of this crime."

Fahmy believes that the images "are a very eloquent testimony to acts of torture and are better than any summary that could be given in court. They would shock people into thinking."

"My strongest argument goes to the logic and spirit of the Freedom of Information Act," he says. "In the Muslim world and elsewhere, much of the anger surrounding the photos stems from the fact the U.S. endorses torture and has failed to hold officials accountable. The government's concealment of evidence only feeds the anger."[38]

And in the end, Judge Hellerstein ruled against the government, saying the images should be released. The photographs stirred up controversy not only in the New York courtroom, of course. Print and broadcast journalists wrote stories and prepared news segments about the photos and the individuals who appeared in them. Like many other things connected with Abu Ghraib, these articles were disputed.

CHAPTER SEVENTEEN

THE OTHER HOODED MAN

A former mayor of Iraq's Al Madifai district, Ali Shalal Qaissi, forty-three, has Andy Warhol–white hair and wears a black, fitted jacket made in Syria that is as stylish as anything seen in Manhattan's Chelsea district. Philadelphia artist Daniel Heyman asks if he can draw a picture of him. Qaissi glances over at a group of German and Jordanian tourists waiting in line at a buffet table adorned with two eighteen-inch–tall meringue swans at the Regency Palace Hotel in Amman on this Friday evening, March 10, 2006.

"Not here," says Qaissi, shaking his head. "It will give the impression that I'm bourgeois."

He is joking, of course. It is hard to believe that Qaissi, an agreeable dinner companion with a dry sense of humor, was once a high-value detainee at Abu Ghraib. Yet his hand—a mass of twisted flesh and scars with a swollen palm and long, oval-shaped fingers in a sci-fi shade of silver—is a vivid reminder of that period in his life. He was arrested in October 2003. The American guards in Tier 1A at Abu Ghraib called him Clawman and believed his hand had been injured while setting off an IED. In fact, says Qaissi, his hand was mangled in a shotgun blast at a wedding as he fired off a rifle in the air—a ritual in Iraqi towns where nearly every man or boy over the age of fifteen seems to have some kind of firearm.

His injury got worse in prison. Hours, even days, of being held in shackles took a toll. One evening, Qaissi says, he was placed on a cardboard box and photographed as he stood with his arms outstretched, wearing a sandbag over his head, and clutching electrodes in his hands, at the prison. Yet he is not the Hooded Man in the famous Abu Ghraib photograph. Unlike that Hooded Man, Qaissi was never an icon. He became instead the focal point of an embarrassing mix-up involving a *New York Times* reporter and several *Times* editors, two human-rights researchers, a Washington journalist, and a Philadelphia lawyer. In this way, Qaissi seems to embody the difficulties faced by reporters and readers in the United States as they try to understand the story of Abu Ghraib.

SYMBOL OF ABU GHRAIB

Qaissi had been known in international circles on the night of our dinner at the Regency Palace. He was featured in a February 2005 *Vanity Fair* article ("The Man in the Hood" by Donovan Webster) and in a PBS program, *Now*, hosted by David Brancaccio, on April 29, 2005.[1] Qaissi is a plaintiff in *Saleh v. Titan*. And he had spoken with United Nations officials about torture in Iraqi prisons. But he was not famous. The following morning, Qaissi appeared on page one of the *New York Times* in a 1,300-word article, "Symbol of Abu Ghraib Seeks to Spare Others His Nightmare," by a *Times* Middle East correspondent named Hassan M. Fattah about Qaissi's imprisonment at Abu Ghraib, the humiliation he experienced, and what it was like to stand on the box.

"Then there is the picture of Mr. Qaissi himself, standing atop a cardboard box, taken 15 days into his detention. He said he had only recently been given a blanket after remaining naked for days, and had fashioned the blanket into a kind of poncho," wrote Fattah. "The guards took him to a heavy box filled with military meal packs, he said, and hooded him. He was told to stand atop the box as electric wires were attached to either hand. Then, he claims, they shocked him five times, enough for him to bite his tongue."

Qaissi's remarks also appear on page two as the *Times*'s "Quotation of the Day:" "I never wanted to be famous, especially not in this way." His name appears below the quote, along with an identifying phrase: "whose torture at Abu Ghraib prison in Iraq was depicted in a photograph that drew worldwide attention." His business card was printed in the *New York Times*. It shows the widely-distributed photo of a hooded man standing on a box, and his cell phone number and three e-mail addresses are legible.[2]

Qaissi sits in front of a laptop in the hotel bar the day after the *Times* story appeared. He is staring, with a bemused expression on his face, at the computer screen. One of his attorneys, twenty-eight-year-old Jonathan Pyle, a University of Pennsylvania Law School graduate, who was raised on constitutional issues, is sitting nearby. Jonathan Pyle's father, Christopher H. Pyle, teaches constitutional law at Mount Holyoke College; at sixteen, Jonathan was a plaintiff in an ACLU suit against the South Hadley School Committee in South Hadley, Mass., that challenged a dress code. (He wasn't allowed to wear a T-shirt that said, "See Dick Drink. See Dick Drive. See Dick Die.") Pyle glances over at Qaissi and watches him scroll through e-mail sent by supporters around the world. It is a triumphant moment for both the lawyer and his client.

CORRECTION BOX

Three days later, Pyle waves me over to a breakfast table in the hotel restaurant. "Did you see this?" he asks. He shows me a printout of a *Salon* article by Washington correspondent Michael Scherer that raised questions about Fattah's *New York Times* piece: the hooded man in the photograph is not Qaissi but a man who has been identified in government documents as Abdou Hussain Saad Faleh. (His nickname was Gilligan.)[3] In sworn testimony with an army investigator, Faleh said he was subjected to a terrifying incident: "Then a tall black soldier came and put electrical wires on my fingers and toes and on my penis, and I had a bag over my head," he said. "Then he was saying, 'Which switch is on for electricity?'"[4]

Fattah's *New York Times* article soon had a "correction appended:" "The *Times* did not adequately research Mr. Qaissi's insistence that he was the man in the photograph. Mr. Qaissi's account had already been broadcast and printed by other outlets, including PBS and *Vanity Fair*, without challenge. Lawyers for former prisoners at Abu Ghraib vouched for him. Human rights workers seemed to support his account. The Pentagon, asked for verification, declined to confirm or deny it.

"Despite the previous reports, the *Times* should have been more persistent in seeking comment from the military. A more thorough examination of previous articles in the *Times* and other newspapers would have shown that in 2004 military investigators named another man as the one on the box, raising suspicions about Mr. Qaissi's claim.

"The *Times* also overstated the conviction with which representatives of Human Rights Watch and Amnesty International expressed their view of whether Mr. Qaissi was the man in the photograph. While they said he could well be that man, they did not say they believed he was."[5]

On March 14 a "Clarifying Article" appeared in the *New York Times* under the headline, "The Struggle for Iraq: Detainees; Web Magazine Raises Doubts Over a Symbol of Abu Ghraib." Chris Grey, chief of public affairs for the Department of the Army Criminal Investigation Command, said, "We have had several detainees claim they were the person depicted in the photograph in question. Our investigation indicates that the person you have is not the detainee who was depicted in the photograph released in connection with the Abu Ghraib investigation."[6] A longer *New York Times* piece about Qaissi, explaining in detail the problems that occurred while reporting on the story, was published on March 18.[7]

That same day, Howard Kurtz wrote a piece about the controversy for the *Washington Post*. An error crept into the story. Kurtz mistakenly thought Faleh—not Qaissi—had a nickname referring to a "claw."[8] Journalists seemed to be piling mistake upon mistake and in their efforts to illuminate the story of Qaissi seemed only to add to the confusion. Eight days later, *New York Times* "Public Editor" Byron Calame weighed in on Fattah's article, describing it as "fatally flawed," especially since previous *Times* articles had already identified the hooded man. "Ethan Bronner, deputy foreign editor, wrote to me in an e-mail that editors had done several searches of the paper's archives using various keywords," wrote Calame. "He said editors now realize that one search—using the terms 'Abu Ghraib,' 'box,' and 'hood'—missed the crucial May 2004 article because it didn't contain the word 'hood.'"[9]

There had been other pieces of evidence that indicated Qaissi was not the hooded man in the photo. "Two slightly different low-resolution pictures, seemingly of the same man, have been released to date," wrote Donovan Webster in his *Vanity Fair* article. "Haj Ali's [Qaissi] lawyers believe he's depicted in the photos, although no one can be sure, given the circumstances under which the photos were taken; [Qaissi] does claim he was subjected to the same abuse. Unless the guards involved shed light on the matter someday, it will likely remain impossible to say for certain who is pictured."[10]

THE TRUTH ABOUT THE HOODED MAN

Officials in the army's public-affairs offices were peeved at Fattah's article. The CID's Grey wondered why he didn't verify the information about Qaissi with him or another army official before publishing his article. "A person comes up and says, 'I was the guy in the car when Kennedy was shot,'" says Grey. "Do you believe him?"[11]

Grey and other military spokesmen sound impatient when discussing detainee stories. Major Wayne Marotto, a Department of the Army public affairs staff officer, for example, says he has had heard many outlandish ones. "Two of them [detainees] said they'd been attacked by lions," he tells me. "Who knows who's been abused or tortured? The word is if you're a detainee and you say, 'I was tortured and abused,' then the military has to investigate it. Now it's a cottage industry."[12]

In another telephone call, Grey interrupts me when I referred to Qaissi as a former detainee. "An *alleged* detainee," he says.[13]

Military officials, journalists, and the American public are understandably skeptical about stories of abuse told by former detainees, many of whom are seen, rightly, as enemies of U.S. troops in Iraq. In addition, the army had been hit with a barrage of unfavorable coverage over the killings of civilians in Haditha and other Iraqi cities. That may explain why army officials reacted strongly to stories about detainee-abuse claims.

"The ACLU and Human Rights First say torture is widespread, and it's systematic, and it's endemic," Marotto tells me. "The U.S. Army has processed over 50,000 detainees since 2001. There have been investigations of [abuse claims of] 1.2 percent of all the detainees. That is not widespread. That is not systematic. Correction. Systemic. Whatever you write, I hope you can be objective and put that in. Few do. They say, 'The army tortures.' Those who have abused detainees have been held accountable. The Army does not tolerate that. I hope you don't believe the government is defending torture."[14]

I admire the diligence of many CID investigators and their persistence in collecting evidence on crimes committed by soldiers. Still, casting doubt on Qaissi's entire story—even whether or not he had been held prisoner at Abu Ghraib—is unwarranted. None of the corrections, clarifying articles, or follow-up pieces in *Salon*, the *New York Times*, or the *Washington Post* had raised questions of that magnitude. Qaissi was issued a prisoner-identification number (151716), and military records show he was held in a U.S.-run detention facility during the time he said he was. Yet he was transformed from being a reliable source for American journalists reporting on detainee abuse and a respected founder of a prisoners'-rights organization into a "a self-styled activist," as the *Times*'s Calame describes him, who may have been guilty of "deception."[15] In short, he became a symbol of crooked storytelling, unchallenged accounts, fraudulent detainee-abuse claims, and sloppy journalism.

I have interviewed Qaissi and more than twenty other Iraqi civilians who claim they were mistreated in U.S. custody, and at times felt skeptical of their claims, especially when they seemed overly interested in financial compensation or in the recovery of lost property. One former detainee, for example, told me that U.S. soldiers had confiscated his possessions during a raid on his house and handed me a list of the missing items on a sheet of paper. I scanned the list and, feeling annoyed at his demands, handed the piece of paper back to him. "No, I can't help you get your machete back," I said. (It had been a long day.)

In other cases, I collected identification cards, photographs or copies of prisoner identification bracelets and medical records, as well as videotapes and photographs of damage done to houses or property, from former detainees. Then I submitted their names, identification numbers, and dates of confinement to the Pentagon to see if military officials could confirm the information. I also tracked down individuals who could tell me more about the arrest and imprisonment of the former detainees. In the case of Selwa, for example, I was granted access to a confidential military file and, through a stroke of luck, managed to find the soldier who had arrested her husband in Samarra. I had multiple sources, too, for the arrest of Haddad. Rahman's description of his detention was consistent with accounts provided by soldiers who had worked at the facility where he was held. (The soldiers were interviewed by a Human Rights Watch researcher.)

When Fattah confused the identity of Qaissi and Faleh in his page-one article in the *New York Times*, he was making a serious error that occurred because he lacked documentary evidence. Yet the basis for the story had seemed sound: Qaissi printed out a copy of the iconic photograph during the interview, as Fattah tells me on the telephone, and said he was the man in the picture.[16] Maybe Qaissi was lying. Or maybe he believed it was true. It is not unusual for people to identify with a powerful photograph and to believe they are, literally, in the picture. As David Friend, an editor at *Vanity Fair*, explained in his book *Watching the World Change: The Stories Behind the Images of 9/11*, ten men claimed to be the sailor kissing the nurse in Times Square on V-J Day in Eisenstaedt's famous photo. "Each one insisting, with convincing evidence—a distinctive hairline, a quirky vein on the right hand, a memory of a newly acquired Quartermaster 1st Class patch visible in the photograph—that he alone was the 'kissing soldier,'" Friend wrote. "Three women wrote in and claimed to be the nurse."[17]

People in Iraq may have identified in some way with the Hooded Man in the picture—and some may have even been treated in a similar fashion at the prison. There was, however, only one Hooded Man in the photograph: Faleh. And thanks to the rigorous reporting Fattah did after his initial piece, and the follow-up articles in *Salon*, the *Washington Post*, and the *New York Times*, we know much more about Faleh, Qaissi, Abu Ghraib, and the CID than we did before. Mistakes occur in every newspaper. Handled properly, they can prompt a higher level of investigative work and a more thorough and nuanced understanding of an issue. The main point in Fattah's article—Qaissi was mistreated at Abu Ghraib—is not in dispute. It never was. Unfortunately, though, Qaissi became "controversial." Whether or not he was the figure in the iconic photograph became the central issue, not the abuse at Abu Ghraib.

Grey and Marotto are right about one thing. Detainees' stories *are* bizarre. (I had heard the one about the lions, too.) Nevertheless, it seems unwise to discount claims of abuse only for that reason. One of the strangest stories ever told in American newspapers concerns a West Virginia woman holding an Iraqi man on a leash, a Pennsylvania soldier who forces prisoners into a human pyramid, and an Iraqi prisoner standing on a box with electrodes in his hand. Yet these are the things, of course, that occurred at Abu Ghraib.

In the end, Americans tend not to believe a story about humiliation and abuse committed by other Americans unless there is hard-and-fast "proof" such as a photograph of the incident. Yet a photograph of an abusive act by itself is not enough to convey the damage; it is most effective when accompanied by a firsthand description of the suffering. "Since it's rare that we can put both together (and the administration doesn't have an interest in helping us do so), this doesn't bode well for our ability to empathize with abused detainees," says Jonathan H. Marks, associate professor of bioethics, humanities, and law at Pennsylvania State University and coauthor of a January 2005 *New England Journal of Medicine* article, "When Doctors Go to War."[18]

"And the worst part about the whole thing is that it's all being treated like some sort of an abstraction," wrote *Vanity Fair*'s Donovan Webster in an e-mail to me. "As if the only thing that happened was a photo session with a box and a hood and some wires; it was part of a far larger chain of events."[19] The controversy over Qaissi shows the difficulties of researching and understanding the incidents of alleged abuse in U.S.-run detention facilities in Iraq while Iraqis and Americans are engaged in armed conflict. Investigating the abuse claims means seeing firsthand how war can distort the perceptions of people on both sides of the conflict.

CHAPTER EIGHTEEN

THE LIST

Iraqi government administrator Dilami is sitting at a table across from attorney Judith Chomsky and me at the Regency Palace Hotel in Amman on this Friday afternoon in March 2006. I ask him about his previous affiliation with the Baath Party, wondering if his political ties had affected how he was treated during his detention and the interrogations (described in chapter eleven). He starts to sketch out a party organization chart on a sheet of paper with a Uniball fine-black pen, and he shows how he and other government employees were promoted to higher positions under Saddam Hussein. As Dilami commits the Baathist organizational chart to paper, Chomsky is tapping impatiently at her keyboard. "It seems you forgot one question," he says, turning to her. "The question was, 'What did you think of the Baath Party?'"

"I didn't forget," Chomsky says.

Dilami looks at her expectantly.

"Do you mind if he answers?" the interpreter asks.

"I do," says Chomsky.

A few minutes later, Chomsky excuses herself from the interview, steps into the hallway and pulls me aside. She explains to me that Baath Party membership is not something she (as an attorney) should discuss with Dilami (client/potential client) with a journalist (that's me) in the room. She has a taut expression on her face, and she leans toward me. "What we're doing is really dangerous," she says. "If he says to you, 'I'm a loyal member of the Baath Party,' they can subpoena you."[1]

She was speaking as an American lawyer. "I was concerned about the appropriateness of you being in the room while I was interviewing a client," she told me later. If I am present during her conversation with Dilami, the attorney-client privilege is compromised. But there were other issues at stake. I wanted to know if he or the other men and women I was meeting in Amman had ties with the insurgency in Iraq, not because it would in any way justify the abuse or mistreatment they had suffered but because it might help me make sense of the events that had led to their arrest or the harsh treatment they said they had received during their detention. Chomsky, Burke, and I had ventured into a complex world: we were dealing with individuals from an occupied country at war with itself, where hatred of America runs deep. Navigating this territory was even more difficult when Chomsky and other attorneys were unwilling to speak with clients about their political backgrounds or allow me to do the same.

One of the biggest problems for prosecutors investigating the abuses at Abu Ghraib has been the reluctance of military police, contractors, officers, and administration officials to support serious inquiries into the crimes. At the same time, some of the former detainees are helpful and forthcoming in presenting their accounts of abuse. Others are less scrupulous about the facts and may be aligned with dangerous individuals. It seemed prudent to find out as much as possible about the former detainees, including their ties with Saddam Hussein, while piecing together the stories.

It was also a troubled time in the Middle East. There had been a measure of success in post-Saddam Iraq in recent weeks. Iraqis voted in their first free election in decades; the parliament met for the first time that month; and Saddam was on trial in Baghdad for war crimes. Nevertheless, the prospects for a vibrant new democracy were not good. Bloodshed, criminality, and ethnic strife plagued the country. Antipathy toward Americans was high. According to Brookings Institute's Iraq Index, 88 percent of Sunni Arabs in Iraq approved of attacks on U.S. troops.[2] Lawyers are not part of the U.S. army, nor are journalists. But the line between civilian and military is not always carefully drawn during war, especially this one.

It had been less than a year since Marla Ruzicka was killed by a suicide bomber in Baghdad and three months since journalist Jill Carroll was seized at gunpoint and held by kidnappers. There were CNN reports on Carroll's whereabouts blaring from a television in the hotel bar along with accounts of the tortured and mutilated body of an American Christian Peacemakers Team activist found in Iraq. Two men implicated in the October 2002 murder of American diplomat Laurence Foley in Amman were to be hanged that week at a desert prison, Swaqa Correctional and Rehabilitation Center, about sixty miles away from the hotel.[3]

THE MISTRESS OF SADDAM HUSSEIN

The decision of Chomsky and the other lawyers not to ask clients about their political views has ideological underpinnings. It is no secret that Dilami, Selwa, and many of the former detainees I interviewed in Amman are supporters of Saddam Hussein. I had served tea to Selwa's daughter Siara and son-in-law, Nabil, in my hotel room and later found out Siara had most likely been Saddam's mistress. I was surprised. When I told attorney Burke the news, though, she seemed unfazed.

"That's really interesting," says Burke, running her fingers through her hair. "Well, at the end of the day, it doesn't have any impact. Regardless of people's past deeds, they shouldn't be tortured."[4]

Assyrian American attorney Khoshaba says she was initially struck by how familiar Selwa seemed. "The way her eyebrows had been plucked very thin and then redrawn—like how my aunt does it," Khoshaba says. "And the color of her hair. Can I tell you how many times my mother has tried to get me to henna my hair like that? There was a push and a pull for me. It was like talking to someone who looks like your aunt. Only she's saying how wonderful Saddam Hussein is. It's very disconcerting. But at the end of the day, our common humanity shone through. First and foremost, our goal is to convince our clients and Iraqis in general that those people— the ones who stomped on their hands and attached electrodes to their bodies—are not us. I hope the Iraqis will see the rule of law does trump everything. Even in a time of war."[5]

Still, as even Burke admits, the information about Siara was unsettling. "It's not helpful," says Burke. "We do want to make sure we don't get schnookered."[6]

THE BLOOD OF A MARTYR

I never got to hear more about Dilami's role in the Baath Party. But I did speak with nine other former detainees, including Alhusain Jassim Ameer, a farmer in Fallujah; Kamil, the seamstress from Baghdad; and Mayah, on that trip. (Their names have been changed for security reasons.) I interviewed Mayah without a lawyer present, and he spoke openly about his views on Iraqi politics and the presence of U.S troops in his country. I had already gotten to know Mayah and his wife over dinner at the hotel. He told me about his experiences at Abu Ghraib (see chapter ten). The following day Daniel Heyman sets up a sketchpad and pencils in Room 705, and an Amman-based interpreter sat on the edge of a bed. The atmosphere is laid-back, casual, even a bit light-hearted. Mayah tells me he is a "modest businessman" who travels to Beirut, Damascus, Tripoli, and Amman and gives talks about the damaging effects of the U.S. military in Iraq. He lets on that he may also be involved in nonbusiness ventures on his trips. He does not say anything explicit about supporting the Iraqi insurgency. But the possibility is there and it puts a damper on my mood, especially when he looks at Heyman and says, "If the picture's not nice, what am I going to do with you?"

Mayah laughs. Heyman and I laugh, too. Nervously. I ask Mayah what he thinks about Saddam.

"Do you want to know how I feel about him as a president of Iraq or as a leader of the people under occupation?" Mayah asks. "When he was the president, he was the idol for the Iraqi people. Everyone liked Saddam Hussein until March 19, 2003."

But he was killing people, I reply.

"I will clarify things," Mayah says. "He challenged the American power and stood up to any nation that was an enemy of Iraq. The Iraqi people would have rather cut off their heads than give up on Saddam Hussein."

I say that many people did lose their heads under him.

"Rather than saying people were killed because of Saddam Hussein, why don't we say it was because of Iran?" Mayah asks, referring to the decade-long war with the neighboring country.

How do you feel about the insurgency? I ask.

"The Iraqi resistance is decent and honest," he says. He tells me there are different ways to support the insurgency, and he had decided not to be part of the armed militia. I make a lame joke. Yes, it's hard to get a job in that line of work, I say. It's very competitive.

He does not look amused.

"One drop of blood of a martyr, or from a wounded man, must be valued," he explains. "This extremely expensive drop of blood cannot be given its true value through words." He slices his hand through the air and puts his fingers on his chest.

It's scary when you talk about the blood of a martyr, I tell him.

"It does not scare me," he says. "As a Muslim, I believe that martyrdom is the ideal stage one can reach because my body is not my own. It is for God."

I guess I don't see things the same way, I tell him.

"So you are hanging on to life," he says.

Desperately, I say quickly.

He laughs. Jabar laughs.

"Me, too," says Heyman. He picks up a hotel promotional brochure from the table and fans himself with it. We all laugh together.

"This is the difference between me and you," Mayah says, looking at me. "If God bought the soul from this humble servant, it must be worth a lot. For me, the true value of the soul is discovered upon entering heaven. Who would not like to go to heaven?"

As I look across the room at him, I am uncomfortably aware of another meaning to his words. He seems to be using the language of martyrdom. It occurs to me, fleetingly, that this is the kind of statement people make while they are discussing a suicide mission. On an impulse, I decide to challenge him.

My heaven is here on earth with my children, I tell him.

The interpreter stares at me. Her eyes widen, and she shifts her weight on the bed. "Honestly, I do not think you should get into it," she says to me, explaining that it is not wise to tell him that I do not believe in heaven or to question his religious views. My sweater becomes damp with sweat, and I have only one thought: God, I want a cigarette.

Moments later, I leave the room, followed by Heyman and the interpreter. I collapse on my bed in nervous laughter, the same uncontrollable laugh I have seen people exhibit when they feel themselves in danger. I make a couple of unfunny beheading jokes, and I consider moving to another floor in the hotel. It seems useless, though. As Khoshaba had told me, as an American, I stick out like a sore thumb in this hotel.

A DEATH IN FALLUJAH

On Friday, April 7, three weeks later, Burke calls me on my cell phone. I am standing in the kitchen at my house in Washington and trying to open a package of soft-shell tacos. Janis Karpinski was coming for dinner.

"One of the detainees was gunned down," Burke tells me on the cell phone.

It was Jassim Ameer, forty-four, the father of five children, ranging in age from four to twelve. He was a farmer in Fallujah, the site of one of the most lethal uprisings against American forces in 2004. He had told me about the time he was held prisoner in a U.S.-run detention facility near his home and watched American guards and soldiers force a father and son to hit each other with their hands.

The son refused, and the Americans made the father dig a shallow grave for his son and bury him in the earth. (The father and son both survived.) Ameer told me how he had tried to protect the father and son, as well as the other prisoners, at the detention camp, but he had not been able to stop the soldiers from hurting the detainees. At the end of our interview, I ask about his name: what does it mean in Arabic?

"It means the line between the good thing and the bad thing," he said.

Which side are you on? I asked.

"The right side, of course," he said and smiled. He had a sense of irony, a useful trait for somebody who had once worked as a police officer under Saddam Hussein and then found himself trying to make a living in the new Iraq. I invited him and his family to visit me in Washington.

"You should come and see us," he said.

Oh, no, I told him. Come to Washington.

"No, thanks," he said, looking straight at me. "You come to Fallujah first."

THE HUG OF DEATH

"Who did you give the list of detainees to?" Burke asks me on the cell phone. Her voice sounds strained. I tell her I gave the names of the former detainees, and their prisoner ID numbers, to the Pentagon so I could verify the dates of their detention. I ask if she thinks somebody had gotten hold of the list of names and was trying to kill the people on it.

"I don't think the DoD's going to assassinate them," she says. "We're wondering if they gave the list to the Iraqis. We're trying to figure out who knew what. We're just completely upset. We're not thinking clearly."

Approximately thirty former detainees in Iraq had planned to meet us in Amman. Two had been killed; one man died before, or perhaps after, he was turned away from the border. "The other was a young person," Burke says. "He was hit by a rocket." Ameer was the third person on the list to die. He and his mother were shot in front of his house in Fallujah. My eyes stung, and my throat felt thick as Burke told me about the killings. Finally, I told her I had to get off the phone, explaining that Karpinski was coming for dinner.

"What do you think of her?" asks Burke. "Is she one of them or one of us?"

I tell her I'm not sure what to say.

"That's right, you're a journalist," she says. "You don't take sides."

After I got off the phone, I wished I had told her I am not against taking sides—in principle. But it's not so simple. Ameer thought he was on the right side. Burke had assured me that his death, and the deaths of the other men, probably had nothing to do with their trip to Amman. I wish I had her confidence.

Karpinski told me about her husband and showed me jpegs of her parrot, Casey, over tacos. I had trouble concentrating on the conversation. I kept thinking about what Human Rights Watch's Kenneth Roth had once said: that reformers in the Middle East speak about America's "hug of death." It is a mistranslation of the phrase "kiss of death." It means, as Roth explained, "the ill effects of Washington's embrace."[7] Many of the Iraqis I had interviewed also made it clear that speaking with me or other Americans put them at risk in Iraq.

Shortly after receiving Burke's call, I visit Jessica Stern, author of *Terror in the Name of God*, at her Cambridge, Massachusetts, apartment, a comfortable home cluttered with books about suicide bombings. I tell her about my interview with Mayah and about the deaths of Ameer and the individuals who had been involved with the lawsuit.

"What you're doing is very dangerous," she says.

But *you* interviewed terrorists, I tell her.

"No, no," she says, shaking her head. "It was nothing like that. I never felt threatened."

I didn't think Mayah was going to slit my throat, I say.

"He has friends," she says. "It's war."

In the months that followed, I thought a lot about the conversations

I had with Ameer, Kamil, Mayah, and the other former detainees. By that time, I was in Washington and no longer worried about possible threats. I wondered, though, who would be next on the list.

On October 10, 2006, I found out.

It was Kamil. "She was kidnapped about a month ago," says Burke on the cell phone. "Her body was found in a morgue. She was badly tortured. We don't know if it had anything to do with her visit to Amman. She was so brave and outspoken—so gutsy in that environment."

I had first spoken with Kamil on the telephone while she was at her home in Baghdad in December 2004. She had been arrested ten months earlier, on February 26, and was taken to Abu Ghraib. She was released on May 24, 2004, and was never formally charged with a crime. I met her in person while I was in Amman in March 2006. She had told me about being shackled and held in a cell and, as I described in chapter ten, how she had tossed pieces of fruit to the hungry children held prisoner at Abu Ghraib.

She shared freely the details of her detention with me. "Not for sympathy, I don't need any sympathy," she said. Instead, she told me, she wanted Americans to know what happened to her and other Iraqis after the fall of Saddam Hussein. When I started writing about her and other former detainees in 2004, I knew about the risks that they faced in their everyday lives in the chaos of Iraq. It would be almost impossible for me to find out what happened to Kamil on the day she was kidnapped or why she was tortured. She is one of the 34,000 Iraqis who were killed in 2006, according to figures compiled by the United Nations, including many without a formal inquiry into the crime, or a pursuit of the people responsible for their deaths, or even an acknowledgment of the tragedy in circles beyond those of friends and family.

PART IV

JUDGMENT

CHAPTER NINETEEN

DISCOVERY PHASE

Kamil was a putatitve plaintiff in *Saleh v. Titan,* the lawsuit that requests financial compensation for the mistreatment and abuse that she and other Iraqi civilians claim they experienced at Abu Ghraib and in other U.S.-run detention facilities. In a section entitled Prayer for Relief, the lawsuit says the following: "Plaintiffs are entitled to any and all remedies available to them as a result of the conduct alleged herein."[1]

For two years, as Kamil recovered from injuries she had received in U.S. custody, the "vexed lawsuit," as Judge Robertson referred to *Saleh v. Titan,* moved among three different parts of the country.[2] (Robertson is a former judge on the Foreign Intelligence Surveillance Court. He resigned from that position five days after the *New York Times* reported in December 2005 the National Security Agency had engaged in warrantless eavesdropping.)[3] The word, "vexed," explained Judge Robertson, "refers to an unfortunate history of relations among counsel for plaintiffs in the related case of *Ibrahim v. Titan Corporation,* Civil Action No. 04-1248, and to this case's odyssey from the Southern District of California, to the Eastern District of

Virginia, to this court, back to the Eastern District of Virginia, and finally back here on January 24, 2006."[4]

Throughout the legal process, the central question remained unaddressed: whether or not Kamil and other Iraqi victims of alleged U.S. torture had the right to seek redress in an American court. Judge Robertson hinted at his views on the subject when he wrote an opinion on August 12, 2005, for the copycat case, *Ibrahim v. Titan*. He stated that the defendants had listed three alternative methods by which plaintiffs might seek remedies for their injuries other than a civil court. These avenues included the Military Claims Act, which provides compensation for claims against the military; the Foreign Claims Act, which also provides compensation, specifically for damages that have occurred in foreign countries, and, as Judge Robertson wrote, "a very general pledge by the Secretary of Defense to compensate detainees mistreated at Abu Ghraib."[5] ("I am seeking a way to provide appropriate compensation to those detainees who suffered grievous and brutal abuse and cruelty at the hands of a few members of the U.S. military," Rumsfeld announced on May 7, 2004. "It is the right thing to do."[6] General Miller, the Guantanamo Bay-based officer who many believe helped introduce the use of harsh interrogation techniques at Abu Ghraib, was put in charge of creating a system for investigating claims and providing compensation for former prisoners in Iraq.[7])

Judge Robertson decided these different avenues—the Military Claims Act, the Foreign Claims Act, and the promise of compensation by the defense secretary—would not necessarily provide a remedy for the former Abu Ghraib prisoners. "The first two on their face are limited to 'noncombat activities,' which would make them inapplicable here if, as defendants argue elsewhere, the activities in question were 'combat activities.' At oral argument, plaintiffs insisted that this court is the only forum in which compensation is available to them. Although the State Department has also stated that relief may be available as defendants describe," he wrote, "the record does not establish that any of these routes is actually viable, and my working assumption is that it is either this court or nothing for plaintiffs."[8]

On June 29, 2006, Judge Robertson dismissed many of the claims against the private military contractors. However, he agreed to let the case go forward in a limited manner, and the case has entered the discovery phase, which means lawyers on both sides are collecting evidence to support their arguments.[9] For Kamil, the prospect of the claims being examined has come too late. The outcome of the case for the surviving plaintiffs and defendants is still months, if not years, away.

CHAPTER TWENTY

THE BRIG

IN MY OPINION, IF SHE'S GOING TO DO IT, SHE SHOULDN'T
HAVE TAKEN PICTURES OF IT.

—A cashier, Dollar General Store,
August 21, 2006, Moorefield, West Virginia[1]

Lynndie England smells like soap. She rubs her hands constantly, and her cuticles are raw and nearly bleeding. Her hair is pulled back in four tortoiseshell clips, and it is streaked with premature gray. She is no longer the waif-like girl with a devilish grin who appeared in the Abu Ghraib photos. On this warm afternoon of August 26, 2006, England, twenty-three, now thirty pounds heavier, wears a short-sleeve army-fatigue uniform with black, waffle-soled boots. Her name is stitched across her chest. Dangling from her waist is a yellow-and-white badge that reads, "PRISONER."

It is England's 332nd day of a thirty-six-month sentence being served in a building surrounded by a thirteen-foot-four-inch fenced topped with concertina wire at the Naval Consolidated Brig Miramar in San Diego. By now, people all over the world have heard of her. She is the "Small-Town Girl Who Became an All-American Monster," as one Australian newspaper described her, or "the lady with a leash," as Mick Jagger calls her in his song "Dangerous Beauty." Yet England has remained a mystery. She was only twenty when many of the Abu Ghraib photos were taken. (Graner, thirty-five, had to buy drinks for her at an officers' club where they used to hang out in Fort Lee, Virginia, before their deployment to Iraq.) She has lived in near-seclusion since the photos appeared on *60 Minutes II*.

MOTHER AND CHILD REUNION

The lawn at the Naval Consolidated Brig Miramar is golf-course thick, and rose bushes are planted alongside the prison's exterior walls. An American flag hanging from an anchor-shaped pole ripples in the breeze.

England's two-year-old son, Carter, and her mother, Terrie, who carries England's metal dog tags in her purse, sit in the prison visitors' waiting room behind thick reinforced glass doors guarded by military officers. A few minutes later, England walks down a narrow hallway toward us. Terrie, who is holding Carter, raises him up high. He is quiet—not wiggling and hollering like he usually does. Mother and son reach their hands toward each other. No tears, no drama. England takes Carter in her arms; he hugs her tight, and England breaks into a smile.

It's mid-afternoon the following day. In a playful mood, England lifts her son in the air. Carter, a husky toddler, rips the prisoner badge from his mother's uniform and hurls it toward the wall. England stares at it, lying on the floor. Her mother and sister stare, too, trying to figure out what to do. Picking up the badge is against the rules. In fact, if England touches anything her family has handled, she will be subjected to a full-body cavity search. As it is, she goes through a strip search after each of our four visits: "If you have your period, and you have a visitor, they make you take your tampon out afterward and squat and cough," she says. "And when the blood comes out on the floor, they say, 'Clean it up.'"

"You think those are mirrors?" England asks me, pointing to a row of reflective glass panes on the side of the room. "Those aren't mirrors. There are people on the other side, watching us the whole time."

Not surprisingly, rules are strict: inmates have to rise at 5:00 AM; they have no choice in what they eat (tonight, macaroni and cheese); and they must perform chores like mowing the lawn, tending vegetable gardens, and folding the American flag. England, however, is not allowed to take the flag down at the end of the day—"because I'm high profile," she explains. "Somebody might be on the golf course [nearby] and see me touching it." And maybe snap a picture. She illustrates, clicking an invisible camera in the air.

Prisoners who break the rules—"push buttons," England calls it—are sent to "DeSeg." (Button-pushing includes engaging in sexual activity with another prisoner.) "In DeSeg, they make you sit by yourself in a windowless room. You can't watch TV or read," she explains. "You have to sit at a desk. You can't sleep from reveille to nighttime."

A sleep plan. It sounds like one of the methods used on prisoners in Abu Ghraib.

"Like a time-out," I add lightly, sensing England's tension.

"You have no idea," she says, giving me a stony look.

REFLECTIONS ON A SCANDAL

Miramar is a Spanish word that means, more or less, "view of the sea." It is the place where the film *Top Gun* was shot—a rugged California landscape with scrub-covered hills, chaparral, and breathtaking vistas. The Miramar Memorial Golf Course is located across the street from the prison building. The prison is unusual not only because of its dramatic backdrop. It is also co-ed. Male inmates pounded across a basketball court during the visit. The other female inmates—roughly forty-five of them—were in their rooms or somewhere else in the brig.

"They all say hi," England tells Terrie.

This afternoon, England has taken the tortoise-shell clips out of her hair. She is wearing her dark-brown hair loose, and it falls around her face. Her hair has gotten long in the brig. As a former tomboy, she doesn't like it. She shakes her head and makes a face.

"Her JAG [military attorney] told her she should let her hair grow out because it will make her look more feminine," Terrie explains. She is sitting at the table with Roy Hardy, her civilian attorney.

It has been two-and-a-half years since the scandal broke. Does England feel differently about what happened at Abu Ghraib? I ask whether she feels guilty or if her opinion about what she did has changed during this time.

"Yeah," she says, nodding her head. "I can't explain why."

She looks down at her hands and is silent. When she speaks, she does so carefully, the way she has been coached. England has confided in Hardy about things she saw or did that never came up in court, and he wants to protect her from any new charges. He told me that he has counseled her to say "I heard," or "There were rumors," or "I was told" when she describes things.

"Some of them were nice," she says, referring to the detainees. "Some of them spoke English. Some of them hated Americans."

Is it true that an American contractor sexually assaulted an Iraqi boy in the prison? I ask her.

"I heard rumors that he did things to boys in the cell," she says.

Were men hung up in the cells with their arms tied behind their back? I ask.

Hardy gives her a stern look. "Remember what I said," he tells her.

"I was told there were hangings of people in the doorways of cells," she says.

She doesn't flinch when she mentions the hangings. It reminds me of her reaction to the mutilated cat and goat corpses in Hilla. In both cases, she seems utterly detached, a slight, awkward smile fluttering across her face.

AWAY FROM THE FLAGPOLE

Terrie and Klinestiver are sitting in a McDonald's off I-68 near LaVale, Maryland. Carter is there, too, chugging chocolate milk, oblivious to the drama his family is caught up in. Graner, England told me back at the prison, "never admitted to being Carter's dad. He's not on the birth certificate," she says. "In order to get that, we'd need a paternity test. That would give him rights, and I don't want him to have any. I don't want him around Carter."

What will she tell him about his father? I wonder.

"I don't know."

Has he asked about him?

"Sometimes."

Inside McDonald's, Carter reaches for a fistful of Chicken McNuggets. "Daddy!" he shouts, as if trying out a new word. Terrie says that's what he's taken to calling her grandfather. Usually the family lets it slide. Nobody wants to tell Carter his father is a prisoner in U.S. Army Disciplinary Barracks in Fort Leavenworth, Kansas, and that he doesn't want to see his son.

England has learned how to repair computer and electronic equipment in the brig. "Now I can fix anything," she says. She has been checking on salaries for electricians in Fort Ashby through a software program that prisoners are allowed to use. "Thirty-five thousand a year," she says. She has also been taking a parenting course. She and the other inmates role-played in the program. One person acts like a parent, and another is the child. A third inmate writes down strategies the "parent" uses.

What is she most looking forward to when she gets out? I ask her.

"Well, I was looking forward to going back and being with Carter," she says. She looks sideways at him and smiles. "Now I'm not so sure," she says, playfully. "I went back to my cell last night and I was like, 'You can throw all that stuff I've been learning in my parenting class out the window.'"

She mentions someone she knows—a prisoner—whose case might be overturned.

"I wish your case would be overturned," says Hardy.

She moves her seat away from the table, and her face darkens. She narrows her eyes.

"That's never going to happen," she says. "I wouldn't want it to."

You wouldn't want a chance to clear your name? I ask.

"They're never going to clear my name," she says. "Everybody knows my name."

"*Change* your name," says Hardy, teasing her gently. "That's the answer."

England doesn't laugh. He leans across the table and looks at her sympathetically. He covers her hands gently with his palms. "Have you read *The Count of Monte Cristo*?" he asks. "It's about this man who escaped from prison, and it has one of my favorite lines in it: 'All human wisdom is contained in these words—wait and hope.' And that applies to you, Lynndie. We try to do everything we can to control our destiny, but all we can do is wait and hope it works out."

She nods her head, but she does not say anything. England is up for parole soon, but chances are, Hardy says, she will serve out her term. She was found guilty of four counts of mistreating detainees, one count of conspiracy, and one count of committing an indecent act. Another soldier, Sergeant Javal S. Davis, was found guilty of battery. Yet he was sentenced to only six months. With the exception of Graner, who was sentenced to ten years, and Frederick, who got eight years, she received one of the harshest punishments of those implicated in the abuse.

England is being punished for what she did. Why she committed the crimes is still not clear—even to her. Now is as good a time as any to mention that some people say England must have been abused as a child. That would help explain her behavior. Terrie and Klinestiver have heard it all before. They tell me she was never mistreated, sexually or physically. But they do banter about sex. In the brig, Terrie makes a joke about the way England's name is emblazoned on the back of her uniform.

"On her ass," Terrie had said. Hardy laughed.

"Show it," Terrie urged, reaching out and pretending to grab her daughter's butt.. "I've been away from it for so long."

It's a joke. England smiles—a little. Certainly Terrie doesn't put a lot of stock in personal boundaries. Still, they are an exceptionally close trio: playfully teasing, quarreling, protecting one another. When they were children, Klinestiver looked out for her little sister, pulling classmates aside in the school cafeteria and telling them to knock it off when they made fun of England's wandering eyes (a medical condition that improved as she got older). These days, Terrie worries about England incessantly; on one afternoon alone Terrie popped three Xanaxes.[2]

Nor does it seem right to call England "overly compliant," as a court psychologist suggested during the trial. He defended her on the basis of "partial mental responsibility."[3] But she stood up to authority figures: her mother, who didn't want her to join the army; her older sister, who disapproved of her affair with Graner; and the chicken-processing plant supervisors when they looked the other way. One thing, though, is certain. England had unexpectedly found herself halfway around the world, in a violent place, and was infatuated with a volatile, manipulative man.

"You have to understand that it builds into a crescendo," says Karpinski. "Lynndie is away from the flagpole, in Abu Ghraib—the most terrible place. You're being mortared every night. You are breathing dust and broken concrete. It's hot. You feel dehumanized. You're drained of every bit of compassion you have. She did it because she wanted to come back from this godforsaken war and say, 'We did this for the government.'[4] And if you apply pressure to the person applying those techniques—in this case, Colonel Pappas, perhaps—and you keep him under pressure, and he is trying to get more, better, faster, sooner, and a clear, critical step in this is finding MPs who will be cooperative," she said. "So you're telling them, 'This is our only ticket out of here,' or 'You talk about this outside of this cell block, and you have compromised national intelligence,' or, 'We know what your record is in your civilian job, and we will take everything from you.'[5] She was made to believe that this was of such importance to national security.

"It was, you know, 'You stick with me, kid, and you might even win a medal.'"[6]

EPILOGUE

DETENTION AND INTERROGATION POLICY ARE AT THE HEART OF
THE PRESIDENT'S COMMANDER-IN-CHIEF POWER TO WAGE
WAR, AND LONG CONSTITUTIONAL HISTORY SUPPORTS THE
PRESIDENT'S LEADING ROLE ON SUCH MATTERS.

—John C. Yoo, "War by Other Means: An Insider's
Account of the War on Terror"[1]

At 9:47 AM on October 17, 2006, President Bush signed into law the
Military Commissions Act, which regulates the treatment of
detainees.[2] The ninety-six-page law is stingy with detail and includes
references to "classified information" that must be withheld from the
public "for reasons of national security."[3] As a result, sections of the
law are shrouded in mystery. Some aspects regarding the treatment of
detainees in the Military Commissions Act, however, have become
transparent in the months that have passed since it became law.

The Military Commissions Act reaffirms the U.S. commitment to
Common Article 3 of the Geneva Conventions. ("Outrages upon
personal dignity, in particular humiliating and degrading treatment,"

according to the Geneva Conventions, are not allowed.) In addition, legal scholars believe that the Military Commissions Act forbids the use of certain types of harsh techniques such as waterboarding, in which suspects are held in water and made to believe they will drown.

Yet the Military Commissions Act encompasses a policy regarding interrogations that many human-rights advocates and legal scholars find problematic. The law grants the president the power to determine how interrogations will be conducted and how detainees will be treated, for example, and whether or not the Geneva Conventions will be honored in certain cases. ("The President has the authority for the United States to interpret the meaning and application of the Geneva Conventions," according to the Act.)

In addition, the Military Commissions Act "in effect," according to Hina Shamsi of Human Rights First, establishes two levels of interrogations for suspects in U.S. custody. CIA field officers may use "enhanced interrogation" techniques. Military interrogators may not.[4] Government officials have declined to specify what kind of aggressive interrogation techniques a CIA field officer can use on suspects in U.S. custody. But human-rights advocates and legal scholars believe the methods include many of those used on Iraqi civilians held at Abu Ghraib and in other U.S.-run detention centers, such as sleep deprivation, stress positions, and the use of military dogs. There may be other methods that are permissible during interrogations that have not been discussed in public. The language of the Military Commissions Act appears to be deliberately vague in part to provide as much leeway, and legal protection, as possible to individuals who have used harsh techniques on suspects in the past or plan on using these methods in the future.

A two-tier system for interrogations, allowing separate rules for CIA officers and military interrogators, has been criticized by human-rights advocates and legal scholars. CIA field officers worked in close proximity to military interrogators at Abu Ghraib. The military interrogators seemed to know what the CIA officers were doing, and vice versa. Many of the interrogation methods were the same. The practical result of the Military Commissions Act may be that the same aggressive methods will end up being used by both CIA officers and military interrogators. In any case, the harsh techniques that were apparently used on civilians in Iraq will continue to play a role during interrogations in the terror war in the future. Now it is the law.

THE LEGAL MEANING OF TORTURE

It is a sultry evening at a bar in Old Town Alexandria, Virginia, in July 2004, and I am asking an army officer questions—okay, interrogating him—about military interrogations. As a high-level officer who was stationed at Guantanamo in 2003 and visited Abu Ghraib frequently in 2004, he knows as much as anyone in the army does about the subject. In his early forties, not too tall, and a little pale, he is a daredevil (and a bit of a showoff) who tells me what it is like to speed through Baghdad in a Hummer and to face down a grizzly bear on an Idaho hunting trip. Still, he is a thoughtful man. He says that a few weeks after he arrived at Guantanamo, he began to have misgivings about the way detainees were being treated at the military installation. He was not specific about what bothered him, but he said he had gone to speak with General Miller about the situation.

"I asked him, 'Are we doing the right thing here?' I was coming to grips with it myself. And he sat down and talked with me about it and assured me that, 'Yes, we're doing the right thing.' It was early on in the global war on terrorism, and we were trying to come to some understanding of the operation."

What did General Miller tell you? I ask.

"It wasn't so much what he said but how he said it. He made tough decisions that he believed were right. Whether or not he regrets it now—" His voice trails off. Then he adds, "You can't diminish the impact of intelligence in the global war on terrorism."

We talk about the role of health professionals such as physicians and psychologists during the interrogation process. Isn't it hard for them to see someone in pain?

"Having observed interrogations, there isn't pain involved," he says. "It's very much a science. You just want to go into it being smarter than the person who's trying to deceive you—if he's trying to deceive you."

Do you really think these techniques are okay to use? I ask.

"[Mohammed al-Qahtani, the "twentieth hijacker," who was held at Guantanamo] obviously has insights," he says. "Are you just going to throw that out the door because he doesn't want to answer questions? As a soldier, I cannot discount that we have tools available to us that may help us prevent future tragedy."

I ask if he knows of examples where the intelligence obtained from harsh interrogations has saved people's lives.

"In real life, there's no quantitative way to state the number of lives saved," he says. "Understanding this loosely affiliated network of terrorists is a game. So were there things that may have been prevented? Yes. I know there were people arrested who were linked back to intelligence obtained from people at Guantanamo."

"As a soldier, I think that the problems that happened at Abu Ghraib—well, it all boils down to leadership. You're trying to lead a chaotic situation and make sense of things. People are making the best decisions based on the information they have. It's part of the whole human equation. You put people in there trying to do the right thing and what's right for the defense of our nation. Hopefully they're falling back on moral values. Do people make mistakes? Yes. There are people who make bad decisions on the spot. There are people involved whose competence I've questioned. But are those mistakes corrected? That's the job of leadership. Is there a place for torture?" he says "No. Is there a place for using the tools available to you? I have yet to hear any alternative, and this is not a situation that's going away. The global war on terrorism is the war of the century."

His professionalism and his ability (after four martinis) to defend the military's harsh interrogation methods were impressive. He believes—and so do I—that the people in charge of detention facilities set the tone for the interrogations and for the handling of detainees and should be held responsible for what takes place on their watch.

Only there is an aspect about the chain of command, and the responsibility for the detention facilities, that he and I did not discuss. In fact, the people in control may not be the military men and women or even officers like General Miller, but individuals at a higher level or located within another organizational chart altogether.

Take John Yoo, for example. He was the man in charge of interpreting the legal parameters for handling detainees in the terror war. He and his White House colleague, Timothy Flanigan, both thought they were doing the right thing. They believed the harsh interrogations provided interrogators with the tools needed to protect the United States from a terrorist attack and that these techniques are necessary for the good of the country. They are not the only ones who defend their position in this manner. In an essay for *Theology Today*, William T. Cavanaugh, a professor at the University of St. Thomas in St. Paul who has studied the Pinochet government, said, "Those who torture tend to think of their work in extremely high moral terms."[5]

"Would limiting a captured terrorist to six hours' sleep, isolating him, interrogating him for several hours, or requiring him to exercise constitute 'severe physical or mental pain and suffering'?" wrote Yoo. "The legal meaning of 'torture' is not as all-inclusive as some people would like it to be. Legally, we are not required to treat captured terrorists engaged in war against us as if they were suspects held at an American police station. Limiting our intelligence and military officials to polite questioning, and demanding that terrorists receive lawyers, Miranda warnings, and a court trial would only hurt our ability to stop future attacks."[6]

Not everybody agrees that methods such as sleep deprivation and forced exercise should be incorporated into interrogations. "These tactics should be considered for what they are from a moral, legal, and medical perspective: torture," said Allen S. Keller, director of Bellevue Hospital's Program for Survivors of Torture in New York.[7]

Yoo and Flanigan, however, have both argued that these techniques should be used as part of the administration's new counterterrorism strategy. The two lawyers have employed different approaches, and personal styles, to defend their positions. Yoo can sound strident, or at least free of doubt, when he states his case. Flanigan is not like that. When I told him that Iraqi women and children were subjected to the harsh methods, including the use of military dogs and sleep deprivation, his tone softened. He spent a long time with me on the telephone, explaining how these techniques were intended only for high-level members of al Qaeda and the Taliban. He, too, regretted that they were used on Iraqi civilians.

Iraqi civilians were protected by the Geneva Conventions and should not have been subjected to the harsh interrogation techniques that were approved for al Qaeda and Taliban members. Yet these methods were used on Iraqis. "These procedures were designed for use on detainees picked up in the Afghan theater and yet they were applied, as the [Taguba and Fay-Jones] Reports included in this volume demonstrate, to alleged terrorists and to prisoners in Iraq," wrote Karen Greenberg in *The Torture Papers*. "The justification for this is hard to find."[8]

How could this happen? That is what I wondered in 2004 when I began to study Yoo's memos, the list of approved interrogation techniques and government documents, as well as to interview people about the subject. It seemed as though the Abu Ghraib scandal could have been so easily avoided. Things at the prison went slightly off course in August and September 2003 and then, by mid-October, turned into a full-blown disaster. If only the military police at Abu Ghraib had followed the law (they weren't supposed to use harsh techniques on Iraqis, as Flanigan said), I would think, the abuse might not have occurred. If only Colonel Pappas had made clear the rules regarding the treatment of detainees, and set a tone for high ethical standards at the prison, the scandal might not have happened. If only General Karpinski had spent more time at Abu Ghraib, the situation might not have spun out of control.

Two years later, my question was different: how could this *not* have happened? The justification for the abuse is embedded in Yoo's writings. He has long had a keen interest in the expansion of presidential powers, and in a September 25, 2001, memorandum to

Flanigan, Yoo explained that the president has broad authority to take military action: "The President may deploy military force preemptively against terrorist organizations or the States that harbor or support them, whether or not they can be linked to the specific incidents of September 11."

"The conflict is with terrorists," Yoo wrote.[9]

Yoo was describing a new paradigm in which harsh interrogation techniques may be used on individuals who seem to pose a threat to United States citizens. Initially, there was no description of the type of terrorist organization—whether it was part of the al Qaeda network or the Taliban—that would receive this kind of treatment. It did not seem to matter. Yoo's goal was to protect the United States from future attack and to pave the way for a broader reach of the executive branch. The president's ability to act without undue restraint was paramount. Defining the types of terrorist organization or terrorism suspect who may be affected by the president's actions was not the point.

Only later did administration officials agree that the techniques would be limited to the interrogations of Taliban and al Qaeda suspects. U.S. officials decided that since these individuals were fighting for shadowy forces or terrorist organizations, and not on behalf of a nation that adheres to international law, they were not protected by the Geneva Conventions. On January 9, 2002, Yoo coauthored a memo regarding "Application of Treaties and Laws to al Qaeda and Taliban Detainees" for William J. Haynes II, a general counsel for the Defense Department. "You have asked whether the laws of armed conflict apply to the conditions of detention and the procedures for trial of members of al Qaeda and the Taliban militia," Yoo wrote. "We conclude that these treaties do not protect members of the al Qaeda organization, which as a non-State actor cannot be a party to the international agreements governing war: we further conclude that these treaties do not apply to the Taliban militia."[10]

By March 2003, the month that American forces entered Iraq, U.S. officials had settled on a policy for the handling of detainees in prisons and jails that would soon be operating in that country. There were, arguably, more important aspects of the invasion and occupation of Iraq. Yet they received only scant attention. "We went into Iraq with no postwar plan. But we did have a detention policy," says Greenberg. "Dude, what about the police? What about the traffic lights?"[11]

Administration officials have blamed rogue soldiers in Abu Ghraib's Tier 1A for using harsh methods on Iraqi detainees and for subjecting them to humiliating treatment. Yet harsh interrogation methods such as stress positions were taught in classrooms at Abu Ghraib. There were guidelines for the implementation of "limited stress—by forcing detainees to assume uncomfortable physical positions, or limiting their sleeping patterns or food," which are the methods Yoo described in his book.[12] These methods were not officially intended for Iraqi prisoners, according to Yoo and other administration officials. Still, they were adopted at Abu Ghraib and in other U.S.-run detention facilities in Iraq during a time when things were going badly in the war. There was intense pressure to obtain information about the insurgency and about the Iraqi forces that opposed the U.S. troops. That may have led in part to the decision to use the harsh methods on Iraqi prisoners.

Army supervisor Steven L. Jordan testified that the interrogation reports from Abu Ghraib were being scrutinized. "I was told a couple of times by Colonel Pappas that some of the reporting was getting read by Rumsfeld," Jordan explained.[13]

One sergeant who was stationed at another facility, Camp Nama, said he recalls watching a PowerPoint presentation on the methods that could be used on detainees. "They were saying things like we didn't have to abide by the Geneva Conventions because these people weren't POWs," he said. "People wanted to go harsh on everybody. They thought that was their job and that's what they needed to do."[14]

"Graner says every time a bomb goes off outside the wire, which is outside the walls of Abu Ghraib, one of the OGA members would come in to say, 'That's another American losing his life,'" one soldier, Ken Davis, told journalist Trish Wood. "'Unless you help us get this information, their blood is on your hands as well.'"[15]

Administration officials claimed, improbably, that the officers or civilian contractors who devised Abu Ghraib interrogation plans (modeled on the Guantanamo Tiger Team approach) were not responsible for the abuse of Iraqi prisoners; nor was Sanchez, the highest-ranking officer in Iraq, though he had approved of the methods. Nor was Defense Secretary Rumsfeld, despite the fact he had encouraged the use of the techniques. Yet conditions for the abuse of prisoners were set early in the terror war by Yoo and other individuals at the White House and in the Justice Department.

The implementation was left to people like Graner, Frederick, and "the muscle," as Provance calls his Robotripping friends. The vast majority of prisoners at Abu Ghraib had no information about the insurgency or about possible future acts of terrorism. Yet American interrogators, guards and contractors applied harsh techniques and then used some of their own methods that did not appear on the approved list. The explanation for this decision is still in dispute. Some things are certain, though. The detainees were hooded and naked. They did not speak English. They had nicknames like "Clawman," "Spiderman," and "Gilligan." It became that much easier to treat them inhumanely.

In addition, high-level administration officials expressed ambivalence over the Geneva Conventions that protected the prisoners at Abu Ghraib—even after the scandal broke. On May 4, 2004, one week after the Abu Ghraib photographs appeared on television, Defense Secretary Rumsfeld told a journalist that the Geneva Conventions "did not apply precisely" in Iraq. Instead, they were "basic rules" for handling prisoners. On May 14, Rumsfeld visited soldiers at Abu Ghraib and said, "Geneva doesn't say what you do when you get up in the morning."[16]

Some military police, contractors, and interrogators refused to implement the harsh interrogation techniques discussed by Rumsfeld, Yoo, and administration officials, however. In the often-cited 1961 Milgram experiment on obedience to authority, 65 percent of subjects follow orders to engage in abusive behavior. (They think they are giving a 450-voltage electrical shock to another person, though in reality there is no electricity transmitted.)[17] The results of the Milgram experiment—distorted through the prism of CNN's *360 Degrees*-style analysis and rapid-fire public debate—can make it seem as though there is a sadist hiding inside all of us.[18] Less discussed, and rarely studied, is the 35 percent of the subjects who refused to harm other human beings. Not everybody is a torturer.

Yet, just as in the Milgram experiment, many of the American women and men at Abu Ghraib showed no such restraint. They brutalized their captives, with impunity in some cases. And were praised for their actions: "'Good job, they're breaking down real fast. They answer every question. They're giving out good information,'" were some of the comments that soldiers heard from officers.[19]

TICK, TOCK

Looking back at Abu Ghraib, it is important to ask what we have learned from the experience. One thing is clear: The scandal has forced Americans to engage in a debate that would have been unthinkable prior to the terrorist attacks—whether or not torture is a viable option. Many people believe there is a compelling argument for its use. Military leaders and government officials should allow, or even encourage, interrogators to torture a suspect under certain circumstances. That's the ticking-bomb theory, a notion familiar to anyone who has watched *24*. The water-boarding of accused al Qaeda suspect Khalid Shaikh Mohammed is used as an example by journalists, members of the military, and scholars who believe torture is—however abhorrent—a method of last resort. If things get out of hand, and an interrogator accidentally kills a suspect, the courts can sort it out.

Human-rights lawyers, physicians, and scholars often claim that torture does not produce the intended results. "I know from years of listening to torture survivors describing their experiences that individuals so brutalized will often say whatever they think the torturer wants to hear in order to stop the nightmare," wrote physician Keller.[20]

The truth is that torture, as well as beatings, assaults, and random arrests, can be effective. Saddam Hussein was tracked down by unraveling a "social network" of friends, relatives, and acquaintances, says John E. Pike, director of Globalsecurity.org, an Alexandria, Virginia–based defense information organization. "Everybody says, 'Well, torture doesn't work,'" he tells me. "It may not work on an individual, but if you put enough people to the question, it can provide information. The people being tortured might not have known where Saddam was, but they would know somebody who might know."

Could other methods have been used? I ask.

"They could have said, 'Pretty please,'" Pike says with a laugh.[21]

The army officer I interviewed says he believes that Americans should use every tool available to us in the terror war and that harsh techniques can be justified under certain circumstances. When criminal acts, going beyond the boundaries of permissible interrogation methods, occur, he says, they should be blamed on poor military leadership. I am not convinced.

Like Yoo and Flanigan, I was in Washington on the day of the terrorist attacks. I left my office building in Rosslyn, Virginia, and ran across Key Bridge to make sure my children were safe, and I looked back and saw the Pentagon in flames. Protecting our country from another attack is important to me, too. But I do not believe that abusive interrogation techniques are an effective tool in the war on terror. It may be possible someday to graph out the results of harsh interrogation methods and discover they are effective in eliciting information from some suspects (despite what human-rights advocates claim). But do we want to live in a society that condones, either explicitly or implicitly, torture? According to the U.S. State Department's 2005 Country Reports on Human Rights Practices, sexual assault, administration of electrical shock, and beatings are used on suspects in Saudi Arabia, Pakistan, Syria, and other countries.[22] We have condemned these nations for their violations of human rights. The United States may have joined their league.

Starting in January 2004, the military initiated a series of inquiries into the abuse at Abu Ghraib and other detention facilities. The reports, which include testimony from hundreds of military personnel and run into the thousands of pages, were prompted by public outcry and congressional inquiries into the mistreatment of detainees. And yet these massive reports have been inadequate, flawed, and, in many cases, overly protective of the military personnel they purport to investigate. None of the investigations have looked at individuals high in the chain of command, despite the fact the Schlesinger Report stated, "There is both institutional and personal responsibility at higher levels."[23] Nor has there been a serious attempt to peel away the layers of secrecy surrounding the CIA at the detention facilities. An independent inquiry into the abuse of prisoners in Iraq, and an examination of the justification for their mistreatment, is overdue. One issue that needs to be addressed is the use of harsh interrogation methods and whether or not they are legitimate in the terror war. A reevaulation of the Military Commissions Act, as well as of the criminal liability of private contractors, is necessary. In examining and debating the question of interrogation methods openly and through a public debate, we will be deciding what kind of country we will become.

There is also the matter of justice. England is currently serving time for her crimes. So is Graner. Many others who were accused of wrongdoing in Iraq have never been put on trial or questioned in a formal manner about their actions. An independent investigation will help establish the necessity of holding individuals accountable for the crimes that occurred—whether those individuals are working for the army, the CIA, a private military contractor, or at the highest level of government.

FURTHER READING

For more information about these issues and to help victims of war and conflict, contact the following organizations:

American Civil Liberties Union (125 Broad Street, 18th Floor, New York, NY 10004) has a Torture Document Search (http://www. aclu.org/torturefoia/search/search.html) that allows researchers to find details about the incidents, decisions, policies, agencies, and leaders behind the treatment of detainees in U.S. custody. The documents available were obtained though the efforts of the ACLU, the Center for Constitutional Rights, Physicians for Human Rights, Veterans for Common Sense, and Veterans for Peace.

Campaign for Innocent Victims in Conflict (CIVIC, 1630 Connecticut Ave NW, Suite #500, Washington, D.C., 20009. info@civicworldwide.org). CIVIC is a Washington-based nonprofit organization founded by Marla Ruzicka. "Our focus is on the human cost of conflict. We advocate on behalf of war victims and their families, working to ensure they receive the attention they deserve in the policies of nations in war and in the public eye," according to their Web site.

Center for Victims of Torture (717 E. River Road, Minneapolis, MN 55455; 612-436-4800; cvt@cvt.org). This private, nonprofit, nonpartisan organization was founded in 1985. "Over half the countries in the world continue to use torture as a strategic tool of repression," their Web site states. "It is our mission not only to heal the wounds of torture, but also to stop its practice worldwide."

ACKNOWLEDGMENTS

I would like to thank my editor, Philip Turner; his successor, Bill Strachan; and Carroll & Graf's vice president and publisher, Will Balliett, for their support and enthusiasm for this project. Many thanks, too, to Adelaide Docx, attorney Alan Kaufman, and to William Morris agent Eric Lupfer. I would also like to thank Karen J. Greenberg, executive director of NYU School of Law's Center on Law and Security, for providing a research fellowship that helped me write the book.

I would like to acknowledge several people affiliated with *The American Prospect*: Bob Kuttner, founding editor; Diane Straus Tucker, publisher; Harold Meyerson, acting executive editor; Michael Tomasky, editor-at-large; and deputy editor Sarah Blustain. I wrote my first article about Abu Ghraib, as well as others about private contractors and interrogation, for the *American Prospect*. *Marie Claire* editor-in-chief Joanna Coles allowed me to pursue investigative work on this subject when she assigned my article, "A Soldier's Tale," and executive editor Lucy Kaylin, deputy editor Julia Savacool, editorial assistant Laurie Campbell, and research editor Chris Moore helped me tremendously. I would also like to thank Joe Conason of The Nation Institute and Betsy Reed, senior editor at *The Nation*, as well as Lincoln Caplan and Nick Thompson, formerly of *Legal Affairs*, for commissioning pieces on related subjects. Sincere thanks to Danny Goldberg and Robert Greenwald for providing assistance for my 2004 trip to Amman, Jordan, and to Errol Morris for sharing with me astute and often funny observations about the subject while he was working on his film about Abu Ghraib. And I am indebted to several journalists for their important articles: Anthony Lewis formerly of the *New York Times*; Canadian journalist Trish Wood; Mark Danner of *The New York Review of Books*; Ray Bonner of the *New York Times*; Seymour M. Hersh and Jane Mayer of the *New Yorker*, and Dana Priest of the *Washington Post*. Allen S. Keller, director of Bellevue/NYU program for Survivors of Torture, has also made a significant contribution to the discussion of detainee treatment in his article, "Torture in Abu Ghraib," for *Perspectives in Biology and Medicine*.

The following individuals were kind enough to read portions of the manuscript and to provide suggestions: Joel Achenbach, Christina Asquith, Nancy Astifo, Ada Calhoun, Jeff Dubner, Karen Greenberg, Jeff Grossman, Aziz Huq, Riva Khoshaba, Christian Lucky, Jonathan Marks, Asra Nomani, Ron Rosenbaum, LaNitra Walker, Judy Warner, and Donovan Webster. Thanks, too, to Peter Schjeldahl and Brooke Alderson for their kindness and generosity; Ren Weschler for reading the book proposal and for his invaluable advice; Karen Greenberg for her editorial suggestions and, best of all, her friendship; Jonathan Marks for sharing notes and sources; Jim Bamford for providing insights on intelligence agencies; Chris Bartlett and Daniel Heyman for their portraits of individuals who appear in my book. Any errors, of course, are mine.

I would like to acknowledge an anonymous Pentagon source who provided background material and gave me the following guidelines for describing him: "whatever sounds sexy in your story and gives me deniability."

Thanks also to Astrid Benedek, Peter Bergen, Matthew Berger,

Max Berley, Doug Brinkley, John Berger, David Corn, Jeremy Edmiston, Caroline Eisner, Alesia Eutsler, Phil Fairclough, Jack Fairweather, Bill Falk, James Fallows, Bill Finnegan, David Friend, Lisa Grubka, Stephen Holmes, Ken Hurwitz, Denise Kersten, Ellen Kampinsky, Robert Kostrzewa, Welmoed Laanstra, Tasha Lance, Belinda Luscombe, Michael Massing, Neal Medlyn, Carol Memmott, Vanessa Mobley, David Rieff, Tim Rieser, Emma Rigney, Rita Rodriguez, Ken Rogoff, Mark Rosenthal, Josh Siegel, Chris Spolar, Jessica Stern, Margaret Townsend, Alan Wade, Brooke Warner, and Eric Wills. Special thanks to interpreters Dana Jabar, Ranya Khadri, and Nancy Astifo (and family members Kamil, Hanna, and Hala) and to ace researcher Amy Marie Shepard.

I owe everything, of course, to my mother, Lee Purcell, and my father, John McKelvey, and a whole lot to my brothers, Kerry and Sean. I would also like to acknowledge my late grandparents—Jean Echols, who was my dearest friend in the world, and Lieutenant Colonel Arch C. Echols. With love and affection, I want to thank Ada Calhoun and Judy Warner and especially Ron Rosenbaum, a brilliant writer, reader, editor, and a true friend. I would like to show appreciation most of all to Lidia Jean, Julia, and Xander. They are equally loving, affectionate, funny, and amazing, and, quite simply, the joy of my life.

Bibliography

BOOKS

Abrahamson, Jennifer. *Sweet Relief: The Marla Ruzicka Story*. New York: Simon & Schuster, 2006.

Bamford, James. *A Pretext for War: 9/11, Iraq, and the Abuse of American's Intelligence Agencies*. New York: Knopf, 2005.

Bergen, Peter L. *The Osama bin Laden I Know: An Oral History of al Qaeda's Leader*. New York: The Free Press, 2006.

Burden, Matthew Currier. *The Blog of War: Front-Line Dispatches from Soldiers in Iraq and Afghanistan*. New York: Simon & Schuster, 2006.

Conroy, John. *Unspeakable Acts, Ordinary People: The Dynamics of Torture*. Berkeley: University of California Press, 2000.

Danner, Mark. *Torture and Truth: America, Abu Ghraib, and the War on Terror*. New York: New York Review of Books, 2004.

Ehrenreich, Barbara. *Blood Rites: Origins and History of the Passions of War*. New York: Owl Books, 1998.

Friend, David. *Watching the World Change: The Stories Behind the Images of 9/11*. New York: Farrar, Straus and Giroux, 2006.

Gilfoyle, Timothy J. *A Pickpocket's Tale: The Underworld of Nineteenth-Century New York*. New York: W.W. Norton, 2006.

Greenberg, Karen J., ed. *Torture Debate in America*. New York: Cambridge University Press, 2005.

Greenberg, Karen J., and Joshua L. Draytel, eds. *The Torture Papers: The Road to Abu Ghraib*. New York: Cambridge University Press, 2005.

Harr, Jonathan. *A Civil Action*. New York: Vintage Books, 1995.

Hersh, Seymour M. *Chain of Command: The Road from 9/11 to Abu Ghraib*. New York: HarperCollins, 2004.

Hillman, Elizabeth L. *Defending America: Military Culture and the Cold War Court-Martial*. Princeton, NJ: Princeton University Press, 2005.

Karpinski, Janis. *One Woman's Army: The Commanding General of Abu Ghraib Tells Her Story*. With Steven Strasser. New York: Hyperion, 2005.

Levinson, Sanford, ed. *Torture: A Collection*. New York: Oxford University Press, 2004.

Lewis, Anthony. *Gideon's Trumpet*. New York: Vintage Books, 1964.

Mackey, Chris, and Greg Miller. *The Interrogators: Task Force 500 and America's Secret War Against Al Qaeda*. New York: Back Bay Books, 2004.

Margulies, Joseph. *Guantanamo and the Abuse of Presidential Power*. New York: Simon & Schuster, 2006.

McKelvey, Tara, ed. *One of the Guys: Women as Aggressors and Torturers*. Foreword by Barbara Ehrenreich. Emeryville, CA: Seal Press, 2007.

Miles, Steven H. *Oath Betrayed: Military Medicine and the War on Terror*. New York: Random House, 2006.

Rieff, David. *At the Point of a Gun: Democratic Dreams and Armed Intervention*. New York: Simon & Schuster, 2006.

Rosenbaum, Ron. *Explaining Hitler: The Search for the Origins of Evil*. New York: Harper Perennial, 1999.

Santos, Michael G. *Inside: Life Behind Bars in America*. New York: St. Martin's Press, 2006.

Singer, P.W. *Corporate Warriors: The Rise of the Privatized Military Industry*. Ithaca, NY: Cornell University Press, 2003.

Solis, Gary D. *Son Thang: An American War Crime*. Annapolis, Md: Naval Institute Press, 1997.

Stern, Jessica. *Terror in the Name of God: Why Religious Militants Kill*. New York: HarperCollins, 2004.

Webster, Donovan. *Aftermath: The Remnants of War*. New York: Random House, 1998.

Weschler, Lawrence. *A Miracle, A Universe: Settling Accounts With Torturers*. University of Chicago Press, 1990.

Wilson, Richard A., ed. *Human Rights in the "War on Terror."* New York: Cambridge University Press, 2005.

Wood, Trish. *What Was Asked of Us: An Oral History of the Iraq War by the Soldiers Who Fought It.* Introduction by Bobby Muller. New York: Little, Brown, 2006.

Yoo, John. *War by Other Means: An Insider's Account of the War on Terror.* New York: Atlantic Monthly Press, 2006.

REPORTS

Jones, Anthony R., Pages 6–33. George R. Fay, pages 34–176. "AR 15-6 Investigation of the Abu Ghraib Detention Facility and 205th Military Intelligence Brigade." July 2004.

Taguba, Antonio. "Article 15-6 Investigation of the 800th Military Police Brigade," March 2004.

U.S. State Department. "2005 Country Reports on Human Rights Practices." Released March 8, 2006, Washington, D.C., http://www.state.gov/g/drl/rls/hrrpt/2005/index.htm.

Notes

PREFACE

1. Wayne Marotto, public affairs staff officer, Department of the Army, Pentagon, Washington, D.C., e-mail interview by author, June 2, 2006.
2. Eric Schmitt, "Iraq Abuse Trial Is Again Limited to Lower Ranks," *New York Times*, March 23, 2006, p. 1.
3. Pew Research Center, *16-Nation Pew Global Attitudes Survey,* Pew Global Attitudes Project, Washington, D.C., June 23, 2005.

CHAPTER ONE

1. *Oxford Universal Dictionary*, third edition, 1955, s.v. "Monster."
2. Chris Mackey and Greg Miller, *The Interrogators: Task Force 500 and America's Secret War Against Al Qaeda* (New York: Back Bay Books, 2004), 289.
3. Samuel Jefferson Provance III, "Seasons of the Abyss" (Unpublished manuscript, 2006).
4. Abu Ghraib prison compound, Abu Ghraib, Iraq, 2003 or 2004. Personal photograph from S. J. Provance.
5. Provance, prepared statement, "Protecting National Security Whistleblowers in the Post-9/11 Era," to the Subcommittee on National Security, Emerging Threats and International Relations, House Committee on Government Reform, Washington, D.C., February 14, 2006.

6. Ibid.

7. Ibid.

8. Scott Horton, in discussion with the author, New York. November 29, 2006.

9. Verbatim Record of Trial, Staff Sergeant Ivan L Frederick II, HHC, 16th MP Bde (ABN) III Corps, U.S. Army, Victory Base, Iraq, by General Court-Martial Convened by Commanding General, Headquarters, III Corps, Tried at Baghdad and Victory Base, Iraq, on 19 May, 21–22 June, 24 August, 20–21 October 2004, page 121. In addition, information was provided on this subject in an article titled "Prisoner of Conscience" by Joe Darby (as told to Wil S. Hylton), *GQ* (September 2006).

10. Joseph M. Darby, acceptance speech, 2005 Profile in Courage Award, John F. Kennedy Library Foundation, Boston, MA, May 16, 2005.

11. Schmitt, "Soldier Reports More Abuses to Senator," *New York Times*, October 5, 2005, p. 8.

12. Alessandra Stanley, "The Slow Rise of Abuse That Shocked the Nation," *New York Times*, October 18, 2005, p. 5.

13. Michael E. O'Hanlon and Nina Kamp, *Iraq Index: Tracking Variables of Reconstruction & Security in Post-Saddam Iraq* (Washington: Brookings Institution, October 30, 2006).

14. "Top Issues," "Small Arms Fire," SECRET/SITREP [Situation Report], 800th MP BDE/ DTG 0117003SEP03, UNIT: 800th MP BDE. Provided by a military source who asked to remain anonymous, September 1, 2003.

15. "Top Issues," "Mortar Fire." SECRET/SITREP, 800th MP BDE/ DTG 0217003SEP03, UNIT: 800th MP BDE. Provided by a military source who asked to remain anonymous, September 2, 2003.

16. Major David W. DiNenna Sr., 320th MP BN, e-mail to [name redacted] MAJ CTTF7-320 MP BN S3, November 9, 2003, "Article 15-6 Investigation of the 800th Military Police Brigade," by Major General Antonio Taguba, March 2004.

17. [Name Redacted], sworn statement, Military Police Battalion. The document was signed by a military notary, USMJ Article 136, Camp Arifjan, Kuwait, May 2, 2004. Obtained from American Civil Liberties Union's Government Documents on Torture Search: http://www.aclu.org/torturefoia/search/search.html. Jennifer Fernandez, "A&T Loses Another in Iraq; Former Political Science Major Lunsford Brown II Was Killed Saturday in a Mortar Attack," *News & Record*, Greensboro, NC, September 25, 2003, p. B1. Sherrie Wheeler Brown, telephone interview.

18. Abu Ghraib prison compound, Abu Ghraib, Iraq, 2003 or 2004. Photographs provided by S. J. Provance.

19. DiNenna, 320th MP BN, e-mail to [name redacted] MAJ CTTF7-320 MP BN S3, October 27 through November 10, 2003, "Article 15-6 Investigation of the 800th Military Police Brigade."

20. Brigadier General Janis L. Karpinski, sworn statement, in Lieutenant General Anthony R. Jones, pages 6–33 and Major General George R. Fay, pages 34–176, "AR 15-6 Investigation of the Abu Ghraib Detention Facility and 205th Military Intelligence Brigade," July 18, 2004.

21. Hydrue S. Joyner, in discussion with the author, Washington. July 12, 2006. He made a similar comment at an August 2004 military hearing in Fort Bragg, NC, that was convened to determine whether or not England would face a court-martial.

22. Carl Levin, United States Senator, "U.S. Military Commitments and Ongoing Military Operations Abroad," Hearing of the Senate Armed Forces Committee chaired by Senator John Warner, Federal News Service, Washington, D.C., September 9, 2003.

23. Major General Geoffrey Miller, CJTF-7 deputy commanding general for detainee operations, "Alleged Detainee Abuse within Iraqi Prisons," Defense Department / Coalition Provisional Authority briefing, Federal News Service, Baghdad, Iraq, May 8, 2004.

24. Miller, "Assessment of DoD Counterterrorism Interrogation and Detention Operations in Iraq," September 9, 2003, Annex, "Article 15-6 Investigation of the 800th Military Police Brigade," Major General Antonio Taguba, March 2004. Karen J. Greenberg and Joshua L. Draytel, Joshua L., eds., *The Torture Papers: The Road to Abu Ghraib* (New York: Cambridge University Press, 2005), 451-456.

25. Leonard Acho, in discussion with the author, Sterling Heights, MI, February 4, 2006.

26. Major General Antonio Taguba, "Article 15-6 Investigation of the 800th Military Police Brigade."

27. "Joe Ryan," Source Watch, Center for Media and Democracy (Madison, WI. February 3, 2006), http://www.sourcewatch.org/index.php?title= Joe_Ryan.

28. Ryan, online diary, provided by Provance, Heidelberg, Germany, July 26, 2006.

29. Acho, February 4, 2006; Abdullah Khalil, in discussion with the author, Vienna, VA, July 2, 2006; Marwan Mawiri, in discussion with the author, Birmingham, MI, February 4, 2006.

30. Summons in a Civil Case, United States District Court, District of Columbia, 2006.

31. Abu Ghraib prison compound, Abu Ghraib, Iraq, 2003 or 2004. Photograph provided by Provance.

32. "JIDC Organization," 23 January 2004, Joint Interrogation & Debriefing Center, Abu Ghurayb, Iraq, PowerPoint presentation. Document provided by Jonathan H. Marks, bioethicist and coauthor, "When Doctors Go to War," *The New England Journal of Medicine* (January 2005).

33. [Name Redacted] of the 519th Military Intelligence Battalion in a sworn statement on May 19, 2004, DOD 00867-71; [Name Redacted] of the 470th Military Intelligence Group in a sworn statement made on May 18, 2004, DOD 000859-63l; [Name Redacted] of the 304th Military Intelligence Battalion in a sworn statement, May 21, 2004, DOD 000598-605; [Name Redacted] of Human Resources Command in a sworn statement on May 24, 2004, DOD 000591-97; International Committee of the Red Cross, October 2003.

34. Provance, "Protecting National Security Whistle-blowers in the Post-9/11 Era."

35. Provance, Heidelberg, Germany, telephone discussion with the author, July 7, 2006.

36. Provance, sworn testimony, January 21, 2004, Baghdad, "Article 15-6 Investigation of the 800th Military Police Brigade."

37. Provance, "Protecting National Security Whistleblowers in the Post-9/11 Era."

38. Provance, in discussion with the author, Carmichaels, PA, November 25, 2006.

39. Frederick, general court-martial.

40. Abu Ghraib prison compound, Abu Ghraib, Iraq, 2003 or 2004. Photograph provided by Provance.

41. Major General Antonio Taguba, sworn testimony, "Article 15-6 Investigation of the 800th Military Police Brigade."

42. Provance, in discussion with the author, Carmichaels, PA, November 25, 2006. He pointed out the location of the building on a GlobalSecurity.org map, http://www.globalsecurity.org/intell/world/iraq/images/040825-d-6570c-007.jpg.

43. Ivan Lowell Frederick II, sworn statement, Camp Arifjan, Kuwait, November 3, 2004, File Number 0003-04-CID149-83130. I was allowed to read an unredacted copy of the document on August 29, 2006, in the

law office of an individual who has provided assistance to Lynndie R. England.

44. Frederick, sworn statement, Camp Arifjan, Kuwait, November 3, 2004.

45. Steven L. Jordan, sworn statement, Camp Doha, Kuwait, February 24, 2004, "Article 15-6 Investigation of the 800th Military Police Brigade," p. 155.

46. Frederick, sworn statement.

47. The Associated Press, July 20, 2002.

CHAPTER TWO

1. "Nomination of Timothy E. Flanigan to Be an Assistant Attorney General," *Public Papers of the Presidents*, Pres. Doc. 623, April 9, 1992.

2. Carl M. Cannon, James A. Barnes, Alexis Simendinger, Bruce Stokes, David Baumann, Marilyn Werber Serafini, and Jason Ellenburg, "The White House Profiles," *The National Journal* (June 23, 2001).

3. Dana Milbank, *Washington Post*, "White House Counsel Office Now Full of Clinton Legal Foes," January 30, 2001.

4. Elisabeth Bumiller, "White House Letter: The Office Where Law Meets War," *New York Times*, September 23, 2002, p. 22.

5. "Federalist Society to Hold Annual Conference in D.C., Nov. 15-17," PR Newswire, November 13, 2001.

6. John Yoo, *War by Other Means: An Insider's Account of the War on Terror* (New York: Atlantic Monthly Press, 2006), 19.

7. In January 2006, the ACLU filed a lawsuit in U.S. District Court for the Eastern District of Michigan that challenged the legality of the National Security Agency's wiretapping program. The ACLU objected to the fact that the intelligence service intercepts telephone calls in the United States without obtaining a warrant when one of the parties is suspected of being a member of al Qaeda or an affiliated group. I have conducted telephone interviews with former detainees in Iraq who were imprisoned because of their suspected ties with terrorist groups as part of research for this book, and Exhibit K in the lawsuit includes a description of my work.

8. Yoo, *War by Other Means*, viii.

9. Dratel, Greenberg, *The Torture Papers* (New York: Cambridge University Press, 2005).

10. Yoo, *War by Other Means*, ix.

11. Ibid., 170.

12. Memo 5, Secretary of Defense, 1000 Defense Pentagon, January 19, 2002, Memorandum for Chairman of the Joint Chiefs of Staff, Subject: "Status

of Taliban and Al Qaeda," declassified on 4 February 2002, *The Torture Papers*, 80.

13. Memo 8, United States Department of State, Memorandum, To: Counsel for the President, Assistant to the President for National Security Affairs, From: Colin L. Powell, Subject: "Draft Decision Memorandum for the President on the Applicability of the Geneva Convention to the Conflict in Afghanistan," *The Torture Papers*, 122.

14. "Status of Legal Discussions re Application of Geneva Conventions to Taliban and al Qaeda," Memo 10, The Legal Adviser Department of State Washington, February 2, 2002, Memorandum to Counsel to the President, From: William H. Taft IV, Subject: "Comments on Your Paper on the Geneva Convention," *The Torture Papers*, 131.

15. Memo 10, The Legal Adviser Department of State Washington, February 2, 2002, Memorandum to Counsel to the President, From: William H. Taft IV, Subject: "Comments on Your Paper on the Geneva Convention," *The Torture Papers*, 129.

16. Memo 11, Subject: "Humane Treatment of al Qaeda and Taliban Detainees" [Signed George Bush], *The Torture Papers*, 135.

17. Donald H. Rumsfeld, "Joint Strike Fighter Signing Ceremony," Defense Department news briefing, M2 Presswire, Washington, D.C., February 8, 2002.

18. Yoo, *War by Other Means*. p. 109, 170.

19. Ibid.,. 170-171.

20. Verbatim Record of Trial, Specialist Megan M. Ambuhl, HHC, 16th Brigade (ABN), III Corps, U.S. Army, Victory Base, Iraq, by General Court-Martial, Convened by Commanding General, Headquarters III Corps, Victory Base/Mannheim, August 11, 23 and 25, 2004.

21. Yoo, *War by Other Means*, 170–171.

CHAPTER THREE

1. Lorraine Boles, in discussion with the author, Fort Ashby, WV, August 24, 2006.

2. Roy T. Hardy, in discussion with the author, San Diego, California. August 25, 2006.

3. Terrie England, in discussion with the author, Fort Ashby, WV, and San Diego, CA, August 20, 21, 24-25, 25-27, 20, 2006.

4. Ibid.

5. Cindy Shanholtz, in discussion with the author, Fort Ashby, WV, August 21, 2006.

6. Jessie Klinestiver, in discussion with the author, San Diego, Californa, August 26, 2006; telephone interview, September 12, 2006.

7. Stipulation of Fact, *United States v. Lynndie R. England,* March 1, 2005.

8. West Virginia. Personal photograph of Terrie England, 2002.

9. Terrie England, in discussion with the author, Fort Ashby, WV, and San Diego, CA, August 20, 21, 24-25, 26-27, 2006; Klinestiver, in discussion with the author, San Diego, CA, August 26, 2006; telephone interview, September 12, 2006.

10. Klinestiver, San Diego, CA; telephone interview, September 12, 2006.

11. Cashier, Dollar General Store, in discussion with the author, Moorefield, WV, August 21, 2006.

12. "Expose: Cruelty in the KFC Slaughterhouse," "What the Investigator Saw: Eyewitness Testimony from PETA's Investigation into a Pilgrim's Pride's Chicken Slaughterhouse," Moorefield, WV, People for the Ethical Treatment of Animals, http://www.peta.org/feat/moorefield/ (Norfolk, Virginia. July 2004).

13. Peter Singer and Karen Dawn, "Echoes of Abu Ghraib in Chicken Slaughterhouse," *Los Angeles Times,* July 25, 2004, p. 4.

14. Elizabeth Williamson, "Humane Society to Sue Over Poultry Slaughtering; Suit Demands That Birds Be Killed or Rendered Unconscious Before Butchering," *Washington Post*, November 21, 2005, p. B2.

15. Klinestiver, in discussion with the author, San Diego, California, August 26, 2006; telephone interview, September 12, 2006.

16. Lynndie England, in discussion with the author, Naval Consolidated Brig Miramar, San Diego, CA, August 26, 27, 2006.

17. Lynndie England, Naval Consolidated Brig Miramar, San Diego, August 26, 27, 2006; Terrie England, Fort Ashby, WV, and San Diego, CA, August 20, 21, 24-25, 26-27, 2006; Klinestiver, San Diego, CA, August 26, 2006.

18. Frederick, sworn statement, Camp Arifjan, Kuwait, November 3, 2004; Stipulation of Fact, *United States v. Lynndie R England,* March 1, 2005.

19. Brigadier General Janis L. Karpinski, in discussion with the author, Newark, NJ, January 23, 2006.

20. Horatio Nimley, *Institution # CY9214, 1040 E. Roy Furman Hwy. Waynesburg, PA 15370-8090 v. Charles A. Graner, correctional officer; 1040 E. Roy Furman Hwy., Waynesburg, PA 15370-8090; Frank Bell, correctional officer; J. Grim, sergeant; Officer Eutsey, correctional officer,* United States District Court for the Western District of Pennsylania, May 25, 1999.

21. Frederick, sworn statement, Camp Arifjan, Kuwait, November 3, 2004; Stipulation of Fact, *United States v. Lynndie R. England,* March 1 2005; Terrie England, in discussion with the author, Fort Ashby, WV, and San Diego, CA, August 20, 21, 24-25, 26-27, 2006.

22. Frederick, sworn statement; Stipulation of Fact, *United States v. Lynndie R. England;* Terrie England, in discussion with the author Fort Ashby, WV, and San Diego, CA.

23. Jonathan Eig, "Inside Abu Ghraib: U.S. military missed red flags from reservists," *Wall Street Journal,* November 25, 2004.

CHAPTER FOUR

1. Lieutenant General Anthony R. Jones, Major General George R. Fay, "AR 15-6 Investigation of the Abu Ghraib Detention Facility and 205th Military Intelligence Brigade," July 2004.

2. Joe Walker, telephone interview with the author, Virginia. April 7, 2006.

3. "Nomination hearing for Robert Gates," Senate Armed Services Committee, Hart Senate Office Building, Washington, D.C., December 5, 2006.

4. P.W. Singer, *Corporate Warriors: The Rise of the Privatized Military Industry,* (Ithaca, NY: Cornell University Press, 2003). Based on information provided by Deborah Avant's "In Focus: Privatizing Military Training," *Foreign Policy,* May 2002.

5. Center for Public Integrity (Washington, D.C.), "Windfalls of War: U.S. Contractors in Afghanistan and Iraq," http://publicintegrity.org/wow/, accessed October 31, 2003.

6. Larry Allen, "Senate Democratic Policy Committee Holds an Oversight Hearing on Contracting Iraq," Senate Democratic Policy Committee, Federal News Service, Washington, D.C., September 10, 2004.

7. Lance Corporal Rajai Hakki, U.S. Marines Corps, in discussion with the author, Washington. May 5, 2006.

8. Haider al-Jebori, in discussion with the author, Detroit, MI, February 3, 2006.

9. Walid Hanna, in discussion with the author, Sterling Heights, MI, February 3, 2006.

10. Karpinski, in discussion with the author, Newark, NJ, January 10, 2006.

11. Khalil, in discussion with the author, Fairfax, VA, January 16 and July 2, 2006.

12. George W. Bush, remarks by the president, The White House, Washington, D.C., March 29, 2006. Al-Jebori, in discussion with the author, Detroit, MI, February 3, 2006.

13. Al-Jebori, in discussion with the author, Detroit, MI, February 3, 2006.

14. Osama A. Siblani, telephone interview, Dearborn, MI, January 30, 2007.

15. Marwan Mawiri, in discussion with the author, Birmingham, MI, February 4, 2006.

16. Lieutenant General Anthony R. Jones and Major General George R. Fay, "AR 15-6 Investigation of the Abu Ghraib Detention Facility and 205th Military Intelligence Brigade," July 2004.

17. Shereef Akeel, telephone interview, Huntington Woods, MI, December 21, 2004.

18. *Saleh v. Titan*, Civil Action No. 05-1165, United States District Court for the Southern District of California, June 9, 2004.

19. CACI, "Latest update on CACI services in Iraq," http://www.caci.com/announcement/Iraq_9-27-06.shtml, accessed September 27, 2006; CACI in Iraq: Frequently Asked Questions, http://www.caci.com/iraq_faqs.shtml. [Attorney John O'Connor's statement does not appear to be currently available on the CACI Web site.]

20. Evan Goetz, e-mail interview, New York, June 5, 2006.

21. Amanda L. Aranowski, "Shereef Akeel: Huntington Woods," "Lawyer of the Year 2004," *Michigan Lawyers Weekly* (Web site, 2004).

22. *Saleh v. Titan*, RICO case statement was filed in July 2004.

23. Susan L. Burke, in discussion with the author, Philadelphia, November 30, 2005.

24. Jones and Fay, "AR 15-6 Investigation of the Abu Ghraib Detention Facility and 205th Military Intelligence Brigade," July 2004.

25. James Robertson, United Stated District Judge, Memorandum Order, Civil Action No. 05-1165, United States District Court for the District of Columbia, Washington, D.C., June 29, 2006.

26. Angela B. Styles, telephone interview, Washington, D.C., March 11, 2005.

27. Christian Lucky, telephone interview, New York, May 4, 2005.

CHAPTER FIVE

1. Trish Wood, *What Was Asked of Us: An Oral History of the Iraq War by the Soldiers Who Fought It*, with an introduction by Bobby Muller (New York: Little, Brown, 2006), 90.

2. Karpinski, in discussion with the author, Newark, NJ, January 23, 2006. A version of this story appears in *One Woman's Army: The Commanding General of Abu Ghraib Tells Her Story*, coauthored with Steven Strasser (Hyperion, New York: 2005).

3. Guy Shields, Briefing, Baghdad, FDCH Political Transcripts, August 18, 2003.

4. Captain Errol A. Huffman, Conference on Prisons, Iraqi Correctional Services (Dept. of Prisons), Ministry of Justice Iraq. Document provided by a military officer who asked to remain anonymous, August 2, 2003.

5. Abu Ghraib, Iraq. Photographs, Joint Forces Intelligence Command document, "Abu Ghurayb Prison Complex," CIA report (#3030452). Document provided by a military officer who asked to remain anonymous, October 2002.

6. "JIDC Organization," 23 January 2004, Joint Interrogation & Debriefing Center, Abu Ghurayb, Iraq, PowerPoint presentation.

7. "Abu Ghraib Prison: Itinerary for the Visit on 18 July 03," Fact Sheet. Document provided by a military officer who asked to remain anonymous, July 2003.

8. Karpinski, sworn statement, in Jones and Fay, "AR 15-6 Investigation of the Abu Ghraib Detention Facility and 205th Military Intelligence Brigade," July 18, 2004.

9. Ibid.

10. Abu Ghraib prison compound, Abu Ghraib, Iraq. Photographs provided by a military officer who asked to remain anonymous, 2003/2004.

11. "JIDC Organization," Joint Interrogation and Debriefing Center, Abu Ghurayb, Iraq, Power Point presentation, 23 January 2004.

12. Karpinski, sworn statement, in Jones and Fay, "AR 15-6 Investigation of the Abu Ghraib Detention Facility and 205th Military Intelligence Brigade," July 18, 2004.

13. "Abu Ghraib Prison.: Itinerary for the Visit on 18 July 03," Fact Sheet. Document provided by a military officer who asked to remain anonymous, July 2003.

14. "CV for Brig. Gen. Janis Karpinski, Commander 800th Military Police Brigade" *The Torture Papers*, 554–556.

15. Karpinski, in discussion with the author, Newark, NJ, January 23, 2006. Portions of the interview also appeared in *One of the Guys*, edited by this author.

16. Camp Ganci. Saddam Hussein was not affiliated with al Qaeda, and he played no role in the terrorist attacks on the United States. Nor were the prisoners at Abu Ghraib involved in the terrorist attacks. Yet American contractors and troops in Iraq repeatedly made connections between the terrorist attacks, Iraqis, and Saddam Hussein. Many people believe that

naming, for example, Camp Ganci in memory of firefighter Peter J. Ganci Jr. is part of an attempt to connect Iraq with the 9/11 attacks.

17. Abu Ghraib compound. Photographs available in "The Abu Ghraib Files," *Salon* (March 14, 2006).

18. Abdul-Sattar al-Kashani, in discussion with the author, Amman, Jordan, March 12, 2006.

19. "JIDC Organization," Joint Interrogation and Debriefing Center, Abu Ghurayb, Iraq, PowerPoint presentation, 23 January 2004.

20. Agent's Investigative Report 0061-04-CID342, Carlisle Barracks Resident Agency (CID), 3d Military Police Group, USACID, Carlisle, PA. Document obtained through the ACLU's Torture Document Search, July 11, 2004.

21. Final Report. Assessment of Detainee Medical Operations for OEF, GTMO, and OIF Office of the Surgeon General Army. April 13, 2005.

22. Steven A. Miles, telephone interview, Minneapolis–St. Paul, MN, February 2, 2007.

23. Report of the International Committee of the Red Cross on the Treatment by Coalition Forces of Prisoners of War and Other Protected Persons by the Geneva Conventions in Iraq During Arrest, Internment, and Interrogation, February 2004.

24. "Policy and Procedures: Disciplinary Measures," Baghdad Central Correc-tional Facility (372nd MP Co (CS)). Document was provided to me by a military officer who asked to remain anonymous, Abu Ghraib, Fall 2003.

25. Agent's Investigation Report 0061-04-CID342, Baghdad Central Correctional Facility, Abu Ghraib. Report obtained through ACLU's Torture Document Search. Carlisle Barracks Resident Agency (CID), Carlisle, PA, July 11, 2004.

26. Agent's Investigation Report 0139-03-CID259-61189, Camp Victory, Iraq; Agent's Investigation Report, 0061-04-CID342. Report obtained through ACLU's Torture Document Search, August 18, 2003.

27. Autopsy Examination Report, Armed Forces Institute of Pathology, Office of the Armed Forces Medical Examiner, Rockville, MD, Autopsy Number 03-366. Report obtained through ACLU's Torture Document Search; Date of Death: August 11, 2003, Date of Report: October 2, 2003.

28. Autopsy Examination Report, Armed Forces Institute of Pathology, Office of the Armed Forces Medical Examiner, Rockville, Maryland, Autopsy Number ME 03-36 (EPW 3). Report obtained through ACLU's Torture Document Search; Date of Death: August 13, 2003, Date of Report: October 24, 2003.

29. Certificate of Death 0147–03–CID255–61195, Abu Ghraib Prison. Documents obtained through ACLU's Torture Document Search; Date of Death: August 20, 2003, Date of Death Certificate: August 21, 2003.

30. CID Report of Investigation, Final Supplemental 0136003–CID259–61187–5H9A, Department of the Army, 22nd Military Police Battalion (CID). Documents obtained through ACLU's Torture Document Search, June 4, 2004.

31. CID Report of Investigation, Final Supplemental–0140–03–CID259–61190–5H9A, Department of the Army, United States Criminal Investigative Command, 12th Military Police Detachment, Baghdad Branch Office. Documents obtained through ACLU's Torture Document Search, January 24, 2004.

32. CID Report of Investigation. Final Supplemental–0147–03–CID259–61195–5H9A, Department of the Army, 22nd Military Police Battalion (CID). Documents obtained through ACLU's Torture Document Search, June 3, 2004.

33. Commander's Assessment, SITREP, 800th MP BDE, Abu Ghraib. Document provided by a military officer who asked to remain anonymous, September 3, 2003.

34. Allen S. Keller, testimony: Hearing, Eminent Jurists Panel on Terrorism, Counterterrorism and Human Rights, Washington, D.C., September 6, 2006, http://ejp.icj.org/IMG/DrKellerTestimony.pdf.

35. Keller, "Torture in Abu Ghraib," in *Perspectives in Biology and Medicine* (Johns Hopkins University Press, Fall 2006).

36. CID Report of Investigation, Final Supplemental 0136003–CID259–61187–5H9A, Department of the Army, 22nd Military Police Battalion (CID). Documents obtained through ACLU's Torture Document Search, June 4, 2004.

37. "Policy and Procedures: Disciplinary Measures," Baghdad Central Correctional Facility (372nd MP Co (CS)), 2.

38. Acho, in discussion with the author, Sterling Heights, MI, February 4, 2006.

39. Security Report, "Smuggling of Messages from VIP Abu Ghraib Prisoners," Baghdad. Document provided by a military officer who asked to remain anonymous, November 12, 2003.

40. Steven L. Jordan, sworn statement, in "Article 15-6 Investigation of the 800th Military Police Brigade," 81.

41. Fallen Heroes of Operation Iraqi Freedom, Army Specialist Lunsford B. Brown II, Fallen Heroes Memorial, http://www.fallenheroesmemorial.com/oif/profiles/browniilunsfordb.html.

42. Fernandez, *News & Record*, Greensboro, NC, September 25, 2003.

43. Fallen Heroes of Operation Iraqi Freedom.

44. Provance, telephone interview, Heidelberg, Germany, July 7, 2006.

45. Fallen Heroes of Operation Iraqi Freedom.

46. Jordan, sworn statement,in "Article 15-6 Investigation of the 800th Military Police Brigade."

47. Provance, e-mail interview, Heidelberg, Germany, July 2003.

48. Fallen Heroes of Operation Iraqi Freedom.

49. Provance, e-mail interview, Heidelberg, Germany, July 2003.

CHAPTER SIX

1. Selwa, in discussion with the author, Amman, Jordan, December 7, 2004.

2. Selwa, in discussion with the author, Amman, Jordan, December 7, 2004. The date was confirmed by an army public affairs officer (detainee operations) in Baghdad.

3. Nadia, in discussion with the author, Amman, Jordan, December 10, 2004.

4. Greg Ford, telephone interview, California, December 28, 2004.

5. Public affairs office, National Guard, telephone interview, California, February 6, 2007.

6. Selwa, in discussion with the author, Amman, Jordan, December 7, 2004.

7. Anthony H. Cordesman, "The Developing Iraqi Insurgency: Status at End–2004," Center for Strategic and International Studies, Washington, D.C., Working draft: updated December 22, 2004.

8. Nabil, in discussion with the author, Amman, Jordan, December 8, 2004.

9. Memorandum for Commander, 104th Military Intelligence Battalion, Subject: "AR 15-6 Investigation Legal Review," Department of the Army, Headquarters 4th Infantry Division Mechanized), Office of the Staff Judge Advocate, Tikrit, Iraq. Document obtained through ACLU's Torture Document Search, October 8, 2003.

10. [Name Redacted], Exhibit H, sworn statement, DCCP, FOB-Ironhorse, Tikrit, Iraq. Document obtained through ACLU's Torture Document Search, October 1, 2003.

11. Memorandum for Commander, 104th Military Intelligence Battalion, 4th Infantry Division (Mechanized), Tikrit, Iraq, Subject: "Rebuttal of [redacted] to Written Reprimand," Department of the Army, 104th Military Intelligence Battalion. Document obtained through ACLU's Torture Document Search, November 9, 2003.

12. [Name Redacted], sworn statement, DCCP, FOB Ironhorse, Tikrit, Iraq,

104th Military Intelligence Battalion. Document obtained through ACLU's Torture Document Search, November 10, 2003.

13. Cordesman, "The Developing Iraqi Insurgency: Status at End–2004."

14. Nabil, in discussion with the author, Amman, Jordan, December 8, 2004.

CHAPTER SEVEN

1. Lieutenant General John F. Kimmons, U.S. Army Chief of Staff for Intelligence, Department of Defense Directive, The Department of Defense Detainee Program and Army Field Manuel 2-22.3, Human Intelligence Collector Operations, Special Defense Department Briefing Studio, Federal News Service Arlington, VA, September 6, 2006.

2. Frederick, general court-martial.

3. Frederick, sworn statement, Camp Arifjan, Kuwait, November 3, 2004.

4. Frederick, general court-martial.

5. Frederick, sworn statement, Camp Arifjan, Kuwait, November 3, 2004.

6. Frederick, general court-martial.

7. Lynndie England, in discussion with the author, Naval Consolidated Brig Miramar, San Diego, August 26–27, 2006. Darby also talked about the animal mutilations in GQ magazine ("Prisoner of Conscience").

8. Karpinski, in discussion with the author, Newark, NJ, January 10, 2006.

9. Frederick, general court-martial.

10. Philip G. Zimbardo, witness for the defense, Ivan L. Frederick II, general court-martial.

11. Justin Cole, "U.S. soldiers offer slack portrait of England, defense focuses on wider abuse," Agence France Presse, August 4, 2004.

12. Joyner, in discussion with the author, Washington, July 12, 2006.

13. Major [Name Redacted], 320th MP Battalion, sworn statement, February 9, 2004, in Taguba Report, "Article 15-6 Investigation of the 800th Military Police Brigade.

14. Colonel Thomas M. Pappas, sworn statement, February 11, 2004, in Taguba Report, "Article 15-6 Investigation of the 800th Military Police Brigade," 59.

15. Karpinski, in discussion with the author, Newark, NJ, January 23, 2006.

16. General Paul J. Kern, Report on Department of Defense Detention Operations, Hearing of the House Armed Services Committee, Rayburn Office Building, Federal News Service, Washington, D.C., September 9, 2004.

17. James R. Schlesinger, Final Report of the Independent Panel to Review DoD Detainee Operations, August 2004.

18. Lieutenant General Anthony R. Jones, Report on Department of Defense Detention Operations, Hearing of the House Armed Services Committee, September 9, 2004.

19. Horton, in discussion with the author, New York, September 2005; telephone interview, New York, February 2, 2006.

20. Sam Provance, telephone interview, Heidelberg, Germany, July 7 and September 22, 2006.

21. Provance, prepared statement, in "Protecting National Security Whistleblowers in the Post-9/11 Era."

22. Chart, Joint Interrogation and Debriefing Center, Abu Ghurayb, Iraq, October 2003, PowerPoint presentation.

23. Karpinski, testimony, in re Criminal Complaint against United States Secretary of Defense Donald Rumsfeld, et al., Berlin, filed by Center for Constitutional Rights, Republikanischer Anwaeltinnen-und Anwaelteverein, et al., Berlin, Germany, October 26, 2005.

24. Hina Shamsi, e-mail interview, New York, July 20, 2006; telephone interviews, New York, July 21, 2006, and February 7, 2007.

25. Pappas, sworn statement, February 11, 2004, in Taguba Report, "Article 15-6 Investigation of the 800th Military Police Brigade."

26. Illustration in Joint Interrogation and Debriefing Center, Abu Ghurayb, Iraq, October 2003, PowerPoint presentation.

27. Karpinski, sworn statement, in Lieutenant General Anthony R. Jones and Major General George R. Fay, "AR 15-6 Investigation of the Abu Ghraib Detention Facility and 205th Military Intelligence Brigade."

28. Joyner, in discussions with the author, Washington, July 12, 2006, and January 29, 2007.

29. Pappas, sworn statement, February 9, 2004, in Taguba Report, "Article 15-6 Investigation of the 800th Military Police Brigade."

30. Joyner, in discussion with the author, Washington, July 12, 2006.

31. "Leadership Failure: Firsthand Accounts of Torture of Iraqi Detainees by the U.S. Army's 82nd Airborne Division," Human Rights Watch, New York, September 2005.

32. Joyner, in discussion with the author, Washington, July 12, 2006.

33. Frederick, sworn statement, Camp Arifjan, Kuwait, November 3, 2004.

34. Ibid.

35. Stipulation of Fact, United States v. Lynndie R England, March 1, 2005.

36. Hardy, in discussion with the author, San Diego, CA, August 25, 2006.

37. Karpinski, in discussion with the author, Newark, NJ, January 23, 2006.

38. Frederick, sworn statement, Camp Arifjan, Kuwait, November 3, 2004.

39. Lynndie England, in discussion with the author, Naval Consolidated Brig Miramar, San Diego, August 26, 27, 2006.

40. Frederick, sworn statement, Camp Arifjan, Kuwait, November 3, 2004.

41. Stipulation of Fact, *United States v. Lynndie R England,* March 1, 2005.

42. Lynndie England, in discussion with the author, Naval Consolidated Brig Miramar, San Diego, August 26, 27, 2006.

43. Richard A. Serrano, "Prison Abuse Ringleader Is Convicted," *Los Angeles Times,* January 15, 2005, p. 1.

44. Frederick, general court-martial.

45. Stipulation of Fact, *United States v. Lynndie R England,* March 1, 2005.

46 Lynndie England, in discussion with the author, Naval Consolidated Brig Miramar, San Diego, August 26, 27, 2006.

47. Frederick, general court-martial.

48. Stipulation of Fact, *United States v. Lynndie R England,* March 1, 2005.

CHAPTER EIGHT

1. Pappas, sworn statement, February 11, 2004, in Taguba Report, "Article 15-6 Investigation of the 800th Military Police Brigade."

2. Provance, sworn statement, January 21, 2004, in Taguba, "Article 15-6 Investigation of the 800th Military Police Brigade."

3. Frederick, sworn statement, Camp Arifjan, Kuwait, November 3, 2004.

4. Pappas, sworn statement, February 9, 2004, in Taguba Report, "Article 15-6 Investigation of the 800th Military Police Brigade."

5. Verbatim Record of Trial, Master Sergeant Lisa M. Girman, Headquarters Company, 220th MP Battalion, U.S. Army, Camp Bucca, Iraq, by General Court-Martial Convened by Commanding General, Coalition Land Forces Component Command, Third U.S. Army, U.S. Army Central Command. Tried at Camp Doha, Kuwait, on November 15, 2003.

6. Taguba Report, "Article 15-6 Investigation of the 800th Military Police Brigade."

7. Karpinski, sworn statement, in Jones and Fay, "AR 15-6 Investigation of the Abu Ghraib Detention Facility and 205th Military Intelligence Brigade."

8. Provance, in discussion with the author, Carmichaels, PA, November 25, 2006.

9. Taguba Report, "Article 15-6 Investigation of the 800th Military Police Brigade."

10. Ibid.

11. Ibid.

12. DiNenna, E-mail Subject: "FOOD," Sent: Sunday, November 2, 2003, 7:48 AM, To: [Name Redacted], in Taguba, "Article 15-6 Investigation of the 800th Military Police Brigade," March 2004.

13. Lieutenant General Anthony R. Jones and Major General George R. Fay, "AR 15-6 Investigation of the Abu Ghraib Detention Facility and 205th Military Intelligence Brigade," July 2004.

14. (1)(U) Incident #25, in Jones and Fay, "AR 15-6 Investigation of the Abu Ghraib Detention Facility and 205th Military Intelligence Brigade," July 2004.

15. Ibid. The incident is also described in a March 21, 2006, article, "Abu Ghraib Dog Handler Found Guilty," by Trish Hoffman, a reporter for Army News Service.

16. Frederick, sworn statement, Camp Arifjan, Kuwait, November 3, 2004.

17. Provance, in discussion with the author, Carmichaels, PA, November 25, 2006.

18. (1)(U) Incident #25, in Jones and Fay, "AR 15-6 Investigation of the Abu Ghraib Detention Facility and 205th Military Intelligence Brigade," July 2004.

19. Frederick, sworn statement, in Jones and Fay. "AR 15-6 Investigation of the Abu Ghraib Detention Facility and 205th Military Intelligence Brigade," July 2004, p. 132.

20. Frederick, sworn statement, Camp Arifjan, Kuwait, November 3, 2004.

21. Incident #15, (24)(U) Incident #24, in Jones and Fay, "AR 15-6 Investigation of the Abu Ghraib Detention Facility and 205th Military Intelligence Brigade," July 2004.

22. (25)(u) Finding: Civilian-11, Interrogator, in Jones and Fay, "AR 15-6 Investigation of the Abu Ghraib Detention Facility and 205th Military Intelligence Brigade," July 2004.

23. Frederick, sworn statement, Camp Arifjan, Kuwait, November 3, 2004.

24. (1)(U) Incident #25, in Jones and Fay, "AR 15-6 Investigation of the Abu Ghraib Detention Facility and 205th Military Intelligence Brigade," July 2004.

CHAPTER NINE

1. Abu Bakr Haddad, in discussion with the author, Amman, Jordan, March 13, 2006.

2. Brigadier General Martin E. Dempsey, Coalition Provisional Authority Briefing, Baghdad, Federal News Service, November 20, 2003.

3. Drew Brown and Jeff Wilkinson, "U.S. Forces Begin 'Iron Hammer' Attacks against Iraqi Insurgency," Knight Ridder Washington Bureau, November 14, 2003.

4. Brigadier General Mark Kimmitt, Coalition Provisional Authority Briefing, Baghdad, Federal News Service, November 17, 2003.

5. Dempsey, Coalition Provisional Authority Briefing, Baghdad, Federal News Service, November 20, 2003.

6. Haddad, in discussion with the author, Amman, Jordan, March 13, 2006.

7. Fulani, in discussion with the author, Amman, Jordan, March 13, 2006.

8. Dempsey, Coalition Provisional Authority Briefing, Baghdad, Federal News Service. November 20, 2003.

9. Sarah Holewinski, in discussion with the author, Washington, D.C., June 8, 2006.

10. Dempsey, Coalition Provisional Authority Briefing. Baghdad, Federal News Service, November 20, 2003.

11. Documents provided by Haddad.

CHAPTER TEN

1. Trish Wood, *What Was Asked of Us* (New York: Little, Brown, 2006), 185–86.

2. Abdul-Hakim al-Mayah, in discussion with the author, Amman, Jordan, March 17, 2006.

3. Memorandum for Commander, U.S. Central Command, Subject: "CJTF-7 Interrogation and Counter-Resistance Policy, Department of the Army, Headquarters." Document obtained through the ACLU's Torture Document Search, Combined Joint Task Force Seven, Camp Victory, Iraq, September 14, 2003.

4. Frederick, sworn statement, Camp Arifjan, Kuwait, November 3, 2004.

5. Guy Womack, telephone interview, May 31, 2006.

6. Wood, *What Was Asked of Us*, 184.

7. Major General Antonio Taguba, "Article 15-6 Investigation of the 800th Military Police Brigade."

8. Mayah, in discussion with the author, Amman, Jordan, March 17, 2006.

9. Case Number: 05-CV-1165, *Saleh v. Titan*, United States District Court, District of Columbia.

10. Acho, in discussion with the author, Sterling Heights, MI, February 4, 2006.

11. Frederick, sworn statement, Camp Arifjan, Kuwait, November 3, 2004.

12. Joyner, in discussions with the author, Washington, July 12, 2006, and January 29, 2007.

13. Acho, in discussion with the author, Sterling Heights, MI, February 4, 2006.

14. Mayah, in discussion with the author, Amman, Jordan, March 17, 2006.

15. Nakhla, Adel, Resume: 1979–1999.

16. Don Eckrod, in discussion with the author, Virginia, April 6, 2006.

17. David Sykes, in discussion with the author, Maryland, April 13, 2006.

18. Nancy Kerr, in discussion with the author, Maryland, April 18, 2006.

19. Tier 1A Photographs, "The Abu Ghraib Files," *Salon*, March 14, 2006.

20. Womack, telephone interview, May 31, 2006.

21. Frederick, sworn statement, Camp Arifjan, Kuwait, November 3, 2004.

22. Taguba, "Article 15-6 Investigation of the 800th Military Police Brigade."

23. Lieutenant General Anthony R. Jones and Major General George R. Fay, "AR 15-6 Investigation of the Abu Ghraib Detention Facility and 205th Military Intelligence Brigade," July 2004.

24. Taguba, "Article 15-6 Investigation of the 800th Military Police Brigade."

25. Lynndie England, in discussion with the author, Naval Consolidated Brig Miramar, San Diego, August 26, 27, 2006.

26. Frederick, sworn statement, Camp Arifjan, Kuwait, November 3, 2004.

27. Karpinski. Sworn Statement. Lieutenant General Anthony R. Jones. Pages 6–33. Major General George R. Fay, pages 34–176. "AR 15-6 Investigation of the Abu Ghraib Detention Facility and 205th Military Intelligence Brigade." July 18, 2004.

28. Final Report. Assessment of Detainee Medical Operations for OEF, GTMO, and OIF Office of the Surgeon General Army. April 13, 2005.

29. Karpinski. Sworn Statement. Lieutenant General Anthony R. Jones. Pages 6–33. Major General George R. Fay, pages 34–176. "AR 15-6 Investigation of the Abu Ghraib Detention Facility and 205th Military Intelligence Brigade." July 18, 2004.

30. Karpinski, telephone interview, January 27, 2007.

31. Joyner, in discussions with the author, Washington, July 12, 2006, and January 29, 2007.

32. Minnah Karam Kamil, in discussion with the author, Amman, Jordan, March 10, 2006.

33. Lynndie England, in discussion with the author, Naval Consolidated Brig Miramar, San Diego, August 26, 27, 2006.

34. Mayah, in discussion with the author, Amman, Jordan, March 17, 2006.

35. Taguba, "Article 15-6 Investigation of the 800th Military Police Brigade," March 2004, in *The Torture Papers*, 478.

36. Christy Hardy, in discussion with the author, Keyser, WV, August 23, 2006.

37. Roy Hardy, in discussion with the author, San Diego, CA, August 25, 2006.

38. Klinestiver, in discussion with the author, San Diego, CA, August 26, 2006.

CHAPTER ELEVEN

1. Trish Wood, *What Was Asked of Us* (New York: Little, Brown), 184.

2. Hisham L. Azzam Dilami, in discussion with the author, Amman, Jordan, March 10, 2006.

3. Paula Span, "The Kids Are All Right: Mom & Dad Were '60s Radicals; Today, Their Children Grapple With the '90s," November 14, 1994, p. D1. Judith Chomsky, telephone interview, January 31, 2007.

4. Vonda Paige, "Attorney Jailed for Refusing to Testify Before Grand Jury," The Associated Press, January 2, 1991. Chomsky, telephone interview, January 31, 2007.

5. The Noam Chomsky Web site, http://www.chomsky.info/.

6. Chomsky, in discussion with the author, Amman, Jordan, March 10, 2006.

7. Dilami, in discussion with the author, Amman, Jordan, March 10, 2006.

8. Cordesman, "Strategies for Reshaping U.S. Policy in Iraq and the Middle East," Senate Foreign Relations Committee, Federal News Service, Washington, D.C., February 1, 2005.

9. Richard B. Myers, "Hearing on the Status of the U.S. Army and Marine Corps in Fighting the Global War on Terrorism," Senate Armed Services Committee, Federal News Service, June 30, 2005.

10. Senior Coalition Official [unidentified], "Release of Detainees," Defense Department Briefing, Federal News Service, Baghdad, January 7, 2004.

11. Dave DaBatto, telephone interview, MA, December 23, 2004.

12. "Leadership Failure: Firsthand Accounts of Torture of Iraqi Detainees by the U.S. Army's 82nd Airborne Division," Human Rights Watch, vol, 17, no. 3(G), New York. September 2005.

13. Dilami, in discussion with the author, Amman, Jordan, March 10, 2006.

14. Anthony B. Sisti, Department of Defense, e-mail interview, March 30–April 4, 2006.

15. Matthew K. Travis, Camp Pendleton, CA, First Marine Division, general court martial, tried at Forward Operations Base Fallujah, Iraq, on August 19, 2004.

16. Department of the Army, United States Army Criminal Investigation Command, 48th Military Police Detachment (CID) (FWD), 3rd Military Police Group (CID), Camp Victory, Baghdad, Iraq, June 17, 2005.

17. Brigadier General Richard P. Formica, Investigating Officer, "Article 15-6 Investigation of CJSOTF-AP and 5th SF Group Detention Operations," November 2004.

18. Dilami, in discussion with the author, Amman, Jordan, March 10, 2006.

CHAPTER TWELVE

1. John Yoo, *War by Other Means: An Insider's Account of the War on Terror* (New York: Atlantic Monthly Press, 2006), 185.

2. Mohammed Rahman, in discussion with the author, Amman, Jordan, December 6, 2004.

3. Lee Siu Hin, "Iraq in the Aftermath: Visions of the Future," National Immigrant Solidarity Network, July 2003.

4. Rahman, in discussion with the author, Amman, Jordan, December 6, 2004.

5. "No Blood, No Foul: Soldiers' Accounts of Detainee Abuse in Iraq," Human Rights Watch. July 2006.

6. Brigadier General Janis L. Karpinski, sworn statement, in Lieutenant General Anthony R. Jones and Major General George R. Fay, "AR 15-6 Investigation of the Abu Ghraib Detention Facility and 205th Military Intelligence Brigade," July 18, 2004. Karpinski telephone interview, January 27, 2007.

7. Rahman, in discussion with the author, Amman, Jordan, December 6, 2004.

8. "No Blood, No Foul: Soldiers' Accounts of Detainee Abuse in Iraq," Human Rights Watch.

9. Rahman, in discussion with the author, Amman, Jordan, December 6, 2004.

10. "No Blood, No Foul: Soldiers' Accounts of Detainee Abuse in Iraq," Human Rights Watch.

11. Chris Mackey and Greg Miller, *The Interrogators: Task Force 500 and America's Secret War Against Al Qaeda* (New York: Back Bay Books, 2004), 289.

12. Rahman, in discussion with the author, Amman, Jordan, December 6, 2004.

CHAPTER THIRTEEN

1. Trish Wood, *What Was Asked of Us* (New York: Little, Brown, 2006), 94.

2. Darby, as told to Wil S. Hylton, "Prisoner of Conscience" *GQ* .

3. Michael G. Santos, *Inside: Life Behind Bars in America* (New York: St. Martin's Press, 2006), 41.

4. S.J. Provance, Heidelberg, Germany, e-mail interview, July 2006.

5. Stipulation of Fact, August 5, 2004, Ivan L. Frederick II, general court-martial, in Darby, "Prisoner of Conscience," *GQ* (September 2006).

6. Brigadier General Janis L. Karpinski, in discussions with the author,
Newark, NJ, January 23, 2006, and telephone interview, January 27, 2007.

7. Klinestiver, in discussion with the author. San Diego, Califor[na, August 26,
2006.

8. Schmitt, "Inquiry Ordered into Reports of Prisoner Abuse," *New York
Times,* January 17, 2004, p. 7.

9. Major General Antonio Taguba, "Article 15-6 Investigation of the 800th
Military Police Brigade."

10. Provance, telephone interview, Heidelberg, Germany, September 22, 2006.

11. Taguba, "Article 15-6 Investigation of the 800th Military Police Brigade."

12. Karpinski, in discussions with the author, Newark, NJ. January 23, 2006,
and telephone interview, January 27, 2007.

13. Taguba, "Article 15-6 Investigation of the 800th Military Police Brigade."

14. Jon R. Anderson, "Home Isn't the Same for Single Soldiers," *Stars and
Stripes*, European edition, February 20, 2004.

CHAPTER FOURTEEN

1. Trish Wood, *What Was Asked of Us: An Oral History of the Iraq War by the Soldiers Who Fought It* (New York: Little, Brown, 2006), 89-90.

2. "Minutes of Iraq Coverage," ABC, CBS, and NBC Evening News, January–August 2004, *The Tyndall Report.*

3. Nabil, in discussion with the author, Amman, Jordan, December 8, 2004.

4. Dora Apel, "Torture Culture," *Art Journal* (Summer 2005): 8. Photograph.
Danner, Mark, et al. Abu *Ghraib: The Politics of Torture* (San Francisco: North
Atlantic Books, 2004).

5. Fareed Zakaria, "Psst . . . Nobody Loves a Torturer," *Newsweek*, November
14, 2005, 36.

6. Wood, *What Was Asked of Us,* 82.

7. Les Brownlee, "Mistreatment of Iraqi Prisoners," Hearing of the Senate
Armed Services Committee, Dirksen Senate Office Building, Washington,
D.C., Federal News Service, May 7, 2004.

8. Lance Smith, "Iraqi Prisoner Abuse," House Armed Services Committee
Hearing, Rayburn Office Building, Federal News Service, May 2, 2004.

9. Yearbook of Frankfort High School, Class of 2001. Office of Mineral
County Schools Psychological Services, Student Services, Keyser, WV,
August 24, 2006.

10. Klinestiver, in discussion with the author, San Diego, CA, August 26, 2006; telephone interview, September 12, 2006.

11. Roy T. Hardy, in discussion with the author, Keyser, WV, August 2006; Terrie England, in discussion with the author, Fort Ashby, WV, and San Diego, CA. August 20, 21, 24-25, 26-27, 2006.

12. Scott Horton, in discussion with the author, New York, November 29, 2006.

13. S.J. Provance, telephone interview, Heidelberg, Germany, July 7, September 22, 2006.

14. Horton, in discussion with the author, New York, November 29, 2006.

15. Provance, e-mail interview, Heidelberg, Germany, July 2003.

16. John Sifton, telephone interview, New York, May 2, 2006.

17. Kenneth Roth, speech, "America and the Rules of War: What Next After Abu Ghraib?" World Affairs Council, Washington, D.C., October 27, 2006.

18. Gary D. Solis, telephone interview, Alexandria, VA, October 23, 2005.

19. Elizabeth L. Hillman, telephone interview, New Jersey, October 23, 2005.

20. William V. Gallo, telephone interview, California, October 27, 2005.

21. Office of the Armed Forces Regional Medical Examiner, Landstuhl Regional Medical Center, Final Autopsy Report, Landstuhl, Germany. Document obtained through the ACLU's Torture Document Search, October 22, 2003.

22. Gallo, telephone interview, California, October 27, 2005.

23. Hina Shamsi, telephone interview, New York, October 25, 2006. She is coauthor of a report, "Broken Chains: Deaths in U.S. Custody in the Global 'War on Terrorism,'" New York, Fall 2005.

24. Deborah Pearlstein, in discussion with the author, Washington, D.C., October 6, 2005.

25. Gallo, telephone interview, California, October 27, 2005.

26. Lieutenant Colonel Mark Ballesteros, in discussion with the author, Pentagon, October 26, 2005.

27. Lieutenant General Anthony R. Jones and Major General George R. Fay, "AR 15-6 Investigation of the Abu Ghraib Detention Facility and 205th Military Intelligence Brigade," July 2004.

28. John Sifton, telephone interview, New York, May 2, 2006.

29. Ballesteros, in discussion with the author, October 26, 2005.

30. Memorandum, Subject: "CID Report of Investigation. Department of the Army," United States Army Criminal Investigative Command, Third Military Police Group, 78th Military Police Detachment. Document obtained through the ACLU's Torture Document Search, Baghdad, September 23, 2004.

31. Mark Corallo, Director of the Office of Public Affairs on Iraq Investigation, statement, Department of Justice Documents, Washington, D.C., May 21, 2004.

32. Matt Kelley, "Civilian interpreter at Abu Ghraib fired, still in Iraq," The Associated Press, Gaithersburg, MD, May 22, 2004.

33. Lieutenant John J. Fitzgerald, in discussion with the author, Gaithersburg, MD, May 1, 2006.

34. Steve Kerr, in discussion with the author, Maryland, April 18, 2006.

35. Report of Investigation (ROI) 0030-04-CID149-83130," CID Form 66, Case Number 0132-04-CID259-80198, SAC 78th Military Police DET (CID). Document obtained through the ACLU's Torture Document Search, May 2004.

36. Kerr, in discussion with the author, Maryland, April 18, 2006.

37. Sifton, telephone interview, New York, May 2, 2006.

38. David Johnston, "U.S. Inquiry Falters on Civilians Accused of Abuse," New York Times, December 19, 2006, p. 1.

39. Valerie E. Caproni, DIV-09, FBI, e-mail, Subject Heading: "Meeting w/DOD Re Prisoner Abuse Investigations in Iraq." Document obtained through the ACLU's Torture Document Search, May 14, 2004.

40. Report of Investigation (ROI) 0030-04-CID149-83130," CID Form 66, Case Number 0132-04-CID259-80198, SAC 78th Military Police DET (CID). Document obtained through the ACLU's Torture Document Search, May 2004.

41. Johnston, "U.S. Inquiry Falters on Civilians Accused of Abuse."

42. Adam L. Rosman, telephone interview, Washington, D.C., May 15, 2006.

43. Susan L. Burke, telephone interview, Philadelphia, July 4, 2006.

CHAPTER FIFTEEN

1. Marla Ruzicka, telephone interviews, New York, February–March 2005.

2. Jennifer Abrahamson, Sweet Relief: The Marla Ruzicka Story (New York: Simon & Schuster, 2006), 236.

3. Tim Rieser in discussion with the author, Washington, D.C., October 2006.

4. Abrahamson, Sweet Relief, 234.

5. Ruzicka, telephone and e-mail interviews, New York, February–March 2005.

6. Cat Philp, in discussion with the author, Washington, D.C., September 2006.

7. Abrahamson, Sweet Relief, 237.

8. Ruzicka, e-mails, Baghdad, March–April 2005.

9. Randa Mukhar, e-mail interviews, Amman, March 2005.

10. Philp, in discussion with the author, Washington, D.C., September 2006.

11. Ruzicka, e-mail interviews, Baghdad, March–April 2005.

12. Abrahamson, *Sweet Relief*, 237.

13. Cliff Ruzicka, telephone interview, Lakeport, CA, May 2005.

14. Robert F. Worth, "An American Aid Worker Is Killed in Her Line of Duty," *New York Times*, April 18, 2005, p. 4.

15. Barry Johnson, in discussion with the author, Washington, D.C., May 2005.

16. Rieser, telephone interview, Washington, D.C., February 5, 2007.

17. Patrick Leahy, U.S. senator, telephone interview, Washington, D.C., May 2005.

CHAPTER SIXTEEN

1. Secretary of Defense Donald Rumsfeld, "Mistreatment of Iraqi Prisoners," Senate Armed Services Committee Hearing, Federal News Service, Washington, D.C., May 7, 2004.

2. Catherine Itaya, in discussion with the author, New York. February 14, 2006.

3. Jameel Jaffer, in discussion with the author, New York, February 14, 2006.

4. Susan L. Burke, in discussion with the author, Washington, D.C., February 15, 2006.

5. Steven H. Miles, "Women Soldiers and Interrogational Abuses in the Terror War," in *One of the Guys: Women as Aggressors and Torturers*, ed. Tara McKelvey, foreward by Barbara Ehrenreich (Emeryville, CA: Seal Press, 2007), 94.

6. Vince Crawley, "'I take full responsibility,' Rumsfeld tells Congress," *Army Times*, May 17, 2004.

7. [Name Redacted], Canine Unit. U.S. Navy, sworn statement, February 1, 2004, in Major General Antonio Taguba's March 2004 report, "Article 15-6 Investigation of the 800th Military Police Brigade."

8. Seymour Hersh, from Daily Kos's partial transcript of a video, July 15, 2004.

9. Chris Suellentrop, "Sy Hersh Says It's Okay to Lie (Just Not in Print)," *New York*, April 18, 2005. ["I actually didn't quite say what I wanted to say correctly," Hersh told Suellentrop. "It wasn't that inaccurate, but it was misstated. The next thing I know, it was all over the blogs. And I just realized then, the power of—and so you have to try and be more careful."]

10. Jim Moran, in discussion with the author, Washington, D.C., January 30, 2006.

11. Lieutenant General Anthony R. Jones and Major General George R. Fay, "AR 15-6 Investigation of the Abu Ghraib Detention Facility and 205th Military Intelligence Brigade," July 2004.

12. "Iraq: The Way Ahead," Senate Foreign Relations Committee Hearing, Federal News Service, Washington, D.C., May 18, 2004.

13. Anonymous, e-mail interview, Washington, D.C., September 29, 2004.

14. Senator Patrick Leahy, "Fiscal Year 2005 Emergency Supplemental," Hearing of the U.S. Senate Committee on Appropriations, Washington, D.C., CQ Transcriptions, February 16, 2005.

15. Selwa, in discussion with the author, Amman, Jordan, December 7, 2004.

16. Riva Khoshaba, in discussion with the author, Amman, Jordan, December 2004.

17. Major General Antonio Taguba, "Article 15-6 Investigation of the 800th Military Police Brigade."

18. Nadia, in discussion with the author, Amman, Jordan, December 10, 2004.

19. Edward Wong, Worth "House in Falluja Seems to Have Been Base for Top Jordanian Terrorist," *New York Times*, November 19, 2004; "Margaret Hassan," BBC News, May 1, 2005.

20. Nadia, in discussion with the author, Amman, Jordan, December 10, 2004.

21. Name withheld for security reasons [From District 36, Baghdad. Formerly employed by Ministry of Higher Education. Held in U.S. custody from November 8, 2003, through May 4, 2004. (Dates confirmed by U.S. military spokesman.)], in discussion with the author, Amman, Jordan, December 5, 2004.

22. Nabil, in discussion with the author, Amman, Jordan, December 8, 2004.

23. Unidentified military official speaking on background, telephone interview, December 21, 2004.

24. Sandra L. Hodgkinson, in discussion with the author, Cambridge, MA, March 22, 2006. Telephone interview, U.S. State Department's Office of War Crimes Issues, Washington, D.C.. February 2, 2007.

25. Unidentified military official speaking on background, telephone interview, December 21, 2004.

26. Sherrie Gossett, "Fake rape photos infuriate Arab world: Iraq prisoner abuse scandal compounded by dissemination of graphic porn images," WorldNetDaily.com, accessed May 9, 2004.

27. Tim Burt, Stephen Donaghy, and Stephanie Kirchgaessner, "Mirror Tells Morgan to Go as Photos Prove Fakes Abuse Claims," *Financial Times*, May 15, 2004.

28. Edward Cody, "Artists Express Iraqis' Anger; Baghdad Exhibit Reflects

Belief that Iraqi Women Were Raped in Abu Ghraib," *Washington Post,* June 9, 2004, p. A14.

29. Wong, "Provincial Capital Near Falluja Is Rapidly Slipping into Chaos," *New York Times,* October 28, 2004, p. 1.

30. Jaffer, in discussion with the author, New York, February 14, 2006.

31. Charles Gardner Mills, telephone interview, Glen Cove, NY, November 8, 2006.

32. Alvin K. Hellerstein, Opinion, *ACLU v. Department of Defense,* U.S. District Court in Manhattan, September 29, 2005.

33. Thomas S. Blanton, telephone interviews, Washington, D.C., November 8, 2005, and February 6, 2007.

34. Brigadier General Janis L. Karpinski, in discussion with the author, Newark, NJ, January 23, 2006.

35. Anthony Romero, telephone interview, New York, November 8, 2005.

36. Jaffer, in discussion with the author, New York, February 14, 2006.

37. State Department official, *ACLU v. Department of Defense,* U.S. District Court in Manhattan.

38. Khaled Fahmy, telephone interview, New York, November 7, 2005, and in discussion with the author, New York. February 14, 2006.

CHAPTER SEVENTEEN

1. Donavan Webster, "The Man in the Hood" *Vanity Fair,* February 2005; David Brancaccio, *NOW with David Brancaccio,* PBS, New York and Guantanamo Bay, April 29, 2005 (transcript).

2. Hassan M. Fattah, "Symbol of Abu Ghraib Seeks to Spare Others His Nightmare," *New York Times,* March 11, 2006, p 1.

3. Michael Scherer, "Identifying a Torture Icon," *Salon,* March 14, 2006.

4. Mark Danner, translation of statement provided by Abdou Hussain Saad Faleh, Detainee #18470, in *Torture and Truth: America, Abu Ghraib, and the War on Terror.* New York: New York Review of Books, 2004), 230.

5. Fattah, "Symbol of Abu Ghraib Seeks to Spare Others His Nightmare" Correction Appended, *New York Times.*

6. "The Struggle for Iraq: Detainees; Web Magazine Raises Doubts Over a Symbol of Abu Ghraib," *New York Times,* March 14, 2006, p. 17.

7. Kate Zernike (Hassan M. Fattah contributed reporting from Beirut for this article, Eric Schmitt from Washington and employees of the *New York Times* from Iraq), "Cited as Symbol of Abu Ghraib, Man Admits He Is Not in Photo," *New York Times,* March 18, 2006, p.1.

8. Howard Kurtz, "Times Says It Misidentified Iraqi as Hooded Prisoner," *Washington Post,* March 18, 2006, p. C1.

9. Byron Calame, "The Wrong Man: Deception, Mistaken Identity and Journalistic Lapses." *New York Times,* March 26, 2006, p. 12.

10. Webster, "The Man in the Hood," *Vanity Fair,* February 2005.

11. Chris Grey, telephone interview, Fort Belvoir, VA, May 23, 2006.

12. Wayne Marotto, telephone interview, from the Pentagon, June 1, 2006.

13. Chris Grey, telephone interview, Fort Belvoir, VA, May 23, 2006.

14. Marotto, telephone interview, June 1, 2006.

15. Calame, "The Wrong Man: Deception, Mistaken Identity and Journalistic Lapses."

16. Fattah, telephone interiew, Dubai. January 31, 2007.

17. David Friend, *Watching the World Change: The Stories Behind the Images of 9/11* (New York: Farrar, Straus and Giroux, 2006), 402.

18. Jonathan H. Marks, e-mail interview, December 19, 2006.

19. Webster, e-mail interviews, March 20, 2006 and December 25, 2006.

Chapter Eighteen

1. Judith Chomsky, in discussion with the author, Amman, Jordan, March 10, 2006.

2. Kamp O'Hanlon, Iraq Index: "Tracking Variables of Reconstruction & Security in Post-Saddam Iraq," Brookings Institution.

3. "Jordan Executes Two Militants for Slaying of U.S. Diplomats," Associated Press, March 11, 2006.

4. Susan L. Burke, in discussion with the author, Washington, D.C., 2005.

5. Riva Khoshaba, telephone interview, Washington, February 15, 2005.

6. Burke, in discussion with the author, Washington, D.C., 2005.

7. Kenneth Roth, speech, "America and the Rules of War: What Next After Abu Ghraib?" World Affairs Council, Washington, D.C., October 27, 2005.

Chapter Nineteen

1. Prayer for Relief, Count XXVI, *Sami Abbas al Rawi, et al. v. Titan Corporation, Adel Nakhla, et al.,* U.S. District Court for the Southern District of California, June 9, 2004.

2. Judge James Robertson, Opinion, Civil Action No. 05-1165, United States District Court for the District of Columbia, *Saleh, et al., Plaintiffs v. Titan Corporation, et al., Defendants,* Washington, D.C., June 29, 2006.

3. Eric Lichtblau, "Bush Would Let Secret Court Sift Wiretap Process," *New York Times,* July 14, 2006, p. 1.

4. Robertson, Opinion, *Saleh v. Titan..*

5. Robertson, *Ibrahim v. Titan,* Civil Action No. 04-1248, United States District Court for the District of Columbia, Washington, D.C., August 12, 2005.

6. Secretary of Defense Donald Rumsfeld, "Iraqi Prisoner Abuse," Hearing of the House Armed Services Committee, May 7, 2004.
7. *Inside the Pentagon*, "Joint Task Force Formulating Compensation Plan for Abuse Victims," vol. 20, no. 21, May 20, 2004.
8. Robertson, *Ibrahim v. Titan.*
9. Robertson, Opinion, *Saleh v. Titan*, June 29, 2006.

CHAPTER TWENTY

1. Cashier, Dollar General Store, in discussion with the author, Moorefield, WV, August 21, 2006.
2. Terrie England, in discussion with the author. Fort Ashby, WV, and San Diego, CA, August 20, 21, 24-25, 26-27, 20, 2006; Lynndie England, in discussion with the author, Naval Consolidated Brig Miramar, San Diego, August 26-27, 2006; Roy Hardy, in discussion with the author, San Diego, CA, August 25-26, 2006; Klinestiver, in discussion with the author, San Diego, CA, August 26, 2006, and telephone interview, September 12, 2006.
3. *United States v. Lynndie R England.*
4. Brigadier General Janis L. Karpinski, in discussion with the author, Newark, NJ, January 23, 2006.
5. Karpinski, sworn statement, in Lieutenant General Anthony R. Jones and Major General George R. Fay, "AR 15-6 Investigation of the Abu Ghraib Detention Facility and 205th Military Intelligence Brigade."
6. Karpinski, in discussion with the author, Newark, NJ, January 23, 2006.

EPILOGUE

1. John Yoo, *War by Other Means: An Insider's Account of the War on Terror* (New York: Atlantic Monthly Press, 2006),185.
2. President George W. Bush, "President Bush Signs Military Commissions Act of 2006," The East Room, The White House, Washington, D.C., October 17, 2007.
3. Military Commissions Act of 2006, Public Law 109-366, October 17, 2006.
4. Hina Shamsi, February 7, 2007.
5. William T. Cavanaugh, "Making Enemies: The Imagination of Torture in Chile and the United States," *Theology Today* 63, no. 3 (October 2006).
6. Yoo, *War by Other Means,* 171-172.
7. Allen S. Keller, testimony, Hearing of the Eminent Jurists Panel on Terrorism, Counter-terrorism and Human Rights, an independent body of

the Geneva-based International Commission of Jurists, Washington, D.C., September 6, 2006, http://www.ejp.icj.org/IMG/DrKellerTestimony.pdf.

8. Karen J. Greenberg, "From Fear to Torture," *The Torture Papers*, xiii.

9. Yoo, Memorandum Opinion for Timothy Flanigan, the Deputy Counsel to the President regarding "THE PRESIDENT'S CONSTITUTIONAL AUTHORITY TO CONDUCT MILITARY OPERATONS AGAINST TERRORISTS AND NATIONS SUPPORTING THEM," September 25, 2001, *The Torture Papers*, 17.

10. Yoo, "MEMORANDUM FOR WILLIAM J. HAYNES II, GENERAL COUNSEL, DEPARTMENT OF DEFENSE," regarding "Application of Treaties and Laws to al Qaeda and Taliban Detainees," *The Torture Papers: The Road to Abu Ghraib*, 38.

11. Greenberg, in discussion with the author, Washington, D.C., June 27, 2006.

12. Yoo, *War by Other Means*, 178.

13. Steven L. Jordan, sworn statement, Camp Doha, Kuwait, February 24, 2004 in "Article 15-6 Investigation of the 800th Military Police Brigade," 112.

14. "No Blood, No Foul: Soldiers' Accounts of Detainee Abuse in Iraq," Human Rights Watch, vol. 18, no. 3(G), New York, July 2006.

15. Trish Wood, *What Was Asked of Us: An Oral History of the Iraq War by the Soldiers Who Fought It* (New York: Little, Brown, 2006), 109.

16. "Leadership Failures: Firsthand Accounts of Torture of Iraqi Detainees by the U.S. Army's 82nd Airborne Division," Human Rights Watch, vol. 17, no. 3(G) (New York: September 2005), 21.

17. StanleyMilgram.com, a Web site maintained by Thomas Blass, professor, department of psychology, University of Maryland, Baltimore County, 1000 Hilltop Circle, Baltimore, MD 21250
http://www.stanleymilgram.com/references.php.

18. CNN's *360 Degrees*, Anderson Cooper interview with John Conroy, author of *Unspeakable Acts, Ordinary People: The Dynamics of Torture*, May 6, 2004.

19. Seymour M. Hersh, "Torture at Abu Ghraib," *New Yorker*, April 30, 2004; Major General Antonio Taguba's March 2004 report, "Article 15-6 Investigation of the 800th Military Police Brigade."

20. Allen S. Keller, testimony, Eminent Jurists Panel, 6.

21. John Pike, telephone interview, Arlington, VA, January 31, 2005.

22. 2005 Country Reports on Human Rights Practices, U.S. State Department, Washington, D.C., March 8, 2006.

23. James R. Schlesinger, Final Report of the Independent Panel to Review DoD Detainee Operations, August 2004.

"above the law" claim, 82

Index